ASPECTS OF ORTHODOX WORSHIP

To the presbyter Richard
Stalwart friend + worthy
priest. Enjoy!

Fraternally in Χ Θεος

+ Lary

ALKIVIADIS C. CALIVAS

ESSAYS IN THEOLOGY AND LITURGY

VOLUME THREE

ASPECTS OF ORTHODOX WORSHIP

HOLY CROSS ORTHODOX PRESS
Brookline, Massachusetts

© Copyright 2003 Holy Cross Orthodox Press
Published by Holy Cross Orthodox Press
50 Goddard Avenue
Brookline, Massachusetts 02445

LIBRARY OF CONGRESS CATALOGING–IN–PUBLICATION DATA

Calivas, Alkiviadis C.
  Aspects of Orthodox worship / Alkiviadis C. Calivas.
    p. cm. — (Essays in theology and liturgy ; vol. 3)
Includes bibliographical references.
  ISBN 1-885652-69-0 (pbk. : alk. paper)
  1. Orthodox Eastern Church—Liturgy. I. Title.
  BX127.C35 2003
  264'.019—dc22
                                    2003017169

In memory of

Archpriest Alexander Schmemann

respected teacher, mentor, and friend

CONTENTS

How the Orthodox Liturgy Was Shaped:
The Byzantine Rite and Its Liturgical Books

The Typikon – A Short Story on the
Development of the Orthodox Liturgy

The Euchologion: A Brief History

The Spirit and Ethos of Orthodox Prayer
as Reflected in the Euchologion

Analyzing the History and Content
of Liturgical Texts: Risks and Challenges

Why Textual Reform Is Necessary – A Case Study

An Introduction To The Divine Liturgy

Invigorating and Enriching the
Liturgical Life of the Parish

Preface

Worship is one of the fundamental activities of the Church. In fact, as Orthodox Christians we understand, believe, and proclaim the Church to be primarily a worshipping community. The grace of God flows through the liturgy to constitute, renew, and sustain the Church in her permanence. Through worship the Church finds her fullest expression and realization, because in worship the community of believers is continually formed to be the mystical Body of Christ. Through her liturgical rites the Church enters into communion with the Triune God, appropriates the gifts of the saving work of Christ, and realizes the inrush of the eschaton in the midst of the anomalies and contradictions of the fallen world.

The ultimate purpose and definitive meanings of life have been revealed by the incursion of God's action in the historical process, and especially by the incarnation of his Son, our Lord and Savior Jesus Christ. In every liturgical event we encounter Christ, who renders present both his past saving acts and their fulfillment. Hence, we affirm that the life of an Orthodox Christian is shaped and nourished, in large measure, by the Church's worship or liturgy, two terms that are used interchangeably to denote the whole range of rites and services that comprise the Church's rule of prayer. Communal worship and personal prayer are the primary and necessary conditions that both establish and define the spiritual experience and nurture the inner life of the Christian. Orthodox Christians come before God first and foremost in joyful adoration to converse with him and to worship him with love and adoration.

The liturgy builds faith and forms identity. It conveys, instills, and imparts a particular vision of faith and way of life.

Through it the people of God are continually fashioned into a new creation, whereby the self-giving, unconditional, and sacrificial love of God becomes the new inner principle, source, and guide of life.

In the liturgy Orthodox Christians, both as persons and as community, live and breathe their faith, learn and affirm their identity, and experience sacramentally their ultimate destiny. Hence, if we are to discern properly the ethos of the Orthodox Church, we have first to acquire a liturgical mind, which is to say we must learn to worship God in spirit and in truth (John 4: 24), thus becoming conscious celebrants of the mystery of redemption. To accomplish this we need to attain a profound appreciation for the transforming power of prayer, a deep love for the liturgy, and sufficient knowledge of the historical, logical, aesthetical, spiritual, and mystical dimensions of the Church's worship. When the liturgy is understood correctly and practiced properly, we are able to hold at bay the deleterious effects of ritual formalism.

The Church is not a grand museum, in which exotic objects and lifeless relics – however lovely or fascinating - are on display. The Church is a living organism and her liturgy is dynamic. What is permanent in the Church are not the institutional structures, disciplinary practices, or forms of worship that she has developed through the centuries, but the one, constant, and changeless truth of the Triune God and of salvation in Christ Jesus, the incarnate Word and Son of God. Liturgical forms and expressions, as the study of liturgy bears out, have undergone a process of development. They have expanded, contracted, and changed sometimes deliberately, other times accidentally, on occasion abruptly, but most often gradually and almost imperceptibly. Proper honor and reverence for our liturgical inheritance is shown not through blind adherence to custom, but in the willingness of the Church to translate the tradition into the living culture of the people in ways that the rituals, language, images, symbols, and art forms of the liturgy carry meaning and power for the worshipper in every age and place.

The essays in this volume are intended primarily for students of theology but also for interested clergy, catechists, and laypeople. They are meant to help the reader appreciate the complexities of Orthodox worship, its rich history, its dynamic character, its capacity to engage the worshipper with the fundamental truths of the faith, and its ability to initiate and sustain the mystical union with Christ; and to do this through an introduction to aspects of the liturgical tradition of the Orthodox Church. The thoughts expressed in the essays are neither definitive nor exhaustive. They are meant to raise questions, foster discussion, and encourage further research and analysis.

Some of the essays are drawn from and are based on my introductory lectures in the course on *Liturgics*, which I have been privileged to teach at Holy Cross Greek Orthodox School of Theology for the past twenty-five years. These are "The Liturgy: The Church's Faith in Motion," "The Nature and Goal of Liturgical Piety," "How the Orthodox Liturgy was Shaped," and "The Typikon: A Short History of the Development of the Orthodox Liturgy."

Other essays in this volume are related to issues of liturgical renewal and reform. They include, "Analyzing the History and Content of Liturgical Texts," "Why Textual Reform is Necessary: A Case Study," and "Probing the Text of the Divine Liturgy: Are Details Important?" The concerns expressed in these essays were objects of inquiry in an elective course entitled *Contemporary Issues* that I taught at Holy Cross several years ago. The aim of that course was to expose the students to a wide range of issues (theological, ecclesiological, pastoral, and liturgical) related to the complex needs and challenges facing the Orthodox Church at the dawn of the twenty-first century, some of which were raised in the essays published in the second volume, *Challenges and Opportunities: The Church in Her Mission to the World*, in the series *Essays in Theology and Liturgy*.

Finally, this volume contains several essays that are, in fact, revised and expanded versions of previously published articles related to a variety of liturgical themes. These are, "The Euchologion," "The Spirit and Ethos of Orthodox Worship as Reflected in the Euchologion," "An Introduction to the Divine Liturgy," "The Penthekte Synod and Liturgical Reform," and "Invigorating and Enriching the Liturgical Life of the Parish."

I am grateful to the publisher, *Holy Cross Orthodox Press*, and the members of the Holy Cross Publications Committee, chaired by Father Theodore Stylianopoulos, for their acceptance of my manuscript and for guiding it into print. I wish, also, to thank Father Nicholas Triantafilou, President of Hellenic College and Holy Cross Greek Orthodox School of Theology, for his kind support and encouragement.

Particular thanks are due to Dr. John Klentos, the "Spanos Professor of Orthodox Studies" of The Patriarchal Orthodox Institute at the Graduate Theological Union in Berkeley, CA, who read the drafts of several essays. He was very kind to provide me with many valuable insights, comments, and suggestions. I would be remiss if I did not acknowledge the assistance of Dr. Lewis Patsavos, Rev. Dr. Pavlos Koumarianos, and Dr. Anton Vrame, who each read an essay and offered helpful advice. Thanks also to Mr. John Metakis and Mr. Herald Gjura of the Holy Cross Orthodox Press for their expert technical assistance. Especially, I owe a debt of gratitude to Presvytera Katherine Sietsema, who diligently read through the entire manuscript and greatly improved it.

The series *Essays in Theology and Liturgy*, as I mentioned in the Preface of volume one, *Theology: The Conscience of the Church*, is due to the generosity of Mr. Alexander Anagnos, a devout Orthodox Christian, philanthropist, and personal friend. I am deeply grateful to him for his many kindnesses throughout the long years of our friendship and most especially for his generous financial support, without which the series would not have become a reality.

Finally, I would like to express deep gratitude to my wife Erasmia for her affectionate care, encouragement, and support. Her enduring trust and abiding love gave me the strength to bring this project to fruition.

I dedicate this volume with profound humility to my most

respected teacher, mentor, and friend, Father Alexander Schmemann of blessed memory, the eminent liturgical scholar from whom I received the priceless treasure, the abiding love for the liturgy of the Orthodox Church.

Brookline, Massachusetts
Feast of the Annunciation
March 25, 2003

1

The Liturgy:
The Church's Faith in Motion

The Church is primarily a worshipping community

Worship is a fundamental and indispensable activity of the Church. It is an essential joyous act of faith, profoundly personal as well as communal in nature. Through her worship or liturgy[1] the Church finds her fullest expression and realization. In worship, the community of believers is continually formed to be the mystical body of Christ and each of its faithful members to be a dwelling place of the Holy Trinity (Jn. 14:23 and Rev. 3:20).

The Church owes her being to Christ. She is his Body. And the Church, as the Body of Christ, depends constantly on the Holy Spirit through whom the eschaton breaks into history, the catholicity of the eucharistic community is manifested, and the mystery of communion is experienced. As Metropolitan John Zizioulas tells us,

> It is important to bear in mind that the Body of Christ, both in the Christological (incarnational) and in the ecclesiological sense, became a historical reality through the Holy Spirit... For creation to lend itself to the Logos of God in order to bring about the incarnation would have been impossible without the intervention of the Holy Spirit... and the same is true about the realization of the community of the Church on the day of Pentecost... That which made (these events) a reality *eph hapax* namely the Holy Spirit, is that which makes them an existential reality, here and now, again.[2]

The Holy Spirit constitutes the Church, which Christ instituted.[3] As the Holy Spirit, to paraphrase Father Boris Bobrinskoy, formed the body and the very humanity of Jesus at the incarnation and raised his body from the dead, so the

1

Holy Spirit forms his mystical Body, the Church.[4] The Holy Spirit animates and vivifies the Church as He filled the entire earthly life of Christ. The Holy Spirit is the source of all prophetic and charismatic gifts and institutional and ministerial services in the Church. He makes us children of God, preparing us to receive the risen Christ and the attributes of divine life. And the Holy Spirit accomplishes this essentially in and through the liturgy and especially through the sacraments of baptism/chrismation, the Eucharist, and ordination, in which the mystery and presence of Christ are contained and communicated.

The liturgy in all of its expressions is a festival of faith, a celebration of the gift of knowledge of the Holy Trinity, and a reaffirmation of the new life that comes from the Triune God.[5] As St. Basil tells it: "The way to divine knowledge ascends from the one Spirit through the one Son to the one Father. Likewise, natural goodness, inherent holiness, and royal dignity reaches us from the Father through the Only-begotten [Son] to the Spirit."[6] All worship – personal as well as communal – is addressed to the Father through the Son in the Holy Spirit, who bears witness with our spirit that we are children of God – joint heirs with Christ – and by whom we cry out, 'Abba,' Father" (Rom 8:15-17). Hence we could say with Father Alexander Schmemann that the liturgy constitutes, shapes, defines, and expresses the Church and her members.[7]

The liturgy sheds light on the Church's tasks, informing her mission to the world and furnishing the basis for the interpretation of situations of daily life that call for decision. The liturgy is, without exaggeration, the face and the voice of the Church, the very expression of her inner self, her essence and conscience, the manifestation of her being the mystical body of Christ.

Through the liturgy the Church expresses her self-identity, preserves her traditions, and manifests the mystery of unity in diversity of her members. Through her liturgical rites – by the power of the Holy Spirit who dwells within her and her faithful members – the church enters into communion with

God and experiences and manifests the realities of the Kingdom to come. She actualizes sacramentally the whole of
God's divine plan for the redemption of the world, making
possible our participation in the mystery of salvation. Hence,
we can say that the Church is primarily a worshipping community.[8] Father Georges Florovsky affirms this truth:

> Worship is the norm of Christian existence... The Church her-
> self is ultimately 'real' precisely as a worshipping community,
> a community or congregation of worshipping members-per-
> sons. She grows in her fullness in the process of worship. The
> process begins in the act of initial dedication, in the act of grati-
> tude and faith, and continues in the sphere of sanctification,
> that is the acquisition of the Spirit. The process is essentially bi-
> focal: it implies both a transformation of persons (sanctification)
> and the growth of the Body in its comprehensiveness and unity.[9]

The Church enacts and celebrates her faith through the liturgy

The Church celebrates the ultimate truths of her faith about
God, about creation, and about humanity in a complex interaction of words, symbols, art, music, and ceremonial
activities that are invested with practical and symbolic significance and efficacy. This interplay constitutes the Church's
rule of prayer, that is to say, her worship or liturgy, her liturgical rites – enacted normally within a particular space and
during a specified time.

Through dogma and prayer, the Church invites us to continually discover, experience, and realize our true and eternal
mode of being. The liturgy is the Church's faith in motion,
the unique setting in which she remembers and celebrates
the revealed truths about God and the created order that she,
by grace, knows, loves, and proclaims. The liturgy conveys,
recommends, instills, and imparts a particular vision of faith
and way of life. It builds faith and forms identity, both personal and communal.

This intimate linkage between dogma and liturgy is especially evident in the Church's liturgical texts, which are
essentially of two kinds, *biblical* and *ecclesial*. The *biblical texts*

include the repertoire of readings from the Old and New Testaments, the Psalms, and the several canticles or songs of the two Testaments. The other texts, which I call *ecclesial texts*, are the compositions of various gifted, inspired, devout, and saintly persons – both known and unknown – that have been received and authenticated by the Church. These *ecclesial texts* include the collections of prayers, hymns, and rubrics that have been incorporated into the liturgical books of the Church.

The essential elements that constitute and shape the content of the liturgy define the way the faith community stands before God. Hence, the liturgy belongs to the whole Church. It is established and regulated not by any one individual but by the *pleroma* ($\pi\lambda\acute{\eta}\rho\omega\mu\alpha$), the entire complement of the Church, which receives it and prays through it (Acts 15:22).

The two ways of prayer – personal devotion and communal worship

Communion with God and neighbor begins with our willingness to see and accept the truth that an authentic human being is above all a worshipping being who feels the irresistible urge to converse with the Author of life, who has loved him first.

Christian worship, as Father Florovsky reminds us, is by its very nature a personal act that finds its fullness only within the community, in the context of common and corporate life.

> Personal devotion and community worship belong intimately together, and each of them is genuine and authentic, and truly Christian, only through the other... Common prayer presupposes and requires personal training. Yet, personal prayer itself is possible only in the context of the Community, since no person is Christian except as a member of the Body. Even in the solitude, 'in the chamber' (Mt. 6:5), a Christian prays as a member of the redeemed community, the Church.[10]

Communion with God is achieved in many ways and on various levels. Most importantly, personal prayer and communal worship are the primary and necessary conditions that both establish and define the spiritual experience as well as nurture the inner life of the Christian. The authenticity and vitality of the spiritual life, which can be defined as the surrendering of one's personal life into the hands of God and as the awareness that Christ dwells in his Body the Church and in each of her members, is centered on these two manners of prayer. It is essential, therefore, that we recognize their inestimable worth, but also their fragility. For, as Father Boris Bobrinskoy points out, "Personal prayer degenerates into individualistic pietism and anarchic ecstasy when cut off from the liturgical rhythm of the Church. Liturgical prayer becomes impersonal, formalistic and superficial, unless it is inwardly experienced and vitalized by the private prayer of believers."[11]

In addition to regular attendance at corporate worship services, the Church proposes and encourages the faithful to cultivate a meaningful personal prayer life, through the use especially of the forms of prayer and the acts of devotion of the Church. In addition to a vibrant prayer life, acts of devotion include, among other things, commitment to the Gospel and loyalty to the true faith, the daily reading of the Holy Scriptures and other edifying texts, the struggle against the passions, fasting, and works of justice, love, and charity.

While Christians, as Father Georges Florovsky said, stand by their personal faith and commitment, they nevertheless recognize and affirm that "Christian existence is intrinsically corporate. [To] be Christian means to be in the Community, in the Church and of the Church."[12] Hence, the personal and corporate dimensions of the new life in Christ are mirrored in worship. Personal prayer and corporate worship are linked inseparably. In fact, private devotions are both "a preparation for and a sequel to corporate worship,"[13] wherein the great mysteries of the faith – God's mighty deeds and promises – are remembered, made present, and communicated to God's People through the sacred rites of the liturgy.

God is present to his people in the liturgy
The liturgy is more than texts, words, gestures, and rubrics. It is the meeting ground of heaven and earth. It is the

place where the people meet the self-giving of God and where, through this encounter, they meet their own human lives in unexpected form.[14]

The liturgy is, first of all, an act of God. This is emphasized, for example, by the words of one of the prayers in the Divine Liturgy which reads, "For you, Christ our God, are the Offerer and the Offered, the One who receives and is distributed." Also, as the clergy prepare to begin the Divine Liturgy, the deacon addresses the presiding bishop or presbyter with these words, "It is time for the Lord to act" (Ps. 118:126).

In the liturgy the Son and Word of God, Jesus Christ, is present to his people, fulfilling his promise to be in their midst when they gather together in his Name (Mt. 18:20). Moreover, as Origen put it, "Anyone who prays shares in the prayer of the Word of God, who is present even among those who do not know him and is not absent from anyone's prayer. The Son prays to the Father in union with the believer whose mediator he is. The Son of God is, in fact, the high priest of our offerings and our advocate with the Father. He prays for those who pray and pleads for those who plead."[15] God draws his people unto himself through the liturgy, in order to communicate to them the gifts of the age to come.

In the liturgy the eternal God, "the unfathomed deep beyond all, takes us to himself as a father his child. He admits us to an area of non-death... His sweetness invades our heart, we thirst for him, we long for all humankind to share this joy of ours, and we pray that all may be saved."[16]

Though he grows ever nearer to us in worship, God remains always the Other, hidden and inaccessible in his divine essence.[17] "The more the Inaccessible shares with us," writes Olivier Clement, "the more inaccessible he shows himself to be... The more unknown, the more he makes himself known."[18] This profound mystery of God's nearness and otherness – the manifestation and the veiling of his divine love, beauty, and holiness – is at the root of our insatiable desire to worship God and to enter into communion with him. The Psalmist is especially aware of these longings of the human heart; indeed the Psalter is replete with passages that refer to God as the proper object of human trust, as the only source of blessings and salvation, and as the very fullness of life. "When You said 'Seek my face,' my heart said to You, 'Your face, Lord, I will seek.' Do not hide Your face from me; do not turn Your servant away" (Ps. 27:8 – 9).

The heart of man, as St. Augustine was fond of saying, finds rest only in God. Our innate attraction to God – the deep yearning for that immaterial reality that is beyond all reason and all intelligence[19] – is rooted in the fact that we have been made in his image. As images, we become the resting-place of God, "τόπος καί ἀνάπαυσις Θεοῦ."[20] Thus, the ultimate truth about who we are as nature and as person is defined not simply by biological, social, economic, and political factors, but by the uncreated Archetype, Christ, "the image of the invisible God" (Col. 1:15).[21]

The liturgy allows us to experience a reality greater than ourselves and greater than death. It brings us before the beauty, glory, and unending life of God. It lifts us up and invites us to become imitators of God as far as possible. Moreover, it helps us to become what Scripture calls 'fellow workers' and reflections of the workings of God.[22] In the liturgy we discover and experience the love of God. Then the Spirit of God enables us to make our confessions of faith and to offer God joyful adoration, praise, and thanksgiving on account of his great goodness, holiness, and glory. He makes it possible for us to offer up petitions, intercessions, and supplications on account of God's tender mercy and compassion. The Spirit makes the reverential lamentations for our sins and transgressions flow forth from our souls, because in God we are certain to gain forgiveness on account of his boundless loving-kindness.

Exercising the priestly office through the liturgy

By drawing us unto himself through his salvific work, Christ has made us into kings and priests, that is to say, into a people who are under the rule of God and are mediators between him and the rest of humanity (Rev. 1:5– 6). Thus, at every Divine Liturgy we pray these words. "We also offer to You this spiritual worship for the whole world, for the holy, catholic, and apostolic Church, and for all those living in purity and holiness" (Anaphora of St. John Chrysostom).

The Church is composed of many members, who form one body, an organic unity of communion, in which, as St. John Chrysostom notes, each member has both a particular and a common activity.[23] The many members of the one Body are knitted together in love (Col. 2:2) and carry out their common activity, including worship, through their different functions, varied duties, and distinct responsibilities. From this perspective, everyone is vital to the liturgy, no one is useless, no one is a spectator, everyone has a role, because the liturgy is the work of all the people. Hence, all who constitute the Church are, by grace, God's own people, a holy nation, a chosen race, and a body of priests upon whom God has poured out his Spirit (1 Pt. 2:9).

The Spirit holds all the members of the Church together and confers upon them different but mutually interdependent gifts. The Spirit teaches them to pray properly (Rom. 8:26)[24] and empowers each of them, according to their order, to exercise the priestly office by proclaiming praises to Him who drew us out of darkness into his marvelous light and by offering up acceptable spiritual sacrifices through Jesus Christ (1 Pt. 2:5). In worship clergy and laity alike stand humbly before the Triune God to thank him for his gracious self-giving and empowering life poured out for the life of the world[25] and to entreat his steadfast love for the world that he might transform the earth and all that is within it, in order to bring about "new heavens and a new earth in which righteousness dwells" (2 Pt. 3:13).

We affirm that Jesus Christ is the one, true priest of the Church. Both the royal priesthood of all believers and the ministerial priesthood have their source in Christ the unique High Priest and Mediator of the New Covenant. The priestly ministry of Christ is perpetuated in the Church by the ministerial priesthood that exists in the three orders of bishop, presbyter, and deacon. This ministerial priesthood belongs to the very essence and structure of the Church. The clergy are set apart by ordination and are bestowed with the authority to lead, teach, and guide the people, to preside at the divine services, and to sanctify the lives of the people through the holy sacraments. The clergy, however, do not possess any individual power apart from or independent of the ministry of the laity. The clergy are members of the same Body, part of the People of God. Hence, every act of the clergy is performed not only on behalf of and for the people, but also with the people because no one order or person stands apart from or above the Church. While the clergy and the laity are both under the rule of God and both share equally the new life in Christ, the striking difference between them is that the clergy are set apart to offer the sacraments, maintain the unity of the community, teach and guarantee the Orthodox faith, supervise the disciplinary rules, and promote the philanthropic activities of the community through the exercise of servant leadership, an all-embracing pastoral concern, care, love, and solicitude for the people.

Through the liturgy, clergy and laity alike enter into an intimate personal relationship with the Triune God, and according to his promise, he comes to dwell in us and we in him so that we may experience a unity that surpasses all understanding, becoming one with him and one with one another (Jn. 14:23, 15:4, 17:21). Thus we pray at the Eucharist, "And unite us all to one another who become partakers of the one Bread and the Cup in the communion of the Holy Spirit" (Anaphora of St. Basil).

True worship draws its power from the Spirit of God. It is primarily an act of faith, the response of the heart to the unfathomable mystery of God's irresistible beauty and love with which he has embraced us through the incarnation of his Son and our Lord Jesus Christ. Hence, the liturgy through which we exercise our priestly vocation, each in and through his/her order, is always an offering in return (ἀντι προσφορά) given to God on account of the riches of his goodness, mercy, and love. At its deepest levels this offering in return is an act of kenosis, a willingness to lose one's life in order to gain it

(Mt. 16:28). This act of self-emptying finds its fullest expression in the Divine Liturgy, when, through the sacramental elements, we offer up our life in order to receive his, so that we may be filled with unfailing love and devotion for the Triune God, becoming unshakable in our fidelity and attention to the commandments, to the values of the Gospel, and to acts of mercy and kindness.

In the liturgy the Holy Spirit draws near to us to enliven us continually, both as persons and as community, that we may be united with the glorified body of Christ, in order to become like him. The Holy Spirit brings us into communion with Christ and forms Christ's mind in us. The Spirit makes possible our confession that Jesus Christ is Lord, the Son of God made flesh, the Savior of the world, and the unique revealer of God.[26]

True worship transforms us into a living sacrifice, that is to say, into persons who live for God, who do not conform to the passing and imperfect standards of this world full of spiritual apostasy and seductive schemes that produce barrenness and spiritual deadness (Rom. 12:1 – 2). The transformation we speak of is not external in nature but internal, a gift of God's indwelling Spirit. It is accomplished by two unequal but equally essential forces, divine grace and human will, and results in the renewal of the human heart, will, intellect, and mind.

The liturgy is a formative, restorative, and transformative experience

The liturgy constitutes what Susan Wood calls the 'formative environment,' which shapes our vision, our relationships and our knowing. She writes,

> Within the liturgy we come to know ourselves and God because the liturgy orders our relationships: my relationship to others within the body of Christ sacramentally constituted within the eucharist, my relationship to God as recipient of God's graciousness, my relationship to the world by being not only sent, but missioned and commissioned to live ethically within history what has been experienced in the metahistorical

time and space of the liturgy. In short, in the liturgy we do not acquire knowledge *about* God; we acquire knowledge *of* God.[27]

The liturgy is not so much an object of knowledge as it is a source of knowledge and understanding, precisely because it is determined by the faith of the Church. It is "grounded in that great vision of accomplished redemption, of that new intimacy of the redeemed man with the Redeemer, which is disclosed and ever re-enacted in the devotional encounter of members with the Head."[28]

The liturgy sets forth the Church's living and authentic tradition. Through the words, actions, and symbols of worship the faithful are continually exposed to the fundamental truths of the faith. The liturgy communicates to people the meaning and purpose of life and helps them to see, understand, interpret, and internalize both the tragedy of the human condition in its fallen state as well as the limitless expanse and potential of the new life in Christ offered freely to all. In this way the liturgy becomes an educative, formative experience, "the great school for Christian living and transforming force,"[29] "our first and best spiritual teacher."[30]

The liturgy is our window onto the spiritual world, our participation in the life of Christ, our fellowship with the Holy Spirit, and the foretaste of the things to come. The liturgy brings to light our failures and errors as it opens us up to the abundant mercies of God. It becomes the vehicle by which we supplicate and beseech God's tender love, express contrition, experience forgiveness, gain hope, reshape feelings, redirect thoughts, and strengthen our will for personal holiness.

Through the liturgy we are in communion with the holy ones of the faith, who have gone before us to their rest in God's eternal realms. The saints teach us about the perennial value and transforming power of the Gospel. We learn from them how to apply the great truths of the faith that the Church celebrates in her worship to our daily activities. Above all, we learn to recognize – as the saints did – the presence of God in the world, in the lives of people, and in the unfolding process of history. The saints came before God in joyful awe to converse with him and to worship him with love and adoration. Their passion for God teaches us the beauty, relevance, and power of prayer. Like the saints, we learn to be "the great celebrants of life," so that life itself is turned into a theology of fervent prayer.

The life of an Orthodox Christian is, in large measure, formed, fashioned, nourished, enriched and, above all, trans-formed by the liturgy. The liturgy, without doubt, is a formative environment. But it is also a restorative and trans-formative environment, in which the mind is illumined and the heart – the center of being and personality – is transfig-ured.

The liturgy is where we simultaneously begin – as well as develop and nurture – our intimate union with Christ and with his mystical Body, the Church. In the liturgy we en-counter Christ, the Archetype of the authentic human being, who has promised to raise us up at the last day (Jn. 6:40). The closer we draw to him the more we become a reflection of him. The clearer the image of Christ is in us, the more perfect we become, because perfection is nothing more than the realization of the purpose for which we have been made. And we have been made to be in Christ and to become like him by grace (Eph. 4:13).

The liturgy calls us to embrace freely the limitless love of God, to "commit ourselves and one another and our whole life to Christ our God,"[31] and to live a life of true piety, both thinking and doing those things that are pleasing to God.[32] In the liturgy we come to experience the radicality of the Gospel, the call to become a new creation. And this newness of life is a gift from God; not something we can accomplish through our own efforts, as noble as they may be.

The liturgy, like the whole of the Christian life, is not a 'fin-ishing school' that seeks to produce people with refined tastes and a good character. Rather, it is the place in which God works to change the very core of our being making us by grace what he is by nature (2 Pt. 1:4). And when this gift is joyfully accepted, as St. Ephraim the Syrian says, "Our mighty Lord gives to bodily creatures Fire and Spirit as food and drink." The Church is the environment in which salvation is apprehended. And the means by which we apprehend? The sacraments especially, and the whole of the Church's teaching, life, and liturgy.

The liturgy brings us to the threshold of another world

The liturgy brings us to the threshold of another world. Through it we reach and cross the ultimate frontier. We encounter the living God. We touch eternity and experience a new reality which transcends us. We enter into communion with the Holy One who alone has life. This communion graces us with the presence of the inexpressible beauty, the searing truth, the boundless love, the indescribable joy and peace, and the deathless life of the Triune God – Father, Son, and Holy Spirit. As a result of this profound relationship with the Author of life, we understand and experience life differently and are united dynamically in a new way to each other and to the world.

In the liturgy we meet Christ, the unique revealer of God (Jn. 1:18), the one who has the words of eternal life (Jn. 6:68). Through the texts, symbols, artistic forms, and ritual acts of the liturgy we remember the Christ-event. In theological language the term 'Christ-event' refers to the decisive moments of the earthly and risen life of Christ, from his incarnation through his passion, death, burial, to his resurrection, exaltation, heavenly intercession, and second glorious Coming. Through the liturgy we share truly in the reality of the Christ-event in a symbolic, iconic, and sacramental manner.[33] In the liturgy, as the ancients were fond of saying, Christ becomes our contemporary. He draws us into his salvific work and makes us to stand before God to bathe in the resplendent, sublime glory of his uncreated divine energies to become, by grace, "partakers of the divine nature" (2 Pt 1:4).

In worship Christ sets our heart on fire. It burns for God and for all of his creation. Worshipping in faith we come to the experience of Cleopas and the other Apostle who encountered the risen Lord on the road to Emmaus. "Now it came to pass, as he sat at table with them, that he took bread, blessed and broke it, and gave it to them. Then their eyes were opened and they knew him; and he vanished from their sight. And they said to one another, 'Did not our heart burn within us while he talked with us on the road, and while he opened the Scriptures to us?' (Lk. 24:30-32).

In Christ nothing remains commonplace and profane, since we – along with the cosmos – are destined for glory, the assured victory that awaits us in the eschaton. Humanity and the whole of the subhuman world – all of creation, once in a state of disorder and abnormality, subject to corruption, dissolution, and death as a result of the ancestral sin – have been liberated from the proclivity to decay by the resurrection of Christ. The liturgy and particularly the sacraments – which are the ἀρραβών, the betrothal, pledge, and guaranty of humanity and creation sharing in Christ's risen life – bear testimony to the fullness of redemption for all who put their faith in him (Rom. 8:11- 39).

The liturgy is a study of life

The liturgy both discloses and also places us within the mystery of God's salvation. In the liturgy we are given access by faith into divine grace, by which we are sanctified and made victors over sin and death. Thus, the prayer of the Church in all of its expressions grounds us in the confident hope of God's immeasurable love. It assures us of his mercy and of the forgiveness of our sins and transgressions. We can say, therefore, that "the liturgy is a set of stories, teachings, and ritual acts that comprise a vision of the good, and that have the power"[34] to help us become servants of redemption, by experiencing a radical conversion of the heart – metanoia, μετάνοια.

In his classic work, *The Shape of the Liturgy*, Dom Gregory Dix reminds us "the study of liturgy is above all a study of life." [35] Indeed, the liturgy is both a celebration of God's mighty acts in history as well as the story of humanity's struggle to live by the vision of life disclosed in the teachings, life, sufferings, resurrection, and glorification of Christ.

Like the Scriptures, the liturgy relates the story of God, about who he is and what he does for the life of the world. But it also tells us the story of who we are and of what God requires of us. The liturgy heightens our awareness of the profound mysteries of life as it increases the depth and breadth of the meaning and the purpose of human existence.

Through word, song, symbol, and ritual, the liturgy narrates the story of the two contrasting realities, the way of death and the way of life.[36] The way of death is the story of the "old man" – "τοῦ παλαιοῦ ἀνθρώπου" – our fallen and unredeemed humanity, which is burdened with the pervasive, seductive, deceptive, and contagious influence of sin that alienates, degrades, enslaves, and kills. It is the story of our vulnerabilities and of our mortality, of the bestial and the irrational forces within us that both plague us and blur the image of God in us. It is the story of our perverted liberty and our inner decadence. It is the story of our moral ambivalence through which all forms of injustice are rationalized and normalized. It is the story of our estrangement from God and our enslavement to the devil through the fear and the reality of death.

The liturgy recounts the sad story of our failed beginnings in Paradise when the progenitors of the race were led into rebellion and betrayed the freely given love of the Author of life (Gen. 3:1-19), which we call the primordial or original sin. The liturgy tells the story of that deadly seduction with all of its tragic consequences. The prayer of the Church confronts us with the universality of human moral failure and names all our collective and personal sins – spiritual, intellectual, and carnal – that estrange us from one another and from the intimate presence of God and make us into impostors.

Sin distorts the image of God in us and forfeits our communion with him. It is the product of a slothful, confused, negligent, and defiant spirit and of an incapacitated will that is reluctant to act decisively on those things that are true, noble, pure, just, good, and lovely. But beyond such personal indiscretions, frailties, and moral failures, there is the reality

of the enslavement of human nature to the Evil One; there is
the ontological condition of corruption and death from which
all personal sins are derived.[37] The Evil One, as the Scriptures attest, rules through the dominion and the fear of death
(Heb. 2:14–15). Christ, however, has healed our dreadful brokenness and tragic unfulfillment. Death has been swallowed
up in victory and life has been liberated (1 Cor. 15:54–55).
Christ, risen from the dead, has taken 'captivity captive' (Ps.
68:19).

Thus, the liturgy tells another story too, the story of God's
glorious victory over his adversaries. It is the story of his
persistent, unfailing providential love. It is also the story of
humanity's response to God's love, manifested as acts of repentance and spiritual vigilance, through which God grants
us forgiveness, reconciliation, redemption, liberation, sanctification, and glorification. The liturgy sings the songs of
divine love and deliverance, of lives transfigured by grace,
and of the mystical experience of the age to come, when all
holiness and righteousness will be fully realized.

The liturgy reminds us that we are not alone in the per-
plexities and complexities of daily life. Christ is with us
always, even to the end of the age (Mt. 28:20). By his death
and resurrection he has overcome the principalities, the powers, and the rulers of the darkness of this age, making us
able to stand against the wiles of the devil (Eph. 6:11–12). In
the liturgy God pours out his Spirit upon his people, so that
they may share in the victory of his Son, our Lord Jesus Christ,
over corruption, sin, and death.

The liturgy enlivens our ecclesial identity

The liturgy recounts and celebrates Christ's salvific work.
Through it the indwelling Spirit of God incorporates us into
Christ and into his new community, the Church, so that we
may appropriate the gifts of redemption and be continually
transformed into a new creation.

Once Christ has liberated us from the consequences of the
primordial sin (i.e., corruption and death), the Spirit supplies us with a new interior principle, mode of existence, and

identity: the ecclesial. As members of a body – the Church – that transcends all manner of biological and social exclusiveness, we subsist in a manner that differs from the biological and historical.[38] In our ecclesial identity, as Metropolitan John Zizioulas says, we exist not as we are, but as that which we will become, not as a result of an evolution of the human race, but as the result of the victory of Christ.[39]

The liturgy tells us that the Christian life is a work in progress. It is a life that is set on things above and is continually moving from weakness to strength, from darkness to light, from death to life, and from glory to glory (2 Cor. 3:18). The Christian is thus anchored in the mystery of God's salvific activity, in God's self-communication in Jesus Christ, in whom his true life is hidden (Col. 3:3). This mystery, however, "is not a puzzle to be solved, but a liberating power of life to be received."[40] And this transfiguring power is none other than the life of Christ in us (Gal. 2:20), which releases us from the bondage of sin, corruption, and death and fashions us into a new creation (Col. 3:1-17).

When Christ is in us, the law of love – the self-giving, unconditional, sacrificial agape of God – becomes the new inner principle, source, and guide of our life. We come to experience this love as the transfiguring power that tears us from our weak earthbound existence, which is under the sway of sin for the fear of death. It brings us under the influence of the Holy Spirit, who is the source of life and the promise of future blessings and glory.

The Spirit – always present yet always anticipated – abides in the Church. He bestows on us the gift of sonship through baptism and empowers us to overcome the debilitating fear of death and the sinful inclinations and desires of the flesh – the irrational, degrading, and divisive forces of sin – to make us children of God and heirs of his Kingdom. At every liturgical event the Spirit is present, thus initiating a dramatic episode of salvation for those whose hearts are afire with the love of Christ.

The tension between the present and the future

Through worship the Church moves beyond all human conventionalities. She realizes her true identity and actualizes herself as the bride and body of Christ. She enters continually into an intimate union with Christ, who is her head, the Mediator of the new covenant and the High Priest of the good things to come (Heb. 9:11, 15). In the liturgy the Church gazes upon God and anticipates the messianic age when he will fully dwell with his people: "This is God's dwelling among men. He shall dwell with them and they shall be his people and he shall be their God who is always with them" (Rev. 21:3).[41]

The Church, in her unity of life with Christ, is oriented towards the eschaton, the end times. She draws her essential self-understanding from them. For this reason the end times both order and fuel the Church's life and ministry, her diakonia to the world.[42] However crucial the eschaton is, it must also be remembered that the Church is rooted in a decisive past event, "which initiated a status of union with God previously unknown,"[43] the incarnation of the Son and Word of God who came and dwelt among us.

Our age is an age of 'dual polarity.'[44] We look back to the central events of the Gospel and forward to the Parousia of the Lord, to the final consummation when "we shall always be with the Lord" (1 Thes. 4:17). The definitive revelation of God's reign began in Christ Jesus our Lord, though its full effect lies in the future. The kingdom of God is already here. The end times have been inaugurated through the incarnation, resurrection, and glorification of Christ. The first fruits (Rom. 8:23) and pledge (2 Cor. 1:22) of the Messianic benefits are already the possession of the faithful.

This fact provides the Church with the courage to endure the long haul of history, to struggle to remain steadfast in the faith, and to "rejoice always" (1 Thes. 5:16), regardless of the trials, tragedies, circumstances, ambiguities, and contradictions of life. Yet, in spite of this great hope, the faithful are fully aware of the apostolic admonition, "Be sober, be vigilant; because your adversary the devil walks about like a roaring lion, seeking whom he may devour" (1 Pt. 5:8).

The liturgy always brings the present and the future into dynamic tension. It holds together the vertical and the horizontal lines of Church life, of our union with God, with each other and with the world.

We are anchored in the realities of God's kingdom. Yet we are not blind to the burdens, tragedies, and calamities of this life. Neither are we blind to discordant tensions, the moral struggles, and the ethical conflicts that afflict men and women of faith who are attempting to live out the demands of the Gospel in a world that is indifferent or even hostile to it. True worship, surely, places us before the limitless love of God. It also takes up the whole range of human frailties that tempt us and make us distort and betray the Christian faith and life. It is unafraid to name all of our inabilities to live in accordance with the demands of the Gospel. This dimension of the liturgy is especially liberating because it keeps every kind of triumphalism at bay and all false righteousness in check.

The liturgy exhorts us to imitate God's love and holiness

Worship, as we have already noted, commends and forms normative patterns of affection and virtue. Worshippers are called to be holy, as God is holy. As Saliers tells us:

> On the other hand, our intentions and actions fall short, and our affections are rarely pure motives for well-doing in actual everyday life. But just at this crucial point, Christian liturgy in its texts, symbols, and ritual acts recognizes this gap, offering truthful repentance and reconciliation.[45]

The liturgy, as an iconic and sacramental enactment of the mystery of salvation, addresses the many elements and features that constitute the mystery of the human being both as nature and as person. The liturgy helps bring clarity of purpose to one's thoughts, emotions, motivations, decisions, and actions.

When we begin to experience the Church's worship at its deepest levels, we come to know that the lingering tragic elements of our fallen existence are being defeated and healed continuously by the grace of God, in order to make us capable of love, freedom and life. Enlivened by the Holy Spirit, we come to realize that being is life, and that life is communion, and that communion is love.[46] What we see, hear, say, and do at worship has serious implications for our life after the liturgy, both as a community and as individuals.[47]

The liturgy exhorts us to think of and to do good things by imitating the boundless love of God. The dispositions of humble love, gratitude, and honor that we bear in our hearts towards the God of our salvation are also due to his creation. The liturgy tells us that our possibilities for life and for goodness are limitless, because God, in whose image we are made, is immortal and infinite in his love.

As the liturgy has the power to form and transform the lives of human beings, so it has the power to shape the life, enliven the mission, and illumine the activities of the worshipping community. "Celebrating the liturgy," wrote Mark Searle, "should train us to recognize justice and injustice when we see it. It serves as a basis for social criticism by giving us a criterion by which to evaluate the events and structures of the world. But not just the world 'out there' that stands under the judgment of God's justice, sacramentally realized in the liturgy. The first accused is the Church itself, which, to the degree that it fails to recognize what it is about, eats and drinks condemnation to itself" (1 Cor. 11:29).[48]

The Church must not only ascend to God, she must also descend into the depths of ordinary life, into the suffering of the world with the settled confidence about the transformation that is to come (Rom 8:19-21). In the words of Father Alexander Schmemann, "The Church must go down to the ghetto, into the world in all its reality. But to save the world from social injustices, the need first of all is not to go down to its miseries, as to have a few witnesses in this world to its possible ascension."[49]

The liturgy is a dynamic event. Consequently, it implies a sense of action and a mission to the world by a people who have experienced the love of God "as a movement from death to life, from injustice to justice, from violence to peace, from hatred to love, from vengeance to forgiveness, from selfishness to sharing, and from division to unity."[50]

Learning to love, know, and live the liturgy

The deepest and most personal of human experiences begin in the heart, with the more responsive and emotional reactions of the intelligent, reasoning self. We are accustomed in modern speech to equating the heart with emotions and feelings. In the Old Testament, however, in the Hebrew idiom, the heart was considered as the organ of reasoning, the seat of intellectual and moral life, of memory and understanding, but of emotion as well, since it is capable of love, grief, suffering, etc. Likewise, in the Orthodox theological and spiritual tradition, the heart is more than the physical organ which is so central to human life. The heart has an all-embracing significance. More than the seat of emotions and feelings, the heart is the spiritual center of the human being's deepest and truest self. The heart is everything that comprises the human person and much more. The heart is the powerhouse that drives our physical, emotional, intellectual, and spiritual life.

The spiritual intellect (νοῦς) dwells in the heart and is its eye. Unlike reason – the analytical and conceptualizing faculty – the spiritual intellect comprehends reality directly. Self-awareness and the conscience dwell in the heart. From the heart come evil thoughts, wicked intentions, and impure desires (Mk. 7:20-23) but also every good and holy thought, desire, and intention (Lk.6:45 and Ezek. 11:19-20). The heart contains untold hidden treasures, and above all, as someone once said, "the real but unapprehended presence of God." The heart has unfathomable depths. The mystery of the union between the divine and the human is achieved and perfected in it.

Emotions often precede understanding. We can say, therefore, that one feels worship before understanding it. Its beauty attracts and moves the soul before one seeks to understand it in all its depth and wonder. What come first are not the lucid and profound explanations of the liturgy – crucial as they are – but the attractiveness, the clarity, the transparency, and the splendor of the ritual in all its expressions, celebrated in faith with solemnity, earnestness, ardor, and joy.

The gathering of the Church for worship is an event much like the epiphanic experience of Moses when he ascended Mt. Horeb (Ex. 3:1-17) and of the three disciples on Mt. Tabor who witnessed the Transfiguration of Christ (Mt. 17:1-8). Moses was attracted to the mountaintop by the remarkable sight of the bush that was burning but not consumed. There, by the burning bush, he came into the presence of God and conversed with him. There he found light, the purpose and the meaning of his life. There he was transformed and became a servant of redemption. Like Moses, the disciples who witnessed the Transfiguration of Christ heard the voice of God and conversed with the Lord. They had a glimpse of the uncreated light of Divinity and proclaimed joyously, " Lord, it is good for us to be here" (Mt. 17:4).

Now, it would be wrong to think that every Christian in every instance experiences the Church's liturgy, in all of its manifestations and expressions, with the intensity described above. Such an assumption fails to take into account the limitations and frailties of human life and the fluctuations the worshipper experiences in his/her spiritual life. We are all subject to the alternations of dryness and inspiration, of dispiritedness and illumination.

The liturgy of the Church presents us with a superb ideal that many times is inadequately realized. Nonetheless, because it is through the liturgy that we live and breathe our Christian faith and reaffirm our ultimate identity, purpose, and destiny, both as persons and as Church, we are obliged to exert every effort of body and soul to acquire a liturgical mind and a prayerful spirit. Hence, the liturgy – in all of its varied components – must not be simply admired and honored, as one admires and honors a cherished heirloom or museum piece. The liturgy must be loved, studied, analyzed, learned, and, above all, lived. This 'living' of the liturgy constitutes the essence and the meaning of liturgical renewal, which, in turn, is the mother of genuine liturgical reform.

2

The Nature and Goal of Liturgical Piety

Our ultimate destiny – entering into a personal
relationship with the living God

God called all things out of nothing into being. He created
the heavens and the earth and everything that is in them. He
made us out of dust, animating and constituting us into living beings, through the breath of life that he breathed into
our nostrils (Gen. 2:7; 1 Cor. 15:47). Outwardly – biologically
and chemically – we are similar to all other living creatures,
which, like us, have the breath of life (Gen. 1:30) and have
been endowed with a certain logic, consciousness, and conscience, be it to a lesser level and varying degrees.[51]

In the very depths of our being, however, we sense that
there is something radically different about us, something
that separates human beings from all other creatures. We are
conscious of a certain grandeur that cannot be explained even
by the most thorough examination of the matter that constitutes our bodies. We sense that we are more than the
wondrous assortment of material, chemical, biological, and
other factors of which our bodies are made. We sense that
we are more than our rational, inquiring, and creative mind
through which we become aware of self. We sense instinc-
tively that the simple creativity of our collective
consciousness is not entirely responsible for the art, science,
and institutions of our varied cultures. If our grandeur is not
to be found in these marvelous things, where then does it
lie; what separates us from the rest of the creatures that God
made; what makes us different and distinct?

Whatever knowledge we may gain about ourselves
through the scientific examination of the untold wonders of
our minds and bodies and of the unfathomable depths of

23

our psyche, it will not explain sufficiently or exhaust fully the mystery of who we are as nature and as person because we are more than the sum of our knowledge. We have been made for something greater than the precarious existence of this world; for something more than conventional morality; and for something beyond the dread finality of death. We long deeply for an encounter with the holy, for an experience of the eternal, for personal union with our Creator. The grandeur of the human being lies not in one's magnificent physical and intellectual powers but in the conscious longing for and pursuit of an intimate personal relationship with the living God. Our hearts, as St. Augustine observed, remain restless until they rest in the presence of God.

This restlessness for God defines the human being's ultimate 'ecstasy,' the movement out of one's self and the desire to reach out for infinite possibilities. More importantly, in God, the human being receives the gift of personhood, which constitutes the total fulfillment of being. In God we discover, by grace, the ultimate truth of our personal unique identity, the deepest self, which is created in God's image and likeness.[52] On the level of the deepest self or the heart, where wisdom and understanding rest and moral decisions are made, we experience the mystery of freedom as love, a love that must be learned from him who alone is love, the Trinitarian God (1 Jn. 4:8).[53]

According to the Christian view of things, as explained by the Greek Fathers, we are radically different from all other creatures not because of our incomparable intelligence or wondrous bodies but because, unlike all other creatures, we have been made in the image of God, a reflection of his own perfect image which is Christ (Col. 1:15-17). Christ is our Archetype and model, our beginning and our end. He defines our true humanity. This great gift, as Panayiotis Nellas says, is at the same time a goal set before us – a possession – but also a destiny, since it really constitutes our being, but only in potentiality.[54] To fulfill all that is most sublime and authentic in our personal embodied existence we must attain "to the measure of the stature of the fullness of Christ" (Ephes. 4:13).

To be complete – which is to say to be an authentic embodied personal existence – we must choose to "bear the image of the heavenly Man" (1 Cor. 15:49). St. Maximos the Confessor describes this crucial choice as follows:

> God in his goodness, creating every soul to his image, brings it into being to be self-moving. Each one (soul), then, deliberately either chooses honor or accepts dishonor by its own deeds... The soul develops according to its free will into either wax because of its love for God or into mud because of its love for matter. Thus, just as by nature the mud is dried out by the sun and the wax is automatically softened, so also every soul which loves matter and the world and has fixed its mind far from God is hardened as mud according to its free will and by itself advances to its perdition, as did Pharaoh. However, every soul, which loves God, is softened as wax, and receiving divine impressions and characters it becomes the dwelling place of God in the Spirit.[55]

The deep longing for the presence of God and the conscious movement towards our Archetype ultimately define our humanity and make us an epiphany of God's rule on earth.[56] The grandeur of man, therefore, lies in his God-given desire to exceed, to transcend the limitations of his creatureliness, and to acquire absolute freedom – not simply for himself but for the benefit of all creation – in his communion with the eternal God who made him in his image and likeness. Of course, as we know, absolute freedom is a divine attribute.[57] Human beings, as created beings, are not absolutely free. They are limited by the possibilities given them. Human beings can choose what they like but they cannot avoid the fact of 'givenness' that limits their freedom, even of choice.

Nonetheless, human beings manifest in so many ways a deep desire for absolute freedom – to reach for infinite possibilities, to transcend the boundaries of creaturehood, to achieve communion with God – a desire that in fact distinguishes them from the animals. The drive for absolute freedom is God-given; it is a manifestation of the image in which man was made. Through it he carries all of creation to its transcendence.

The primal wound of the original sin

Man retains his claim to absolute freedom even in his negative attitude to God, albeit – as Metropolitan John Zizioulas says – against his own good and that of creation.[58] Indeed, man is capable of using his freedom for the good or for the bad. Our creativity is ambivalent, capable of great things but also of ruinous deeds and diabolical acts. Despite the unparalleled successes that humanity has had in the arts and sciences, its history is also identified with unspeakable wickedness and is filled with countless failures and tragedies, lost opportunities, and unfulfilled potentialities and promises, both personal and collective.

However strong our claim to freedom is, we are also conscious of another reality that rages in our soul, the hidden psychic drama that places limits on all our claims. Our inner world is beset by a profound sense of alienation and failure. It is in a state of continuous unrest, deeply wounded by the hereditary cosmic corruption that resulted from the revolt against God by Adam and Eve, the Progenitors of the race. In the language of our theology we call this prideful and corruptive revolt against God the 'Fall' and the inherited state of estrangement, discontent, and confusion the 'original sin.' In our deepest heart we are conscious of the dreadful consequences of the Fall and the deleterious effects of the original sin, even though we are unable to comprehend them fully. We sense that life is out of focus and out of joint.

As a result of the sin of our Progenitors, the image of God with which we have been endowed is broken, disfigured, and distorted. The tyrannizing power of death and corruption holds sway over us. Terrified of our mortality, we are 'subject to life long bondage' to the devil who has the power of death (Heb. 2:14-15). We are driven by an arrogant, demanding subjectivity, the irrational desire to be the center of the world, to possess all power, knowledge, and life.[59] The will to self-preservation with all of its negative impulses and irrational attitudes beclouds our judgment, leads us to wrong decisions and destructive choices, and betrays the promise and joy of self-giving love. An egotistical, rebellious, prideful, and self-centered spirit haunts and consumes us. The pervasive influence of sin subverts and destabilizes the God-given drive for absolute freedom, real transcendence, and authentic love. In such an unredeemed state, the desire for transcendence, deification, and the absolute union with God remains an elusive promise and an unfulfilled possession.

Christ – Church – Deification

However, that which man has failed to do, God accomplished through the incarnation of his Son and Word, Jesus Christ. The primal wound of original sin was healed and the absolute union with God was achieved once for all through God's own initiative. God himself bridged the essential gulf between created and uncreated nature through the incarnation of the Word and Son of God, our Lord and Savior Jesus Christ. Christ, the God-Man (Θεάνθρωπος), has two perfect natures, the divine and the human, united 'without confusion, without change, indivisibly and inseparably' in the one person of God the Word, according to the famous doctrinal formula of the Fourth Ecumenical Synod. Christ, "who Himself bore our sins in his body on the tree [cross], that we might die to sin and live to righteousness" (1 Peter 2:24), destroyed the deadly tyranny of the devil. He raised us up again. And healing all our psychic, moral, and emotional wounds, he has not ceased doing everything until he has led us to heaven and granted us his Kingdom to come.[60]

Christ takes us unto himself and renders us members of his Body, the Church (Eph. 5:30). And the Church is 'the place of our deification.'[61] It is the milieu in which we apprehend salvation and share in the mighty, salvific, and life-giving acts of Christ. Through prayer and the sacraments "Christ settles himself in [our] heart – the center of [our] being... [As we] progress in prayer [and] live according to the holy commandments, [we] are made worthy of divine grace and taste the sweetness of God's communion."[62] United with the glorified human nature of Christ through the holy sacraments, we continuously fulfill our ultimate destiny, to become gods by grace, to transcend all the limitations of our creatureliness, a gift made possible through the grace and love of God.

Through the liturgy the Triune God – Father, Son and Holy Spirit – is actively present to the Church and to each of her faithful members, that all may discover their true vocation, which is to transcend the limitations of creaturehood, to share in the plenitude of divine life and joy, and to fill their lives with hope, purpose, and meaning. In the Church we realize the ultimate purpose of life. We die continuously to everything that is old, corrupt, and moribund. We become a new creation and taste the gifts of the age to come. We put on Christ, in order to become like him.

Appropriating the saving grace of God

God, hidden in us, reveals himself to the heart that is open to discovering him. The quest for a personal relationship with the Triune God is complex and multiform. We encounter him in many ways, on various levels, and in different circumstances. Mostly however, Orthodox Christians tend to live their faith essentially and especially through worship. The liturgy becomes the essential environment – though not the exclusive one – through and in which we come to understand, respond, and relate to God's redemptive economy, that is to say, his all-embracing providential love for the world.

It is not difficult then to see why the liturgy is so central to Christian life and identity. It constitutes the primary and fundamental way by which faithful persons appropriate the saving grace of God and share in the life and faith of the ecclesial community. The liturgy nourishes and enlivens our relationship with the Author of life, who becomes our sole refuge and hope.

The liturgy also molds our inner world and our outward actions, inasmuch as it reminds us that in Christ humanity has been fashioned anew and is empowered by grace to fulfill the plans of God for the world. In the liturgy we learn what it means to be Christian and we are enabled by grace to conduct our lives accordingly. The rebellious spirit deeply ingrained in the human heart is transformed through faith and life is liberated. The steadfast love of God and the abundance of his compassion lead us in the path of righteousness that we may dwell in the house of the Lord forever (Psalm 22/23). In the liturgy we experience the ultimate break-through: God is present to his people; eternity touches our finiteness. Our soul rests in God.

The meaning and aims of liturgical piety

Prayer is the fundamental activity of the Christian life. Liturgical piety is based on this fact, inasmuch as it understands the liturgy as the unique way in which Christ's saving acts are always remembered, renewed, and partaken of by the Church and her members. Liturgical piety recognizes worship – in both its corporate and personal expression – as the distinctive Christian mode of existence and as the main source of spiritual direction, because in its structure, content, and style Orthodox worship is replete with biblical themes, doctrinal teachings, and moral exhortations. Worship is, in fact, the Church's primary spiritual guide and teacher as it provides the worshipper with a fundamental understanding of the deeper meanings of the Scriptures and of the life of faith.

Liturgical piety is formed, nourished, sustained, and enriched by the prayer of the Church in its several expressions and forms, and by the objective content of the Orthodox faith. Orthodox worship springs from the full understanding of the Christ event – the Mystery of God's creative and redeeming love – from both the highest sources of Tradition that contribute to the real understanding of the Mystery, and from the human response to the Mystery, that of praise for his awe-inspiring majesty and our thanksgiving for his loving compassion and mercy. The Mystery, which was once for all delivered to the saints (Jude 3), is permanently embodied in the liturgy: in the sacraments, especially in Baptism and the Eucharist, in the Daily Office, and in the feasts of the liturgical year.[63]

The aim of liturgical piety is to help nourish the spiritual life of Christians by making the prayer of the Church an integral part of their lives and by helping them navigate the various levels of the spiritual landscape as they seek to perfect their lives in faith.

The degrees or stages of prayer

In conformity with the spiritual tradition of Orthodoxy, the Christian at prayer – whether it is personal or corporate – through quiet attentiveness is always aware of the degrees or stages of prayer, which in the teaching of the Church are usually referred to as the prayer of the lips, of the mind, and of the heart. The Christian is always mindful to turn the prayer of the lips into the prayer of the mind, and to make the prayer of the mind into the prayer of the heart. In other words, all prayer must grow increasingly inward: recited consciously and meaningfully with one's whole being.

Prayer is not mindless and thoughtless speech, a mere repetition of words and sounds that have no meaning. Intelligible and intelligent speech is characteristic of the human being. Hence, every prayer is first of all oral. It is bodily speech or the prayer of the lips, through which one gives expression to the thoughts and emotions of one's inner world. The prayer of the lips, whether it is the recitation of the formal prayers of the Church or other extemporaneous prayers, is usually accompanied by bodily postures that underscore the mood of the prayer, such as making the sign of the cross, standing, the raising of hands, the bowing of the head, kneeling, or prostrations.

However, to be truly effective the prayer of the lips must ascend to the mind, which is to say, it must become a conscious act, part of one's mental awareness. Unless the mind is centered on prayer, it wanders off into any number of irrelevant things. Hence, the mind must be trained to pay attention the to the words of prayer. The more intense the prayer becomes mentally, the greater its efficacy.

To be complete, however, the prayer of the mind must descend into the heart, into the very depths of one's being.[64] When the prayer of the mind is gathered into the interior parts of the self, in the innermost chambers of one's being and penetrates the conscience, the whole person – body, soul and spirit – is engaged and feels the presence of God's Spirit, who "himself makes intercession for us with groanings which cannot be uttered" (Rom. 8:26). In this way the liturgy becomes more than words, sounds, and rituals. It becomes an illumination of the mind and heart, an inward journey, and a deep attraction towards God, out of which all authentic prayer is born.

Levels of the spiritual life

If liturgical piety helps us to decipher the presence of God in the everyday experiences of life through prayer (Phil. 4:4-9) and the practice of philanthropy (Matt. 25:31-46), it also helps us to understand and engage the spiritual life and learn to traverse its landscape and pass through its several levels.[65]

The liturgy helps us to know that the pure of heart can obtain the vision of God from now, from here on earth, even though the fullness will be given in the age to come. The liturgy makes us aware of God's inaccessibility, transcendence, otherness, and holiness. It also makes us aware of his accessibility and closeness; aware of the astonishing, radical, transforming love with which he embraces us, a love that is given freely to all who would accept it. God never ceases to be the friend of all, even of those who hate him or are indifferent to him. He desires that all might be saved; that all might partake of the divine nature. The liturgy reminds us that on the last day all will come before God, the righteous judge. Then the just and the sinners alike will see and experience God. The just will see him as light and experience him as life, while the sinners will see him as eternal fire; they will be cast out into outer darkness where there will be weeping and gnashing of teeth (Matt. 8:12).

The spiritual life is engaged on different levels. There are people who relate to God out of fear, others out of need and expected rewards, and still others out of sheer love. God is present to all his people on whatever spiritual level they may be and provides them – to the capacity they are able to bear it – with a vision of the Kingdom which is to come.

Some Christians relate to God as slaves (δοῦλοι) in the narrowest sense. They accept his will and obey his commandments and do what is required of them out of fear, out of the impending judgment, of the wrath to come (Matt. 3:7-12). But the spiritual life is not managed only through fear. Other Christians enter into the spiritual warfare as hirelings (μισθωτοί), as laborers or as soldiers in the pay of the king, as people who give themselves to God as for hire, accepting the responsibilities of the Christian life for the sake of reward (Lk. 6:35). Unlike the slave who acts out of fear, the hireling acts out of duty and obligation. He joins the ranks of God's army to wage battle against the passions, against the evil forces of darkness that are in him and around him in the fallen world, because he is assured of God's faithfullness to fulfill his promise to pay him his just reward (1 Cor. 3:8; 2 John 8).

But greater perfection is expected of us. To be complete one must become, by grace, not only a slave or a hireling but also, and above all, a child of God, a brother – by adoption – and a friend of Christ (φίλος Χριστοῦ). As a friend Christians accept God's call with gladness of heart and act in all things out of love for the Master, who has loved them first (1 John 4:10). Friendship with God is unconditional because God's love is unreserved, free, and absolute. Friends of Christ enjoy a deep, intimate personal relationship with him and come to know the hidden truths of the Gospel. They obey the commandments out of love, expecting nothing in return. "You are my friends if you do whatever I command you. No longer do I call you servants, for a servant does not know what his master is doing; but I have called you friends, for all things that I heard from my Father I have made known to you" (John 15:14-15).

Embracing Christ as faithful servants

The beauty of God is beyond description. His holiness is awesome. Before the greatness of his righteousness we find ourselves always wanting, aware of our deficiencies and conscious of our sinfullness. Therefore, we approach him with fear and trepidation. We stand before him humbly in awe of his majesty and power and submit ourselves to him as slaves or servants. When we submit ourselves to Christ, we no longer belong to ourselves but to the Holy Spirit, the divine Fire within us who purifies our heart purging it of all vainglory and self-conceit.[66] Whoever desires God must first become a slave of God. He must deny himself (Mk. 8:34); he must overcome his delusions of self-sufficiency by renouncing the false values of the fallen world and the influences of its culture, habits, and addictions.

Because God's majesty is beyond our endurance, we are always 'slaves' before him. Indeed, there is no greater name or sweeter identity – beside our given name – than to be called a slave or servant of God. In fact, in every sacramental act and in every prayer made on our behalf the priest addresses us as "the servant ($\delta o\hat{v}\lambda o\varsigma$) of God (Name)." This relationship, however, should not be construed as servitude and bondage because we enter into it freely. God is not a cruel taskmaster, but a loving Father, gentle and lowly in heart, a lover and a friend of all. His yoke is easy and his burden is light (Matt. 11:29-30). In fact, as St. Nicholas Cabasilas puts it, God "possesses us by a double right, as slaves whom he has made his children."[67]

Since the condition for entering the Kingdom is to put on Christ, the ultimate goal of the spiritual life is to embrace Christ and be like Christ. God, who is plenteous in mercy and boundless in love, has imprinted his righteousness, goodness, and holiness on us whom he made after his image, who is Christ. The spiritual life born of and in the liturgy is none other than the actualization of our union, through faith, with Christ crucified and risen. And this union consists of an infinite ascent towards fullness that is never obtained, inasmuch as the life of God is inexhaustible.

The ultimate end of the spiritual life is for each one – according to his capacity and the grace given to him – to make the union with Christ an abiding condition of life, so that he may hear in the deepest recesses of his heart the words that Christ spoke to St. Symeon the New Theologian, "I am God

who became man for your sake. And since you have sought
me with your whole soul, this is why from now on you will
be my brother, my co-heir, my friend."[68]

Four activities

The spiritual tradition of the Church also tells us that worship does not exist in isolation. First of all, worship is enacted
within the faith community and, secondly, it is intimately
linked to three other activities that are also essential to a
meaningful and vibrant interior life, namely, *ascesis, watchfulness, and philanthropy.*

These four activities – worship, ascesis (spiritual exercise
or discipline through which we acquire dispassion, the state
of reintegration, and spiritual freedom), watchfulness (vigilance or spiritual sobriety), and the practice of charity
(philanthropy) – that form the basis for a rich interior life are
founded on a certain ethos that was especially characteristic
of the early Church. This ethos emphasizes the eschatological
nature and character of Christian worship, faith, and life.

The eschatological ethos of liturgical piety

In the early Church, Christian life and worship were
marked by a deep sense of wakefulness and expectation. All
of life drew its identity from and was illumined and judged
by the eschaton – the end times. The Church at prayer sought
to prepare the faithful for the 'risen life' while simultaneously
making that life a living reality in this present age, especially
through the sacraments. The faithful experienced the Church
both as the visible, historical community of those who abide
in Christ, and in whom he himself dwells by the Holy Spirit,
and as an organism of divine grace that draws its identity
from the Kingdom of God, bearing witness to the new life
disclosed in Jesus Christ.

In the early centuries the worship of the Church emphasized the soteriological value of the Christ event more than
its historical framework.[69] Thus, the liturgy stressed the cosmic significance and the theological dimensions of the 'once
for all' more than the historical fact upon which it was based.
The great feasts of the Church, as Anton Baumstark has

shown, are celebrations of saving events rooted in history but also expressions of fundamental theological truths through which we come to know the will and plan of God for the salvation of the world.[70] For the early Christians the great feasts of the Church, as Father Schmemann says, were more than mere historical commemorations. They were first and last "the entry of the Church into the lasting reality created by Christ through his death and resurrection." [71] And so, as Robert Taft notes,

> Christmas is not just about coming to Bethlehem, but about the coming of Christ to me, and about my going out to others. And Easter is not about the empty tomb in Jerusalem 2000 years ago, but about the reawakening here and now of my baptismal death and resurrection in Christ... The festal cycle is but one facet of the life of the Church, one way of expressing and living the mystery of Christ that is radically one in all aspects of its Christian expression.[72]

Essentially, the function of the liturgy is to make the Church that which she really is, the presence in this world of the Kingdom to come. In worship the faithful become more than witnesses to the saving events of sacred history. They are participants in the new life that has resulted from God's saving activity. As Jean Danielou has said,

> The Christian faith has only one object, the mystery of Christ dead and risen. But this unique mystery subsists under different modes: it is prefigured in the Old Testament, it is accomplished historically in the earthly life of Christ, it is contained in the mystery of the sacraments, it is lived mystically in souls, it is accomplished socially in the Church, it is consummated eschatologically in the heavenly kingdom... The whole of Christian culture consists in grasping the links that exist between Bible and liturgy, Gospel and eschatology, mysticism and liturgy.[73]

As truth is not merely a philosophical proposition but a Person (Jn. 14:6), so too, the resurrection and the eschaton are not future events to be realized at some distant time and place, but instead a Person, Jesus Christ (Jn. 11:25-26). Whoever is in Christ has already passed from death into life (Jn. 5:24), for the mission of the Son of God is to give life to those who believe.

The early Church was not indifferent to history, and neither are the prayers of the Church void of references to the events of sacred history. This is especially evident in the various priestly prayers that are filled with anamnestic material. Indeed, God's promises and mighty acts in history are not simply remembered, but they also become the point of departure for most petitions and supplications. God is sure to hear the prayers of his people, because he is certain to fulfill his promises (Ps. 64/65).

Interest in time and eternity, history and eschatology have been part of the fabric of Christian life from the beginning. After all, our faith and hope are anchored in sacred history, in the mighty acts of God enacted in the unfolding process of the world's history. Time is always important to the Church, but it is viewed from an eschatological perspective because the end times have already been inaugurated in Christ Jesus. God is now present to his creation in a new and distinctive way through his abiding presence in the Church, "Lo, I am with you always, even to the end of the age" (Mt. 28:20). By his personal incursion into human history through the incarnation, as Father Georges Florovsky notes,

> God is now guiding his people as it were from the inside, and no more from the outside... (The) mysterious presence of Christ – in the Church and within the world – has been inaugurated in history by a sovereign intervention of God, by a decisively revelatory 'earthquake,' to use the bold expression of St. Gregory the Theologian. The acknowledgement of the Presence (of Christ) is inseparably coupled with the memory of the Past. This paradoxical coincidence of Past and Present constitutes the distinctive and unique character of Christian memory, which reaches its culmination in the Eucharistic anamnesis or commemoration.[74]

The saving nature of certain historical events have made it possible for us to taste here and now the wonders of God's Kingdom, which is yet to come in glory. The purpose of all creation and history has been realized in the hypostatic union of the God-Man (Θεάνθρωπος), Jesus Christ. The promise is already a possession of those who live by faith in the Son of God. And the liturgy is the accomplishment of the good news, the manifestation of the transforming work of the Triune God upon the world. The prayer of St. Symeon the Translator (ὁ Μεταφραστής), who lived in the latter part of the 10th century, provides us with an eloquent example of how a person of faith takes possession of the benefits of Christ's saving work. The prayer is included in the 'Service of Holy Communion –᾽Ακολουθία τῆς Θείας Μεταλήψεως' found the Horologion and the Ieratikon.[75] It reads as follows:

O Lord the only pure and incorruptible, who in the ineffable mercy of your love toward humankind did assume our nature, being incarnate by the Holy Spirit of the Virgin Mary, by the good will of the eternal Father; O Jesus Christ, Divine Wisdom, Peace and Power, who took upon yourself the life-giving and redeeming passion of the cross, the nails, the spear, death itself, destroy the bodily passions that slay my soul. By your burial you despoiled the regions of Hades, bury my evil counsels with good thoughts and dissipate the spirits of wickedness. By your life-giving resurrection on the third day you restored our fallen progenitor [Adam], raise me – for sin has made me slip down – and show me the ways of repentance. By your glorious ascension you made human flesh divine and honored it by sitting at the right hand of the Father, make me worthy through the communion of the Holy Mysteries to stand at your right hand among them that are saved. By the descent of the Comforter-Spirit you made your holy disciples honorable vessels, likewise declare me to be a receptacle of the same Spirit. You are coming again to judge the world in righteousness. In your good pleasure let me meet you, my Creator and Maker, in the clouds with all your saints: That I may unceasingly glorify and praise you, together with your eternal Father and your all-holy, good and life-giving Spirit, now and forever and to the ages of ages. Amen.

Liturgy – Time – Kairos

In the liturgy we experience time as *kairos* (καιρός), as a time filled with divine grace and salvation. Kairos is the criti-

cal and decisive moment; the framework within which all
people are called to salvation and the Body of Christ – the
Church – is being built up. Through worship and other acts
of devotion and genuine, self-giving love, ordinary time (χρό
νος) is continually changed into kairos (καιρός), into an experience of the presence of God and of his work of salvation.

Since the ultimate purpose and meaning of life was revealed in the incursion of God in the historical process, time
– as kairos – is understood especially to be a preparation for
and lived in joyous expectation of God's Kingdom, already
upon us and yet to come in power and in glory.

Father Alexander Schmemann especially emphasized the
eschatological ethos of the Church and her liturgy. He wrote,
for example, the following perceptive words about the liturgy, through which the Church reveals and communicates
the gifts of the eschaton and also realizes her own
eschatological nature and vocation:

> The essential function of the eschatological character of the
> Christian cult is to realize the Church by revealing her as the
> epiphany of the Kingdom of God. In this sense the Christian
> cult is unique, without analogies and without antecedents
> within the universal phenomenon of religious cult…. This King-
> dom, which for this world is yet to come and forms the ultimate
> horizon of its history, is already present (revealed, communi-
> cated, given, accepted) in the Church. And it is the liturgy which
> accomplishes this presence and this parousia, and which in this
> sense (in its totality) is the sacrament of the Church and thus
> the sacrament of the Kingdom. Whether it be the sacraments,
> or the liturgical year – from Pascha to Pascha – or the week
> lived in remembrance of and waiting for the Eighth Day, the
> Day of the Lord; it is always this eschatological reality, this fore-
> taste, this anticipation of the Kingdom of God, which is offered
> to us by the liturgy. But it is the Eucharist, which, by all evi-
> dence, constitutes the heart and center of this eschatological
> experience. In it and through it the Church realizes herself in
> her ascension to the table of the Lord in his Kingdom in order
> that she might have the power to bear witness to that Kingdom
> in this world. As the Fathers said, the Eucharist is the sacra-
> ment of sacraments.[76]

Church – Eucharist – Eighth Day

Of the many valuable contributions of Father Schmemann to liturgical studies, perhaps two are the most significant. The first, called by Thomas Fisch the hallmark of Schmemann's thought, is his understanding of liturgical theology.[77] The second contribution is Schmemann's rediscovery of the eschatology inherent in the Orthodox liturgy and his articulation of the early Church's deep awareness of the integral relationship between Church, Eucharist, and the Eighth Day.

The Eighth Day is outside of time; it has nothing coming after it. It is after the seven-day week, outside of the time measured in weeks, which constitutes the recurring cycle of time in the fallen world. While the week stands for time (χρόνος), the Eighth Day stands for eternity, for the world to come. The Eighth Day defines the unending First Day of the new creation. It is the Day of the Lord – the Κυριακἡ Ἡμέρα – the day of Christ's resurrection, the fulfillment of time and the beginning of another world.[78] It is the Day of the Kingdom, which Christ introduced into the world through the defeat of sin, corruption, and death by his incarnation, passion, resurrection, and glorification.[79]

The Church, as Father Schmemann said, belongs to the new Day, to the Kingdom, which is yet to come in fullness. Indeed, the Kingdom exists already in the Church through the Eucharist, at which the Church is actualized as the Body of Christ. The Eucharist is the presence of Christ and therefore the manifestation of his Kingdom in the flow of time of this age, which is destined to pass away. Through the Eucharist the members of the Body of Christ, who have become one with Christ through Baptism and through him one with one another, receive the new life of the age to come.[80] They become, in the words of St. Peter, "partakers of the divine nature" (2 Peter 1:4).

Thus, every Sunday – the first day of the week on which Jesus rose from the dead – the Church gathers to realize her eschatological fullness through the celebration of the Eucharist by which the unending Day of the Lord, the hope and salvation of the world, is revealed in time. These profound mysteries, Church, Eucharist, and Eighth Day, are integrally related to one another and from the earliest times to Sunday, the day of rejoicing, which the early Christians renamed the Lord's Day or Κυριακή Ἡμέρα (Rev. 1:10), on account of the fact that through Christ's resurrection the perpetual First Day of the new creation was made manifest to the world.[81]

Liturgical theology and piety and the Church's eschatological vocation

Father Schmemann's two fundamental insights – his re-discovery of the eschatological character of Orthodox liturgy and his understanding of the liturgy as a living theology – led him to claim correctly that the liturgy is the primary source of "the Church's comprehending of her own nature and eschatological vocation."[82]

For Father Schmemann, liturgical theology – and I would add by extension, liturgical piety – is "first of all and above everything else, the attempt to grasp the theology as revealed in and through the liturgy... The essence of the liturgy is ultimately nothing else but the Church's faith itself, or better to say the manifestation, communication, and fulfillment of that faith... It is, to be sure, faith that gives birth to and shapes liturgy, but it is liturgy, that by fulfilling and expressing faith, bears testimony to faith and becomes thus its true and adequate expression and norm: *lex orandi est lex credendi.*"[83]

The essential ecclesial function of the liturgy, as Schmemann was fond of saying, is to reveal the faith of the Church by the means which are proper to it and which belong only to it.[84] In other words, the *rule of faith* finds its principal criterion and standard in the *rule of prayer.*[85] Hence, "the liturgy in its totality is not only an object of theology, but above all its source."[86] Liturgical theology is based on the recognition of this fact.

The fundamental task of liturgical theology is to translate the fundamentals of the faith into genuine liturgical piety. By genuine liturgical piety I mean piety which is focused on the fundamentals of the faith and the essentials of the liturgy, by which words, sounds, symbols, and rituals become an epiphany. This epiphany draws us into the mystery of salvation to encounter the Trinitarian God, so that we may learn to live by the Holy Spirit the life of Christ, through faith dying daily to sin and rising again to a new life.

I contrast this piety to an ambiguous, pietistic approach to liturgy – an inauthentic liturgical piety – that is sentimental, often sad and gloomy, and revels mainly on the peripheral and external aspects of the liturgy, whereby ritual and symbol become opaque, an end unto themselves, serving no purpose beyond them. A living celebration, however, as one theologian put it, depends not only on the exactitude of rites, but primarily on the spirit in which they are performed.

Genuine worship is more than ritual trappings and rubrical details. It is more than a self-indulgent nostrum and a personal sanctuary, a refuge from anxiety and distress. It is more than a sentimental journey, a way to recapture experiences of one's youth or a vehicle for maintaining or renewing cultural ties.[87] Authentic worship is an act of faith. It is the life of Christ in us lived and celebrated, rooted in Baptism and the Eucharist and drawing its purpose and meaning from the age to come. Thus, we can say that Orthodox spirituality is fundamentally both biblical and liturgical precisely because Word and Sacrament, as the Fathers have taught, constantly nourish and renew the life of Christ in us.

The essential purpose of liturgical theology is to help people celebrate the faith of the Church through the acquisition and nurture of an authentic liturgical piety; a piety that is capable of restoring to us "that unique eschatological energy and perspective which makes us the people of God, acquainted with the true sense of the ancient formula, 'in this world but not of the world.'"[88] It is this eschatological vision – the remembrance of the Kingdom – that should mark the faith, the activities, and the liturgy of the Church and the life of her people. In other words, to paraphrase Fr. Schmemann, Christians should live in time by that which is beyond time. They live by that which has not yet come in fullness, but which they already know by faith and possess through the sacraments and the liturgy.[89]

The eclipse of eschatology and the shift to historicism and allegory

At an early point in the history of the Church, as Father Schmemann has shown, the eschatological dimension and foundation of the Christian faith and liturgy was eclipsed by other emphases. This was especially true of the fourth century as the Church emerged upon the empire to shift from a persecuted minority to an official state religion. As a result, the decline in eschatological vigilance became more pronounced as another understanding of worship came to the surface, which prompted a new emphasis in liturgical piety, the one Father Schmemann calls *mysteriological piety*.[90] A confluence of events and interests helped to create the atmosphere for the appearance of the new piety, namely, a new interest in time and history, the more immediate encounter with pagan culture, and the deep concern for doctrinal integrity.[91]

The emphasis in worship was now placed on external festal solemnity and on the allegorical explanations of the sacred rites suggesting, in one way, that the Lord could be grasped by the imagination as well as by faith.[92] The liturgy was now understood primarily – though not exclusively – as a sacred solemn ceremonial.

The eclipse of eschatology and the shift to historicism, allegory, and ceremonial splendor was dramatic. This is not to say, however, that the cult of the early Church lacked in ceremonial beauty. To the contrary, the early Church's system of worship was both organized and elaborate, as the writings of the Apostolic Fathers, the Apologists, and the early Church Orders indicate.[93] What changed, according to Father Schmemann, "was not worship itself in its objective content and order, but rather the reception, the experience, the understanding of worship."[94] The liturgy was beginning to be understood less in an eschatological, sacramental way and more in a dramatic, symbolical, and representational way.

The new mysteriological piety placed greater emphasis on the representational and allegorical nature of the liturgy rather than the eschatological. The sacred rites were seen more as an imitation or reenactment of the saving acts of Christ's life rather than as an anticipation of the Kingdom. For example, several medieval liturgical commentaries explain the Divine Liturgy mostly in terms of a sacramental representation of the life of Christ rather than as a sacrament of God's Kingdom.[95] According to Father Schmemann, these commentaries raise some serious concerns, the crucial one being the shift in how symbols in relationship to theology and worship came to be approached, understood, and used. Although this is much too complex an issue to deal with it properly here, a very brief comment is nevertheless required.

For the early Christians, as for most people of the ancient world, symbols were not empty figures or substitutes for reality but the embodiment and the expression of the reality that they disclosed and conveyed. Water, for example, is a primary symbol. By its very nature it lends itself completely to the mystery of Baptism, of which it is the essential sacramental matter, embodying and expressing the essential meanings of the sacrament. Mircea Eliade, the historian of religion, tells us:

> The waters symbolize the universal sum of virtualities; they are *fons et origo,* 'spring and origin,' the reservoir of all the possibilities of existence; they precede every form and support every creation... On the other hand, immersion in water signifies regression to the preformal, reincorporation into the undifferentiated mode of preexistence... In whatever religious complex we find them, the waters invariably retain their function; they disintegrate, abolish forms, 'wash away sin;' they are at once purifying and regenerating.[96]

Water cleanses, water destroys, water regenerates; it is life-giving. These realities constitute the essence of Baptism, which is at once a purification of sins, a participation in the death and resurrection of Christ, and a new birth, the making of a new creation. Theodore of Mopsuestia describes the mystery with these words:

> You have now received baptism which is the second birth; you have fulfilled by your baptism in water the rite of burial, and

you have received the sign of the resurrection by your rising out of the water; you have been born and have become a new man; you are no more part of Adam, who was mutable and burdened and made wretched by sin, but of Christ who was completely freed from sin through resurrection.[97]

Symbols differ from allegorical interpretations. While primary symbols are linked to reality, allegorical interpretations arbitrarily impose meanings upon an act or an object. Allegorical interpretations lead us to another reality only because someone has directed us to attach a special meaning to a particular act or object.

The medieval liturgical commentators used allegorical interpretations extensively. By vesting the ritual actions and objects of the liturgy with various allegorical meanings, they turned them into signs of the life and ministry of the Lord. In the process, at least to some degree, symbols as well as ritual actions began to loose their authentic identity and resulted in a discontinuity in the understanding and in the experience of the Church's liturgy.[98] Worship became "more and more a sacred action in itself, a mystery performed for the sanctification of those participating;"[99] as something being done for the faithful rather than what the faithful – clergy and laity together – do in response to the redemptive work of Christ to experience the presence of his saving grace and the realities of the age to come.

Though the early commentators of the Divine Liturgy sought to express a consistent Eucharistic theology through the symbolic interpretations they employed, the later commentaries with their one-symbol-per-object correspondence represent what Robert Taft calls "the decomposition of the earlier patristic mystery-theology into a historicizing system of dramatic narrative allegory."[100]

Allegorical explanations usually have little, if any, relation to the text of a given service and pay little, if any, attention to the historical development of a particular liturgical action. In fact, they impose upon the liturgy meanings that are neither suggested nor intended by the texts. Let me cite the 'Small' Entrance of the Divine Liturgy as an example.

Briefly stated, today's entrance rite with the Gospel Book (Εὐαγγέλιον), which is performed with a circuitous route by the clergy who exit and re-enter the sanctuary, is a remnant of the ancient entrance rite introduced into the Divine Liturgy after the persecutions ended. The original rite of entrance constituted the formal procession of the clergy and the people into the Church for the celebration of the Divine Liturgy. Before entering the Church, the clergy recited a prayer at the doors of the nave and then entered the Church followed by the people. After the eighth century when the Antiphons began to be added to the Divine Liturgy to create a new enarxis (ἔναρξις) or introductory rite, the Entrance gradually lost its original shape and significance.

In the *Barberini Codex* – an eighth century manuscript – the Liturgy of St. John Chrysostom has its own Prayer of Entrance.[101] The present Prayer of Entrance, which is common to both Liturgies, is from the Liturgy of St. Basil in the same *Codex*. It reads as follows: "Master and Lord our God, You have established in heaven the orders and hosts of angels and archangels to minister to Your glory. Grant that the holy angels may enter with us that together we may serve and glorify Your goodness. For to You belong all glory, honor, and worship to the Father and the Son and the Holy Spirit, now and forever, and to the ages of ages. Amen." From its content, it is clear that the prayer reflects the original purpose of the Entrance, the entry of the clergy and the people into the Church – in the company of the heavenly hosts – in order to worship and to glorify the Triune God.

However, the medieval liturgical commentaries assign very different meanings to the Entrance, which are unrelated to the original purpose of the Entrance or to the Prayer of Entrance. Instead, they interpret the Entrance allegorically in terms of a dramatic representation of an episode in the life of Christ. For example, St. Germanos of Constantinople in his commentary on the Divine Liturgy gives the following explanation of the Entrance. "The entrance of the Gospel signifies the coming of the Son of God and his entrance into this world... And we proclaim the coming which was revealed to us in the grace of Jesus Christ."[102]

The allegorical interpretations, however, are not without some value, especially as a catechetical tool. They were used to communicate the truths of the faith to the surrounding culture, which employed widely the language of symbol, image, and drama. In short, as Paul Meyendorff notes, the purpose of the medieval liturgical commentaries with their system of allegorical interpretations was to help the people "understand the meaning of what they were supposed to experience in the liturgy, as well as to inspire in them the feeling of awe and fear. This latter element began to be increasingly emphasized in reaction to the large numbers who participated only nominally in church life, and who therefore needed prodding."[103]

The allegorical interpretations of the liturgy were popular in their time and continue to have the same attraction for people today. Their value as a teaching tool remains constant. However, it is important to stress that allegorical explanations have their limitations. They should not be used as the sole method of interpreting and understanding the sacred rites, especially to the exclusion of the sacred texts and the knowledge of the historical evolution of the various components of the liturgy. To do so would reduce the liturgy to allegory, depiction, and drama. It must be remembered, however, that the Gospel was proclaimed as a saving faith – not as a saving drama.

The mystery of the faith is not found in arcane symbolisms but in the inrushing of God into human history for the salvation of the world. The liturgy is indispensable to the Church not because of its quaintness and mysteriousness, or of its aesthetic and cultural value, or of its ability to fulfill the religious needs of people, but because it expresses, shapes, and actualizes the Church as the Body of Christ. Without this understanding of the liturgy the Church – or if you will the local parish, through which the people experience the mystery of the Church – ceases to be Church and remains a limited human community.[104] The liturgy, as Father Schmemann noted, establishes the reality of the Church. "Its purpose is not the individual sanctification of the members [of the Church], but the creation of the people of God as the Body of Christ, the manifestation of the Church as new life."[105]

The emergence of liturgical historicism with its renewed interest in history and geography produced another phenomenon, the historical reconstruction and expansion of feasts. Paul Bradshaw, among others, attributes this development, at least in part, to the same apologetic factors that gave rise to the liturgical commentaries with their allegorical explanations. Bradshaw writes:

> A multiplicity of feasts and commemorations began to emerge in the fourth century in a way they had not done earlier... The Church now needed to communicate the tenants of its faith to a barbarian world, which was willing to listen, and to defend its doctrinal positions against a variety of heretical attacks; and what better means could be found than the promotion of occasions that publicly celebrated aspects of what the Church believed... The so-called Constantinian revolution did not so much inaugurate new liturgical practices and attitudes as create conditions in which some preexistent customs could achieve a greater measure of preeminence than others.[106]

The expansion of liturgical feasts commemorating separate events in the earthly life of Christ was meant to highlight the redemptive significance of sacred history. These commemorations take each event out of the past, so that for the liturgical assembly it becomes an immediate and present reality. The feasts of the Theotokos, also essentially theological in nature, reveal aspects of the mystery of the divine economy in which she played a central role. The commemorations of the saints also serve to celebrate the grace that flows from Christ for the sanctification of human life. As forerunners and the first fruits of the Kingdom, the saints call us to imitate their devotion and holiness of life and, by grace, to establish righteousness in the midst of our moribund world.

The feasts of the Church serve to underscore the historical reality of the Christian faith. Far from being mythical, the events occurred in real historical times and the persons are real historical figures. In addition, through her feasts the

Church seeks to lead the faithful to the fullness of the truth and the right participation in the mysteries of the faith.

The shift towards historicism and allegory, as already noted above, was to have a profound and lasting effect on every aspect of the Church's worship. However, the gradual eclipse of eschatology, according to Father Schmemann, produced some negative results. "When eschatology was relegated to the end of the theological manuals into a chapter that was exclusively personal and futurist, the sacraments were defined and understood as so many means of personal sanctification. Ecclesiology was reduced to a total institutionalism, and piety to an individualism complete in and closed upon itself."[107] This sobering assessment requires further exploration. It should trouble the Church and prompt her pastors and theologians to examine the facts, carefully making the necessary adjustments both in the practice of liturgy and in the theological explanations and definitions related to the sacraments and ecclesiology. Already, much valuable work is being accomplished in these fields, shedding new light and new perspectives on these matters.

Another shift in liturgical piety – the ascetical

Monasticism of the middle and late Byzantine periods created yet another understanding of worship and a new liturgical piety that could be called ascetical. Early monasticism sought to realize what Father Schmemann calls the 'eschatological maximalism' of the early Church through the formation of monastic communities separate from the Church in the world. However, this departure from the world was not a repudiation of either the Church or her worship. In fact, the monastics were ardent subscribers to the doctrinal, canonical, and liturgical rule of the Church. Yet in spite of its eschatological orientation, the monastic movement brought yet another change both in the emphasis and the understanding of the Church's liturgy.

If, as Father Schmemann notes, in the early Christian perspective every undertaking could become a prayer, in later monasticism prayer itself became the most significant undertaking and central focus of life, practically replacing all others. He writes:

> The command to pray constantly was of course not new in Christianity – 'pray without ceasing' (1 Thess. 5:17). What was new [in monasticism] was the idea of prayer as the sole content of life, as a task, which required a separation and a renunciation of the world and all its works. In early Christian understanding prayer was not opposed to life or the occupation of life; prayer penetrated life and consisted above all in a new understanding of life and its occupations, in relating them to the central object of faith, the Kingdom of God and the Church... Work was controlled, enlightened and judged by prayer, it was not opposed to prayer. And yet monasticism was a departure out of life and its works for the sake of prayer.[108]

According to the monastic perspective, prayer is essentially an ascetical act, an aid in the struggle against the passions. Devotional rules – the very core of ascetical liturgical piety – are meant to train the monk in the life of prayer, through which the heart becomes purified and the mind is not distracted with worldly things – good or evil – but is engaged only with God. For the monastics prayer is meant to bring inexpressible joy and profound peace to the soul by generating tears of repentance through which temptations are overcome and divine illumination is granted. Prayer thus becomes an ascetical act and a form of individual piety. This, according to Father Schmemann, is best understood through the act of private Communion as practiced by monastics. He writes:

> Without being noticed the receiving of Communion [by monastics] was subordinated to individual piety, so that piety was no longer determined by the Eucharist (as in the early Church). Instead the Eucharist became an 'instrument' of piety, an element of asceticism, an aid in the struggle against demons, etc... The change here was not a reduction of the place and significance of Communion, but a change in the way it was experienced and understood. It was included within the general scheme of monasticism as an ascetical act and a form of individual self-edification. In this sense the view of the Eucha-

rist as the actualization of the Church (as the people of God) and as the eschatological feast of the Kingdom was not denied or disputed. The emphasis simply shifted to the view of Communion as a beneficial ascetic act. The Eucharistic service was now seen as an opportunity to receive spiritual succor. This was in fact a change in liturgical piety.[109]

It must be noted that the practice of reserving the consecrated Eucharistic elements for private Communion was not invented by monastics. Early Christians practiced it in several ways. St. Justin the Martyr (ca. 150 AD), for example, tells us that the deacons brought Communion to those absent from the Sunday Liturgy, presumably the sick and those other faithful members of the community who for good reason were unable to attend the Liturgy.[110] Some years later, Hippolytus, in his treatise *Apostolic Tradition*, informs us that it was customary for pious Christians to reserve the Eucharist in their homes for private Communion on weekdays when the Eucharist was not customarily celebrated.[111] St. Basil the Great (+379) provides us with similar information:

> All solitaries in the deserts, where there is no priest, keep the communion by them and partake of it by themselves. At Alexandria too, and in Egypt, each one of the laity, for the most part, keeps communion at home, and whenever he wishes partakes of it himself. For after the priest has completed the sacrifice and distributed it, he who then receives it in its entirety... must believe that he duly takes and receives it from the hand that first gave it. For even in Church, when the priest distributes each portion, he who receives takes it into his complete control, and lifts it to his mouth with his own hand. It comes to the same thing, whether one or many portions at a time are received from the priest.[112]

The practice of private Communion was finally disallowed by the Church probably for practical and doctrinal reasons, in order to forestall abuses and mistaken interpretations of the meaning and purpose of Communion. Nonetheless, the practice, in part, gave rise to the creation of the Divine Liturgy of the Pre-Sanctified Gifts[113] and to the celebration of the Divine Liturgy on days of the week other than Sunday.

The issue here is not so much the practice of private Communion, but its meaning and purpose. For devout Christians in the early centuries, private Communion was a way of extending into the days of the week the Sunday Eucharistic experience – the joyous feast of the Kingdom – and a way of renewing their ecclesial identity. For them private Communion was never understood as an ascetical act of personal devotion, nor as a substitute for the weekly Eucharistic assembly, only as its extension.[114]

Prayer is an essential component of a Christian's life. From the earliest days Christians were instructed to pray often throughout the day, so that they may not undergo temptation nor perish, as Hippolytus of Rome wrote in the *Apostolic Tradition*, since they will have Christ always in memory.[115] Frequent or continual prayer, however, is not meant to exclude work and other essential human activities. As Origen wrote in his treatise *On Prayer* (XII, 2), "That man 'prays without ceasing' who combines with prayer the needful deeds and the prayer with the fitting actions. For thus alone can we accept 'pray without ceasing' as a practicable saying, if we speak of the whole life of the saint [Christian] as one unbroken prayer: of which prayer that which is commonly called prayer is a part. This ought to be engaged in not less than three times a day..."

Every devotional act of the Christian is meant to emphasize one's personal relationship to Christ in and through his Body the Church, of which one is member. A Christian at prayer, whether in the privacy of the 'cell' or in the company of the assembly, never prays as an individual but as a member of the Body of Christ, the Church. Moreover, prayer for a devout Christian is more than an activity; it is a state of being that is defined by an abiding love for and trust in God. St. Basil makes this point in a beautiful passage on prayer, which reads, in part, as follows:

> Ought we to pray without ceasing? Is it possible to obey such a command? ... Prayer is a request for what is good, addressed by the devout to God. But we do not rigidly confine our petition to words. Nor yet do we imagine that God requires to be

reminded by speech. He knows our needs even though we ask him not. What do I say then? I say that we must not think to make our prayer complete by syllables. The strength of prayer lies rather in the moral attitude of our soul and in deeds of virtue reaching every part and moment of our life. 'Whether you eat,' it is said, 'or drink, or whatever you do, do all to the glory of God' [1 Cor. 10:31]... Thus will you pray without ceasing; if you pray not only in words, but also by uniting yourself to God through all the course of life, so that your life becomes one continuous and uninterrupted prayer.[116]

The Byzantine synthesis – An integrated liturgical piety

There is a final, significant development in the story of liturgical piety. Father Schmemann calls it the Byzantine synthesis. In essence, this synthesis consists of the creative integration of the several layers, strands, and emphases in liturgical piety into a general theological principle and rule of prayer, the basis of which are the revelatory and eschatological dimensions of Christian liturgy reflected in the official liturgical books of the Church. According to this basic principle, the Church essentially actualizes herself as the Body of Christ – as the eschatological community that reflects the final stage of things – at prayer and most especially through the preeminent sacraments of baptism and the Eucharist. The Eucharist, as the expression of the Church's eschatological fullness, occupies a special place in the life of the Church.

In daily prayer and in the sacraments, and especially in the Eucharist, "we discover our body to be a liturgical body."[117] In worship the body of death becomes the body of the Resurrection. Worship and the Eucharist nurture the seed of immortality, sown inside the body through baptism.

Power and life flow from the liturgy. Our biological mode of existence – with its limitations, contradictions, and insufficiencies – is being continuously transformed into a sacramental, Eucharistic hypostasis that reflects ever more clearly the realities of the new life in Christ. The liturgy takes hold of each one personally and of the liturgical community we constitute. The liturgy holds everything together. It both reveals and gives us our true identity. It embodies the invisible and uncreated realities and brings into us the gifts of the age to come.

The end time – the eschaton – has already begun in the resurrection, exaltation, and glorification of the God-Man, Jesus Christ. The eschaton, which will usher in God's eternal Kingdom in power and in glory, forms the point of constant reference for both the faith community and its individual members. All else is preparation and expectancy. No matter the circumstance and the occasion, every prayer and sacrament of the Church reflects something of the Paschal mystery. For Olivier Clement this is especially true of the Byzantine synthesis. He writes:

> Having preserved the eschatological theology of time as its foundation and principle of formulation, the Byzantine synthesis has also preserved the ecclesiological significance of the Church's rule of prayer. No symbolic explanation, no mysteriological piety and no ascetical individualism could obscure completely the unchanging essential nature of worship as the Church's act of self-revelation, self-fulfillment, self- realization.[118]

The genius of the Byzantine synthesis is that it brings the various strands of liturgical piety – the eschatological, mysteriological, and ascetical – into a dynamic relationship of complimentary balance. This creative integration has been translated into the tangible realities of the Byzantine Rite with its profound spiritual, mystical tradition and its complex ritual splendor of communal and personal prayer. In and through the various components of this rite, "men and women, according to their capacity and desire, are caught up into the adoring worship of the redeemed cosmos, where dogmas are no barren abstractions but hymns of exulting praise."[119]

How the Orthodox Liturgy Was Shaped: The Byzantine Rite and Its Liturgical Books

Encountering God in worship

The fullness of revelation is Christ Jesus, the incarnate Son and Word of God. The Church, which is his Body, has been appointed to be the guardian and custodian of revelation and the permanent witness to the fullness of truth. The perennial message of the Gospel is reflected in the life and structures of the Church. It is kept alive and summarized in her creeds, dogmas, canons, and liturgy, which constitute in part the living apostolic tradition. The liturgy of the Church is the doxological expression of "the faith, which was once for all delivered to the saints" (Jude 3). Thus, we can say that the liturgy is the essential context for the reception and transmission of the truth, which the Church believes, formulates, and reflects upon.

In worship the Church encounters the living God. Through worship God is present to the Church. Stated in another way, worship – the liturgy – constitutes the fundamental way by which the Church stands before God. And the Church's stance before God is always one of joyous-sadness (χαρμολύπη), watchfulness (νῆψις), and expectation (προσδοκία). The liturgy is the very expression of the Church's life and at the same time a manifestation of the age to come. Through the liturgy the Church becomes the temple of the Holy Spirit, actualizes herself as the Body of Christ, and becomes the witness to the eschaton, the age to come. The sacred rites of the Church celebrate the Kingdom of God already come and already given as the very pledge of salvation.

Through age-old rites we keep vigil before God, in order to celebrate in faith the glorious mysteries of his divine economy and, according to the capacity and desire of each, behold the glory of God and the coming splendor of the redeemed and transfigured cosmos.[120] Thus, the liturgy – in its setting, content, and ritual action – becomes the gateway to heaven, a place of mystery, flooded by the presence of God. It brings us to the threshold of another world.[121] The earth encounters heaven; God embraces his creation. This was the way, according to the legend recorded in the *Russian Primary Chronicle*, that the emissaries of Prince Vladimir of Kiev experienced the Orthodox liturgy at the great Cathedral of St. Sophia in Constantinople (ca 987):

> And the Greeks led us to the edifices where they worship their God, and we knew not whether we were in heaven or on earth. For on earth there is no such splendor or such beauty, and we are at a loss how to describe it. We only know that God dwells there among men, and their service is fairer than the ceremonies of other nations. For we cannot forget that beauty.[122]

The Byzantine Liturgical Rite

The essential elements and basic structures of modern Orthodox worship are rooted in the liturgical tradition of the early church. Ritual and text developed gradually over the course of many centuries. The Byzantine Rite (Βυζαντινός Λειτουργικός Τύπος) constitutes the final unification of liturgical practice in the Orthodox Church. This rite or form of worship takes its name from Constantinople. The great imperial city, established in 324 by St. Constantine, the first Christian emperor, was inaugurated in 330 as the new capital of the Roman Empire. Constantinople, named after its founder, was built on the site of the small port town of Byzantion or Byzantium, an ancient Greek colony founded in the seventh century B.C. by Byzas of Megara, located strategically on the shores of the Bosporus, the strait between Europe and Asia Minor connecting the Black Sea and the Sea of Marmara. The great empire that emerged out of the foundation of Constantinople came to be known as the Byzantine Empire; and the complex civilization it spawned was formed, as historians tell it, by the Roman imperial tradition of law

and government, the Hellenic tradition of language, litera-
ture, and philosophy, and the Christian Orthodox tradition
of faith, dogma, liturgy, morals, and practice.[123] The continu-
ator, guardian and cultivator of this great heritage was and
still is the Ecumenical Patriarchate of Constantinople.

The city of Constantinople (or New Rome) grew in power
and prestige and became the center of a glorious civilization
– the Byzantine – that lasted over one thousand years.
Constantinople became the primary See of the Christian East
and developed into a renowned liturgical center. The liturgy
of the city gradually spread far and wide. The dioceses dependent on the Patriarchate of Constantinople in Greece, the
Balkans and in Asia Minor embraced it. Through the missionary efforts of the Patriarchate of Constantinople,
beginning at the end of the eighth century, the liturgy of the
city was also diffused among the Albanian and Slavic people
of the Balkans, then among the Romanians, and finally among
the Russians.[124] Then, gradually, during the Middle Ages, the
other ancient Orthodox Patriarchates of the East – Alexandria, Antioch and Jerusalem – adopted the liturgy of
Constantinople.[125] Thus, by the thirteenth century the Rite of
Constantinople had become the common inheritance of all
the Orthodox Churches, albeit with minor local variations.
And this happened not by imposition, force, or synodical
legislation, but simply by practice.

The Rite of Constantinople or the Byzantine Rite represents
both the intermingling of cathedral and monastic practices
and the reception, assimilation, and synthesis of the liturgical riches of Eastern Christianity. Constantinople, as Father
Alexander Schmemann was fond of saying, became the magnificent 'crucible,' the great receptacle of the liturgical
traditions of the leading liturgical centers of the East: Antioch
(Syria), Jerusalem (Palestine), Ephesus (Asia Minor), Caesarea
in Cappadocia (Pontus), and Heraclea (Thrace).[126] The influence of these centers on the liturgy of Byzantium can be
attributed, in part, to the fact that many of the early clerics of
Constantinople – patriarchs, bishops, and presbyters – came
from these cities and regions. Also, many of the poets and

the authors of prayers whose works were incorporated into the liturgical books of the rite lived and flourished in these areas. In fact, the Byzantine Rite is part of the largest ancient liturgical family of rites, the Antiochene, which derives its name from the ancient city of Antioch, one of the first great Christian centers whose influence spread throughout Syria, Palestine, Asia Minor, Armenia, and other regions of the Middle and Far East.[127]

The Byzantine Rite passed through various stages of development and is "renowned for the sumptuousness of its ceremonial and liturgical symbolism, and heritage of the imperial splendors of Constantinople before the eighth century."[128] The rite as we know it today is basically, as Robert Taft points out, "a hybrid of Constantinopolitan and Palestinian rites, gradually synthesized during the ninth to the fourteenth centuries in the monasteries of the Orthodox world, beginning in the period of the struggle with Iconoclasm."[129] The printing of the Greek liturgical books in the sixteenth and seventeenth centuries was a defining moment in the evolution of the shape of the rite, when the divine services became more or less fixed. And, although adaptations, revisions, and modifications of varying degrees have been introduced, the basic shape of the rite has changed little since then.

Like all classical liturgical rites, the Byzantine Rite is constituted by several basic components and by certain characteristic theological and ritual attributes. The rite features highly developed and distinctive forms of the liturgical arts – architecture, iconography, hymnography, and music[130] – and has a wide range of liturgical services, including Eucharistic liturgies, sacramental rites, other occasional services, and a daily office. It also has a lectionary system and a calendar of feasts and fasts. A brief description of these fundamental components of the rite follows.

Constantinople was the great crucible in which several liturgical traditions of the East converged. Out of this synthesis came three Divine Liturgies – or sacred rites by which the Orthodox Church celebrates the sacrament of the Eucharist

– which are distinctly Constantinopolitan. *The Divine Liturgy of St. Basil* was, until the twelfth century, the chief Eucharistic liturgy of Constantinople. Now it is used only ten times a year. *The Divine Liturgy of St. John Chrysostom*, which was probably the weekday Liturgy of Constantinople, gradually superseded and replaced the Liturgy of St. Basil. It is now celebrated at every Eucharistic assembly, except on those occasions when the Typikon designates the Divine Liturgies of St. Basil or of the Pre-Sanctified Gifts. *The Divine Liturgy of the Pre-Sanctified Gifts* is now celebrated on Wednesdays and Fridays of Great Lent and on the first three days of Holy Week. It is comprised of Vespers, the transfer of the Eucharistic Gifts consecrated at the Divine Liturgy the previous Saturday or Sunday, and the order of the distribution of Holy Communion as in the other Liturgies.

Although they are not of the Byzantine Rite, in some places three other Greek Divine Liturgies are occasionally used on the feast day of the saints whose name they bear. These Liturgies are St. Iakovos (James) the Brother of the Lord (Antioch/Jerusalem) whose feast is on October 23, St. Mark the Apostle and Evangelist (Alexandria) whose feast is on April 25, and St. Gregory the Theologian (Alexandria/ Cappadocia) whose feast is on January 25. The latter, which is rarely celebrated, is distinct among the classical Divine Liturgies, inasmuch as the Anaphora (Eucharistic Prayer) is addressed to God the Son and not to God the Father as in all the other Liturgies.

In addition to the Eucharistic liturgies, the Byzantine Rite has sacred rites for the other sacraments: Baptism, Chrismation, Penance, Holy Orders, Matrimony, and Holy Unction. The Byzantine Rite also has other occasional services such as Burial Rites, the Making of Monastics, The Great and Small Hagiasmos (Blessing of Water), the Kneeling Service of Pentecost, various Supplicatory Canons, Doxologies, Akathists, and assorted prayers and services of blessings.

The received Daily Office of the Church is of monastic origins. It contains seven prayer intervals with eight services. The liturgical day begins at sunset with the service of Vespers ('Εσπερινός). It is followed by the Compline or Apodeipnon ('Απόδειπνον), the Midnight Office (Μεσονυκτικόν), the Orthros ("Ορθρος) and the First Hour (Πρώτη "Ωρα). These are followed by the Third (Τρίτη "Ωρα), Sixth ('Εκτη "Ωρα), and Ninth ('Ενάτη "Ωρα) Hours. The fixed elements of these services are contained in the *Horologion* ('Ωρολόγιον) or Book of the Hours. [131]

Writing about 150 AD, St. Justin the Martyr in his *First Apology* (chapter 67) is the first to attest to the public reading of the Scriptures at liturgical assemblies. Over a period of time the Church developed an organized system of readings (also called lections, lessons, or pericopes) from the Old and New Testaments, called the Lectionary.[132] The Lectionary currently in use dates to at least the tenth century, if not much earlier. The Lectionary consists of assigned readings from one of the four Gospels, the Book of Acts, and the twenty-one Epistles for each day, so that in the course of one year the entire New Testament – except for the Book of Revelation – is read publicly in the liturgical assembly.[133] In addition to the daily, Saturday, and Sunday cycle of lessons, a recurring cycle of eleven Gospel pericopes related to the resurrection appearances of Christ is assigned to the Sunday morning Orthros. New Testament readings are also designated for the annual cycle of feasts, the sacraments, and other occasional services. After the fifth century the readings (ἀναγνώσματα) at the Divine Liturgy, the sacraments, and the other occasional services were limited to two: Gospel and Apostolos (Book of Acts or Epistles). The Old Testament lections are limited in number and are assigned for the weekdays of the Great Lent and Holy Week and for the feasts of the Lord and his holy Mother, the Theotokos, and for the feasts of certain saints.[134] These Old Testament lections are generally read at the Vesper service of the feasts. From this brief description it is clear that "the Bible lives in the Church. It is an essential element of the organic wholeness of the Church."[135]

The *festal calendar* is a result of continuous development. Its essential purpose is to keep alive the memory of past events and future promises and to make these memories and promises – the saving acts of God – a present reality to the worshipping community. The feasts vary in importance and are divided into two main categories: fixed and movable. The movable feasts are related to the celebration of Pascha (the date of which changes from year to year), while the fixed feasts occur on the same date each year. The liturgical year is marked with feasts that commemorate events in the life of the Lord, his Mother (the holy Theotokos), and St. John the Baptist. The Church also honors the Holy Apostles, the Prophets, the great Hierarchs and Teachers of the faith, and the Martyrs. The Church also honors and commemorates each day many other friends of God, imitators of Christ and models of Christian living, saintly men, women, and children – emperors, clerics, monastics, physicians, and other lay people in all walks of life – whose life was (is) a witness to the perennial value of the Gospel. In addition, the Church commemorates important events of Church history, such as the Triumph of Orthodoxy over iconoclasm (the First Sunday of Lent) and the convocation of Ecumenical Synods.

The liturgical calendar also contains a number of *fast days* and several *fast periods* of varying lengths and degrees of importance. The weekly fast on Wednesday and Friday, the fast of Holy Week, and the forty-day fast of the Great Lent are the oldest and most important fast days and periods of the Church. Gradually, several other fast periods were added to the calendar: those for the feasts of Christmas, the holy Apostles, and the Dormition of the Theotokos. The Church also observes a Eucharistic fast, a practice that originated in the late first century when the Eucharistic elements were consumed before the meal. By the end of the first century and the early part of the second century the original evening Eucharistic synaxis was transferred first to the pre-dawn hours and later to the 'third' hour (mid-morning) of the day, no longer connected to the agape meal. As a result of these changes, the Eucharistic fast became a fixed prerequisite for participation in the Eucharist. Thus, whoever is prepared to receive Holy Communion at the Divine Liturgy must remain fasted from the night before and partake of the Eucharist as the first food of the day.[136]

The Orthodox Church also has a *weekly cycle* of feasts, which succinctly but ingeniously summarizes the entire annual festal calendar. The weekly festal calendar begins with Sunday, the first day of the week, which Orthodox Christians call the Lord's Day (Κυριακή Ημέρα), on which the Church celebrates weekly the Lord's resurrection. On Monday the Church honors the Angels, on Tuesday St. John the Baptist, on Wednesday and Friday the combined mystery of the Cross and the Theotokos, on Thursday the Holy Apostles and St. Nicholas, and on Saturday, the martyrs, the ascetics, and all who have fallen asleep in the hope of the resurrection.

The liturgical books of the Byzantine Rite

The various elements of the liturgical services are codified in the liturgical books of the Church. These books express the mind and faith of the Church in doxological, poetical, and rhetorical language and are considered authoritative.

With a combined doctrinal, ethical, and devotional purpose, these books consist mainly of prayers, litanies, hymns, Psalms, lectionary readings, and rubrics. The prayers and hymns represent and interpret the central truths and core values of the Orthodox faith, conveying the fundamental vision of the Church in a given rite. By proclaiming the promise of salvation, the prayers and hymns of the liturgical books evoke devotional responses of the mind and heart and provide the faithful with direction for their continued edification and growth in the life of faith and guidance and inspiration for their activity and mission in the world.

Each book, with its own complex history of development, falls into one of four major categories. The **first category** includes the books that contain the prayers and petitions that are used by the clergy for the various divine services. These are the *Euchologion* (*Εὐχολόγιον* – Service Book or Book of Prayers) and its derivatives, the *Small Euchologion* (*Μικρόν Εὐχολόγιον*), the *Archieratikon* (*Ἀρχιερατικόν* – Pontifical or Bishop's Book), the *Ieratikon* (*Ἱερατικόν* – Priest's Book), and the *Diakonikon* (*Διακονικόν* – Deacon's Book).

The **second category** includes the books that contain the fixed and variable elements of the Daily Office. These are the *Horologion* (Ὡρολόγιον – Book of the Hours), the *Octoechos* or *Parakletike* (Ὀκτώηχος or Παρακλητική – Book of the Eight Tones), the *Triodion* (Τριῴδιον – Book of the Three Odes or the Lenten Triodion), the *Pentekostarion* (Πεντηκοστάριον – Book of Paschaltide), and the *Menaia* (Μηναῖα – the 12 Books, one for each month containing the services of the fixed feasts).

The **third category** includes the books that contain the lectionary readings of the Holy Scriptures. These are the *Evangelion* (Εὐαγγέλιον – Gospel Book), the *Apostolos* (Ἀπόστολος – Book of the Acts and the Epistles), the *Psalter* (Ψαλτήριον – Book of Psalms), and the *Prophetologion* (Προφητολόγιον – Book of the Prophecies).

Finally, the **fourth category** contains the *Typikon* (Τυπικόν) and the *Diataxeis* (Διατάξεις), which are books of directives and rubrics. The Typikon presupposes the existence of the other liturgical books and serves several purposes. It contains the basic calendar of the rite and the rubrics for the divine services of the daily cycle of worship and of the feasts of the year. It gives the order of service by providing directives about what should be said and done. It specifies the Scripture lessons for the different liturgical celebrations. Finally, the Typikon underscores the essential fact that the liturgy is an act of the Church. The Typikon is meant to provide continuity in liturgical practice and ethos, secure recognizable standards and good liturgical order, and maintain a balanced and healthy tension between tradition and life, protecting the liturgy from whimsical experimentations, fanciful archaisms, and arbitrary decisions.

4

The Typikon – A Short Story on the Development of the Orthodox Liturgy

The Typikon, as mentioned above, does not create the liturgy; it presupposes its existence and secures for the Church recognizable standards of usage. The history of the Byzantine Rite – its origins, formation, and development – is intertwined with the history of the Typikon in its various manifestations, not because the Typikon is the source of the Rite but because it reflects the various stages of its development and brings to light the forces that shaped it. For that reason a brief review of its history is appropriate.

The precursors of the Typikon: two examples from Christian antiquity

The sacred rites are an essential part of the life of the Church. They are windows unto another reality: the Kingdom of God already come and yet to be realized in all of its fullness. These sacred rites celebrate the Kingdom of God already given as the very pledge of salvation. Spiritual worship, clothed in form and language, must be performed with sober splendor and joyfulness. Hence, respect for tradition and good order are essential qualities of established Orthodox liturgical practice. It has been so from the beginning.

From all that is said about prayer and worship in the New Testament (1 Cor. 14:26, 40; and 2 Thess. 2:15) and in the writings of the early Church Fathers, we can assume safely that the Church favored orderly prayer and developed a well-organized system of worship from the start. Two first century texts, the *Didache* (or Teachings) *of the Twelve Apostles*, an early Church Order[137] and the *First Letter to the Corinthians*, written by St. Clement of Rome, support these claims. In both of these ancient texts we find the earliest forms of a Typikon, that is to say, a book or manual of liturgical directives or rubrics.

The *Didache* (Διδαχή τῶν Δωδεκα᾽ Αποστόλων), the earliest of the Church Orders,[138] was discovered in Constantinople in 1873 by Metropolitan Philotheos Bryennios in an eleventh century manuscript and was published by him in 1883. Some scholars believe it to be a composite document that developed in stages, beginning as early as 50-70 A.D.[139] The document is made up of two parts. The first deals with Christian morals and the second with liturgical practices, including valuable directives related to baptism, the Eucharist, penance, the ministry, fasting, and the Lord's Day. It also gives the text of the Lord's Prayer, which is to be prayed three times a day. By way of example, let us look at several directives in the *Didache*:

> Regarding baptism, baptize thus. After giving the foregoing instructions, baptize in the name of the Father, and of the Son, and of the Holy Spirit in running water. But, if you have no running water, baptize in any other;[140] and if you cannot in cold water then in warm. But, if the one is lacking, pour the other three times on the head in the name of the Father, and Son, and Holy Spirit. But, before baptism, let the one who baptizes and the one to be baptized fast, and any others who are able to do so. And you shall require the person being baptized to fast for one or two days (chapter 7).

> But do not let your fasts be with the hypocrites; for they fast on Monday and Thursday; but you shall fast on Wednesday and Friday. And do not pray as the hypocrites, but as the Lord directed in his Gospel, "this shall you pray: Our Father in heaven..." Three times in the day pray thus (chapter 8).

> And on the Lord's Day, after you have come together, break bread and offer the Eucharist, having first confessed your offenses, so that your sacrifice may be pure (chapter 14).

In the *First Letter to the Corinthians* of St. Clement of Rome, written about 96 A.D,[141] we find another brief passage (chapter 40), which reads like a basic 'manual of directives' for a rudimentary liturgical rite. The occasion of Clement's Letter was a schism in the Church of Corinth. In the course of his lengthy appeal to the Corinthians to put an end to their fierce strife, Clement provides us with valuable information about the liturgical practices of the Church in the first century. Chapter 40 of the Letter is of particular interest to us:

> Since all these things are clear to us, and we have looked into the depths of divine knowledge, we ought in proper order to do all things, which the Lord has commanded us to perform at appointed seasons (times) (καιρούς τεταγμένους). He has commanded offerings (προσφοράς) and ministrations (λειτουργίας) to be carried out, and not carelessly or disorderly, but at fixed seasons and times/hours (ὡρισμένοις καιροῖς καὶ ὥραις). He has himself fixed according to his surpassing counsel where and by whom he desires them to be performed, in order that all things may be done in holy fashion (ὁσίως) according to his good pleasure and acceptable to his will. Those who make their offerings at the appointed times, therefore, are acceptable and blessed, for they err not, following the ordinances of the Lord. For the high priest (τῷ ἀρχιερεῖ) has been allotted his proper ministrations, and to the priests (τοῖς ἱερεῦσιν) their proper place has been assigned, and on the Levites (Λευΐταις) their own duties are laid. The layman (ὁ λαϊκός ἄνθρωπος) is bound by the lay ordinances.

This text is important for several reasons. It tells us that the Church in the first century had already developed a rule of prayer that consisted of different services that may be classified as eucharistic (προσφοραί) and non-eucharistic (λειτουργίαι). The text also refers to fixed prayer-times (ὧραι) and to a rudimentary calendar (καιροί). In addition, it speaks about liturgical space and a variety of liturgical ministries and roles (πού τε καί διά τίνων ἐπιτελεῖσθαι θέλειν – where and by whom). Moreover, the text claims without hesitation that the liturgical practices that the author champions are based on a received tradition that comes from the Lord; and that these customs and ritual activities are appropriate to the Church and should be observed with due care and conducted in proper order. One may, therefore, reach the conclusion that this text provides us with the foundational elements that would in time constitute a liturgical rite and a manual of directives (the Typikon).

In addition to these important pieces of information about the shape of the liturgy in the first century, the Letter of St. Clement also gives us important data about the organizational structures of the Church and includes a lengthy prayer of thanksgiving, which many scholars believe is an ancient form of the Anaphora, or great Eucharistic Prayer.[142]

The Daily Office and the Typikon

The liturgical cycle moves on four interrelated planes: the day, week, month, and year. Of these, the day is the most fundamental unit, inasmuch as all of the other planes collapse into it and are defined by it.

In the liturgical tradition of the Church, we reckon the beginning of the day using two different methods, one Semitic in origin, the other Roman-Byzantine. The Semitic, according to which the day starts at sunset, is the older of the two and is the dominant method. It is based on Hebrew traditions and is reflected in the Old Testament, especially in the Genesis account of creation (Gen. 1:5). The Roman method, according to which the day begins at midnight, was part of Roman law and passed into the civil law of the Byzantine Empire and, in fact, is the method used today throughout the world in civil law. Nonetheless, the Orthodox Church, in keeping with the tradition of the ancient Church, continues to reckon the liturgical day from sunset to sunset. On the other hand, the fast on a given day is reckoned according to the Roman-Byzantine method, from midnight to midnight.[143]

The liturgical day, then, begins at sunset and has a prescribed order of services, often referred to as the Daily Office or Divine Office ('Ημερονύκτιος 'Ακολουθία ή 'Ακολουθίαι του Νυχθημερου). The Daily Office designates the Church's system of public communal daily prayer. It is celebrated through a series of services at certain fixed intervals of the day and night. These services – of varying length, content, and purpose – consist of both fixed and variable elements.

The festal or variable elements contained in the liturgical cycles of the week, month, and year are linked to the constant elements and the fixed structures of the Daily Office. The feasts of the Church – except for rare occasions – do not have an independent or self-sufficient service apart from the Daily Office. And when they do, these extra services, such as the Great Blessing of the Water on the Feast of Theophany (January 6) or the Elevation of the Cross on the Feast of the Exaltation of the Cross (September 14), are usually celebrated in conjunction with the Daily Office, at least in theory if not in practice.

The Typikon is the liturgical book that contains the directives and rubrics that regulate the use and the order of the variable elements in the Daily Office for each ordinary and festal day of the year and prescribes the Scripture lessons and the other variables in the Divine Liturgy on any given day. Thus, to put it succinctly, the directives or rubrics in the Typikon are related essentially to the Daily Office and the Divine Liturgy.

As we shall see below, the Divine Liturgy is not part of the Daily Office and its celebration is not determined by the fixed hours of prayer of the Daily Office.[144] The Divine Liturgy, the way by which the Orthodox Church celebrates the sacrament of the Eucharist, belongs to a totally different category of prayer. Baptism and the Eucharist are the preeminent sacraments of the Church. Through the Eucharist the Church celebrates and actualizes the one unrepeatable event, the "once for all" – (ἐφάπαξ) – sacrifice of the Cross (Rom. 6:10) and realizes herself as the Body of Christ. Hence, "the time of its celebration is unimportant, since what is being accomplished in the service introduces and incorporates us into a reality which is no way subject to time."[145] Nevertheless, the Divine Liturgy is not celebrated haphazardly. Though it is not part of the Daily Office, its celebration is not entirely independent of time. According to the Typikon, it is celebrated after the Orthros or after the Sixth Hour or in conjunction with a Vesper Service.

The Daily Office, on the other hand, is intimately related to time, to fixed hours and periods of the day and night. It is rooted in a theology of time, which contrasts the time of this world and the time of the age to come. Our common, everyday experiences of time – sunset and sunrise – have been integrated into liturgical time, in order to express and signify God's life in us and our life in him. Key events of salvation history have been tied to certain times and periods of the day, filling them with meanings and sanctifying them with the memory of God's transforming presence in the unfolding history of the world. Indeed, through worship – in all of its manifestations and expressions – and the Gospel, the Church keeps alive the memories of sacred history and the promises that were once for all delivered to the saints. Hence, the Church has organized her liturgy around time and the sacraments, or as someone put it, around a calendar (day, week, month, year) and a set of acts that make Christ and his saving acts – of the past and the future – a present reality.

The Daily Office, through its cycle of services at different intervals of the day, incorporates us into the mystery of Christ, in order to transform the time ($\chi\rho\acute{o}\nu os$) in which we live into the time ($\kappa\alpha\iota\rho\acute{o}s$) of our salvation through the remembrance of the Christ event.[146] Prayer, practiced consciously in truth and in the Spirit, transforms ordinary time into a decisive moment, into an opening and an opportunity, into a moment or day of grace. In the liturgy time acquires a new significance, a new urgency, and a new solemnity. Each day can become a shared existence with eternity, with the Risen and Reigning Christ, the Lord of history.

Though it is difficult to draw definitive conclusions about the forms of daily prayer in the early Church, it is safe to assume that the practice of daily worship goes back to apostolic times, as evidenced by the many references to prayer in the New Testament. Christians, like the Jews before them, adopted the custom of praying at certain fixed times during the day and night. Clear evidence of a pattern of daily prayer-times emerges during the course of the second century. By the middle of the fourth century the Church had in place several public communal services.[147]

The Daily Office developed chiefly along two lines, the cathedral and the monastic. The cathedral rite represents the form of services that were developed and practiced in the parochial or secular churches. The monastic rite, as the name indicates, originated in monastic communities. Scholars have further divided the monastic rite into two forms: the desert monastic (which originated in Egypt) and the urban monastic (which began in Capppadocia and Syria). Robert Taft has suggested that within the urban monastic types, it is possible to distinguish between two kinds of offices, one that is basically monastic in character but has absorbed cathedral elements, and one that is originally cathedral in its pattern but has added monastic elements.[148]

The cathedral and monastic offices, each with its own distinctive characteristics and features, coexisted for many centuries. This early distinction, however, came to a gradual end in the post-iconoclastic period with the eventual demise of the cathedral office.

In the aftermath of Iconoclasm (723-843), the monasteries – as the guardians of Orthodoxy during that long, unsettling and disruptive period – began to exert a larger influence on church affairs. The 'monasticization'[149] of ecclesial and liturgical life in the Eastern Church, beginning with the Penthekte Synod (691-692) which introduced celibacy as a requirement for the episcopacy (canon 12), was reinforced during the iconoclastic controversy. It grew progressively through the ensuing centuries until modern times.

The history of the Byzantine Rite and of the Typikon is intimately related to the history of the cathedral rite and to the rise and subsequent domination of the monastic rite.

The Cathedral Rite of Constantinople

We continue our review of the history of the Byzantine Rite and of the Typikon with a brief description of the cathedral rite of Constantinople. It should be remembered that the monastic movement, as a community of persons committed to personal sanctification living apart from the Christian community in the world, originated in the third century, long after the establishment of the Church. Thus, the parochial forms of communal worship of the early Church, which would eventually evolve into the cathedral rite, predate the monastic.

Anton Baumstark, the noted German liturgical scholar, was the first to use the terms *'cathedral rite'* and *'monastic rite'* to distinguish the parochial communal form of worship and especially the Daily Office, from the monastic.[150] In the Greek liturgical sources the cathedral rite is usually called the *Sung* or *Secular Office* ('Ασματική ἤ Κοσμική 'Ακολουθία). The term Sung Office comes from the fact that almost everything in it was sung or intoned. The other term, Secular – which has now fallen into disuse – (from the Latin *saecularis*, temporal, related to the world), is meant to denote the Office performed by the people assembled in parish churches in the world (in the cosmos – κόσμος and hence κοσμική – the adjective of cosmos, ἀκολουθία).

The label 'cathedral rite' comes from the bishop's church, known as the cathedral, which from the earliest times was the center of the Church's liturgical life. During the first two centuries, the people gathered around one Eucharist united under the leadership of one bishop.[151] When individual parishes began to emerge in the middle or late third century under the leadership of presbyters,[152] the liturgical usages of the bishop's church (the cathedral) were reproduced in and practiced by the parishes. What was done at the cathedral was also done in the parishes, although on a smaller scale.

In the East, the Cathedral of St. Sophia – Hagia Sophia, 'Αγία Σοφία – in Constantinople emerged as the single most significant church and its usages played a decisive role in the formation of the liturgical rites of the imperial city and eventually of the whole of the Orthodox Church. To quote Robert Taft:

> In no liturgical tradition is liturgical space such an integral part of the liturgy as in the Byzantine, and in no tradition has one edifice played such a decisive role as Justinian's Hagia Sophia... Hagia Sophia was the cathedral church of the city where the Byzantine Rite was molded and celebrated, and where the vi-

sion of its meaning, enacted elsewhere on a smaller stage, was determined and kept alive.[153]

As one might expect, the cathedral rite of Constantinople, as we noted above, included the whole array of elements that constitute a rite: Eucharistic liturgies, sacramental rites, a lectionary system, a calendar, and a daily office, which consisted of four services: Vespers, Pannychis (Παννυχίς – a type of vigil), Orthros, and Trithekte (Τριθέκτη – a service for the late morning hours). The cathedral daily office of Constantinople differed from its monastic counterpart, as we shall see below, both in the number as well as in the content, structure, order, spirit, and purpose of its services.

The ceremonies of the rite in all its myriad details were determined and regulated by the *Typikon of the Great Church*, the earliest extant manuscripts of which date from the ninth and tenth centuries.[154] The title of the book is derived from the name of the church built by St. Constantine and dedicated in 360 to serve as the cathedral of the City: the *Great Church – Ἡ Μεγάλη Ἐκκλησία –* which was also called *Hagia Sophia*. This church was severely damaged in 404; in 532 it was razed to the ground. In the same year the emperor Justinian I ordered the erection of a far more glorious church, the new Hagia Sophia or Great Church that was dedicated in 537.

The cathedral daily office of Constantinople was usually celebrated only twice a day, in the evening (Vespers) and the morning (Orthros). When a nocturnal vigil was indicated for a given feast, the Pannychis followed the Vespers. On fast days especially, when the Divine Liturgy was not celebrated, the service of the Trithekte was performed in the mid-morning hours. The psalms in the services were chosen for their suitability to the hour and the feast.[155] The same was true for the chant (antiphons, responsories, and hymns). The repertoire of hymns and responses was limited and select. Some hymns were complex, meant for the choir and the soloists, while other hymns were simple and recognizable, easy for the people to sing together with the choir. Instances of this type of singing survive in our liturgical texts, as, for example, the Antiphons in the beginning and the Alleluia before the Gospel at the Divine Liturgy; the Amomos (Psalm 118/119) in the Funeral Service; and the troparia between the Old Testament Readings in the Great Vespers of Christmas and Theophany. To illustrate, let me cite the troparion after the second Reading at the Christmas Vespers:

> The Choir (or soloist) sings: *You have shown forth from a Virgin, O Christ, spiritual Sun of Righteousness (Malachi 4:2). And a star showed You, whom nothing can contain, contained within a cave. You led the Magi to worship You, and joining them we magnify You: O Giver of life, glory to You.*

> Reader or Soloist (intones): *The Lord reigns, He is clothed in majesty; the Lord is clothed, He has girded himself with strength.* (Ps. 92/93:1).

> People (led by the singers): *You led the Magi to worship You, and joining them we magnify You: O Giver of life, glory to You.*

Several more verses of the Psalm are intoned and the people respond as above. At the conclusion of the Psalm, the people say the Glory, and the singers sing the entire hymn again.

The cathedral office was also characterized by the diversity of ministries: a bishop, who presided at the service; presbyters, who offered prayers and blessings; deacons, who said the petitions leading the people in prayer and who did the censing; sub-deacons, who kept order and assisted the clergy; readers and chanters, who read the Psalms and the lessons and led the singing.

The cathedral Vespers and the Orthros on most occasions did not have Scripture lessons, which emphasized their essential character as services of extensive intercession and praise.[156] As Paul Bradshaw says, "the cathedral office had a strong ecclesial dimension: here was the Church gathered for prayer, exercising its royal priesthood by offering a sacrifice of praise and thanksgiving on behalf of all creation and interceding for the salvation of the world."[157]

The cathedral or sung office of Constantinople had many other striking characteristics, one of which was the stational liturgy, which featured a grand procession, a Christianized element borrowed from the imperial ceremonies of the Roman Empire.[158] As John Baldovin tells us, liturgical processions through the streets of the city on a regular basis were in vogue in Constantinople by the early fifth century.[159] Stational liturgies were used to celebrate feasts and commemorate important events with prayer and solemn processions. More precisely, according to Boldavin's definition, a "stational liturgy is a service of worship at a designated church, shrine, or public place in or near a city or town, on a designated feast, fast, or commemoration, which is presided over by the bishop or his representative and intended as the local church's main liturgical celebration of the day."[160]

The *Typikon of the Great Church* lists sixty-eight such stational liturgies and processions, thirty-two of which involved the patriarch and some even the emperor. Stational liturgies were conducted on Palm Sunday, on the feast days of the Theotokos, St. John the Baptist, and a number of popular saints, and on the memorials of several earthquakes and enemy sieges.[161] On many – if not all – of these occasions the commemoration began on the eve of the feast in a designated church. This night assembly was called the *paromone* – παραμονή (station or watch). It included Vespers with Scripture readings (ἀναγνώσματα) and the Pannychis. The Orthros was also conducted in a designated church or shrine. From there, the clergy and the people processed through the city streets using antiphonal psalmody and stopping at one or more places (stations) to invoke God with litanies and prayers. The terminus of the procession was always a church in which the Divine Liturgy was then celebrated.

The following entry is from the Feast of the Dormition of the Theotokos on August 15. It gives the directives for the various ceremonials of the feast, through which we can gain a perspective on the contents of the *Typikon of the Great Church* and on the manner by which feasts were conducted and celebrated. First, the entry gives the date of the month and the title of the feast together with the general directives regarding the place where it is to be observed; and when and where the procession of the stational liturgy will begin. Second, the entry gives the essential details of the Service (ἡ Ἀκολουθία). It starts by telling us where the Vespers and the Pannychis are to be held and some details of the Vesper service, at which the patriarch presides. This is followed by another general directive about the troparion of the feast and some details about the morning services. The patriarch arrives at the designated place for the start of the procession at "early dawn" when the Orthros has ended. The Prayer of the Trisagion is said and the procession begins with song. The procession winds through the streets of the city and arrives at the Church of Blachernae, where the Divine Liturgy will be celebrated. The Typikon provides the details:

> On the fifteenth of the month (August) the commemoration of the holy Dormition (Μετάστασις – passing over, death) of our undefiled Lady Theotokos and ever-virgin Mary is celebrated... The synaxis of the feast[162] is celebrated in her venerable temple, which is at Blachernae,[163] and in her holy churches in every place. The procession (λιτή)[164] begins at early dawn at the Martyrium (a martyr's shrine) of St. Euphemia in Petrion and departs for the aforementioned synaxis.

The service (ἡ Ἀκολουθια) is conducted as follows. At the Vespers (Λυχνικόν – the hour of lamp-lighting),[165] that is to say, at the paramone (παραμονή) of the feast, the patriarch, as is customary, comes to [the church of the Theotokos of] Chalkoprateia;[166] and after the entrance, the prokeimenon is said in the third tone (ἦχος γ): 'My soul magnifies the Lord.' The verse (is): 'For he has regarded the low estate.'[167] And after the three small antiphons, petitions and prayer are made,[168] and three lections (ἀναγνώσματα – or passages, lessons, readings) are read. The first (is) from Genesis: 'And Jacob went out from Beersheba,' ending with, 'and this is the gate of heaven.' The second lection (is from) the prophecy of Ezekiel: 'Thus says the Lord: it shall be, that upon the eighth day,' ending with 'and, behold, the glory of the Lord filled *the house of the Lord.'* The third (is from) Proverbs: *'Wisdom has built her house,'* ending with, *'and the years of your life shall be increased.'*[169] Then, at the amvon (pulpit) the chanters (ψάλται) sing the troparion (hymn) in the first tone (ἦχος α). The hymn given in the text is the same as the apolytikion (dismissal hymn) of the feast in the Menaion, " Ἐν τῇ γεννήσει – In giving birth, O Theotokos, you have retained your virginity, and in falling asleep you have not forsaken the world. You are the Mother of Life who has passed over into life, and by your prayers you deliver our souls from death." And after the hymn the deacon says: Sophia. And the Pannychis is celebrated according to the order.

In the morning, both at Psalm 50 (51) (in the Orthros service) and the Entrance of the Liturgy, the same troparion (hymn) is sung. After the apolysis (dismissal) of the Orthros, the patriarch comes to the Martyrium of St. Euphemia in Petrion. The Prayer of the Trisagion is said, and the chanters ascend the ambon and begin the troparion of the procession in the plagal fourth tone (πλ. δ.). The hymn in the *Typikon* appears as the *hypakoe* (ὑπακοή) in the Orthros of the feast in the Menaion. "Μακαρίζομέν σε πᾶσαι αἱ γενεαί – From all generations we call you blessed, O Virgin Theotokos: for Christ our God who cannot be contained was pleased to be contained in you. Blessed also are we in having you as our succor: day and night you intercede for us, and the scepters of kings are strengthened by your supplications. Therefore, singing your praises we cry aloud to you: Hail, you who are full of grace, the Lord is with you." And the procession enters the church at Blachernae and there the chanters glorify (δοξάζουσιν – they sing 'Glory to the Father...').

The antiphons are not said, but immediately the Trisagion (is sung). The prokeimenon is in the third tone. (The prokeimenon and the verse are given; and are the same as those in the Vespers). The Apostolos (Epistle is) to the Philippians: *'Let this mind be in you'* ending with *'that Jesus Christ is Lord, to the glory of the Father. Amen'*. The Alleluia is in the first tone and the verses are: *'Listen, O daughter, consider and incline your ear'* until *'your beauty.'*[170] The Evangelion (Gospel lection) is according to Luke, paragraph (κεφάλαιον) 128: *'At that time, Jesus entered a certain village,'* and he reads until, *'which shall not be taken away from her;'* and jumps ahead to paragraph 131 and says, *'and as he spoke these things,'* ending with, *'and keep it.'*[171] The Communion hymn (Κοινωνικόν) is 'I will receive the cup of salvation – Ποτήριον σωτηρίου λήψομαι.'[172]

The act of processing – the drama of liturgical movement, a sign of the Church on the pilgrimage toward the Kingdom – was also incorporated into the Divine Liturgy and the daily office of the cathedral rite. For example, the first part of the Vespers and the Orthros was conducted in the narthex. Then, at a given moment in a dramatic forward movement, the clergy and the laity entered the church together singing hymns and occupied the center of the nave around the amvon. As the service progressed towards its conclusion, the clergy processed into the sanctuary to occupy the synthronon, while the people pressed forward toward the sanctuary. Finally, in the order with which they entered, the clergy and the people processed out of the church singing hymns. Similarly, at least prior the eighth century, the Divine Liturgy began with prayer and song and a solemn entrance of the clergy and the people into the church, the clergy moving into the sanctuary and the people occupying the nave. At the Great Entrance, the deacons and the servers performed a grand procession, carrying the sacramental gifts to the sanctuary. At the end of the Divine Liturgy, after the Prayer Behind the Amvon ('Οπισθάμβωνος Εὐχή), the clergy and the people processed out of the church together singing hymns joyously.

While in many respects the Sung Office of Constantinople was impressive and striking, it lacked the large body of hymnody that had come to characterize the revised monastic daily office in the post-iconoclastic period (the Studite synthesis). The elaborate cathedral office had now become, by comparison, the more staid of the two, thanks to the profusion and infusion of new hymnody in the monastic office. Another factor that helped bring about the decline of the cathedral office was the simplicity of the monastic office. One priest (and if available, one deacon) and one chanter/reader could perform the service. The cathedral office on the other hand required a group of clergy – bishops, presbyters, and deacons – together with singers, readers and servers to effectively perform the service. These and other reasons that are lost to history brought about the gradual demise of the cathedral office.

The Monastic Office

From the earliest times in the history of the Church certain men and women of faith felt a special calling to lead an intense interior life through the recasting of their relationships and their existence. They gave themselves up to the ideal of voluntary virginity as an effort to realize union with Christ. They nourished their new way of life with ceaseless prayer. They became monastics (μοναχοί). A monastic (monk or nun) "was simply a Christian, and more precisely a devout layman, who limited himself to taking the most radical means to make his Christianity integral."[173]

In the early years, monastics – Christians who voluntarily made themselves eunuchs spiritually for the sake of God's kingdom (Mt. 19:12) – lived in the world within the general Christian community and shared its life. By the middle of third century, however, monastics began to depart from the world, living at first in the outer edges of towns and villages and later withdrawing further into the deserts in search of greater solitude. They became anchorites and hermits (ἀναχωριταί καί ἐρημῖται), living alone or in small desert colonies, renouncing evil. Secluded from the world, they gave themselves up to grace to be possessed by the Spirit of God. The retreat to the desert, however, was neither an escape from responsibilities nor a "desire for tranquility, for leisure and for extended contemplation in the sense of Greek philosophy. If the (good) monk buried himself in the desert, it was with the intention of fighting against the devil… It was simply the means of effectively gaining integral charity."[174]

The ascetic effort – the disengagement from the bonds of the flesh and the world – involved poverty, prayer, vigils, fasting, the study of and meditation on Scriptures, acts of charity, and honest work for both a simplified livelihood and for the practice of charity. For the monastic the reformation of the soul begins with the body, not by showing contempt for it or for anything in the created order, but by mastering it and liberating it from its passions. The ascetic effort was and continues to be essentially instrumental. It is not an end unto itself but a means to something greater and higher, as St. John Cassian (+435) informs us. "Our fastings, our vigils, meditation on Scripture, poverty, and privation of all things are not perfection, but the instruments for acquiring it."[175]

Early in the fourth century, St. Pachomios (+346), a soldier convert to Christianity who became a monk in the deserts of Egypt, began to introduce reforms into the monastic communities of the desert. These changes altered radically the primitive forms of monasticism, and especially its free-spiritedness. He organized the monks into hierarchical cenobitic (κοινόβιον—common life) communities with codified rules and regulations under the undisputed authority of an hegoumenos (ἡγούμενος – abbot), to whom the monks pledged complete obedience. These innovations, which sought to protect monasticism from anarchy and decline, did not gain universal approval at first. However, within decades it became the standard practice to organize monastics into cenobitic communities or into a lavra, i.e., into a community of anchorites and hermits who lived alone during the week but shared prayer, the Eucharist, and meals in common on Saturday and Sunday and on feast days. Each community, whether cenobitic or lavra, had its own rules and regulations regarding their forms of communal life, governance, and prayer.

The early cenobitic communities of Pachomios, for example, were organized around small houses, each with a number of monks under the obedience of an abbot. In these communities, prayer in common consisted especially of the recitation of Psalms and was conducted three times a day, in the morning, at midday, and in the evening. Prayers were also said at bedtime and again in the night during which the monks kept vigil. During the vigil the Scriptures were read at length and were interspersed with psalms and prayers to break the monotony and to increase attentiveness.

Monks were laymen. Though they had a vigorous personal and communal prayer life, they depended on the local churches and the local clergy for the Eucharist and the other sacraments. Thus, monks were obliged to go to the nearest villages or towns for the Eucharist or they would invite village priests to their colonies to celebrate the Eucharist. In the course of the fourth century, however, monastic communities, under the supervision of the local bishop, began to have some members of their brotherhood ordained to the diaconate and the presbyterate to meet the sacramental needs of the community.[176] As this occurred, the monastic communities became totally 'self-sufficient' sacramentally.

Organized monasticism had become a reality throughout the East by the middle of the fourth century.[177] St. Basil the Great (330-379), wholly imbued with an evangelical spirit, was another of the great reformers of monasticism. He had a definite preference for the cenobitic form, which is to say a sharing of life together in community. "Nothing is as proper to our nature," he wrote, "than as to enter into one another's society, to have need of one another, and to love man who is of our race." He put forward a monastic Rule in two forms, *The Longer Rules* and *The Shorter Rules* (Ὅροι κατά Πλάτος καὶ Ὅροι κατ' Ἐπιτομήν).[178]

For St. Basil, the ideal monastic community had to be integrated into the life of the Church and had to be small. A small community allowed for the growth of personal relationships and for an orderly life under obedience to the abbot. It also provided each monk with the opportunity to achieve a high level of solitude, honored above all even within a cenobitic community, so that he might come to experience the gift of ceaseless prayer.

St. Basil's Rule, among other things, cautioned against extreme forms of asceticism, encouraged manual labor, prescribed chastity and poverty, established community life under obedience, required care for the poor and other social work, and laid down the liturgical hours of prayer. The Rule of St. Basil was to become the cornerstone of Eastern Orthodox monasticism.

Yet as highly influential as the Rule of St. Basil was in shaping Eastern monasticism, it was not the only one and it did not supplant entirely the spirit of the primitive desert monasticism, that is to say, its interior charismatic and anchorite character, its free-spiritedness and solitariness.

There were times, however, when monastics abused their free-spiritedness and meddled in church and civil affairs, causing strife and divisions. Sometimes monastics established private foundations to circumvent the immediate supervision of the local bishop and the oversight of civil authorities. As a result, ecclesial and civil legislation was formulated to bring unregulated monasteries and unruly itinerant monks under the control of civil and ecclesial authorities. Canon 4 of the Fourth Ecumenical Synod was the first official account of the status of monastics in the structure of the institutional Church. It reads as follows:

> Let those who truly and sincerely lead a monastic life be honored as is proper. But because certain persons, for whom the monastic life is only a pretext, sow trouble in the affairs of the Church and state by inconsiderately roaming around in the cities trying even to establish monasteries for themselves, it seemed good and proper that no one be allowed to build or establish a monastery or an oratory anywhere without the consent of the bishop of the city. In each city and country area, let the monks be subject to the bishop; let them seek peace and only apply themselves to fasting and prayer, remaining in the place where they made their profession of renunciation; let them not cause any troubles in the affairs of the Church or state; and let them not get mixed up in such affairs by leaving their monasteries, except if eventually they are permitted to do so by the bishop of the city for some grave necessity... We have decided that whoever goes against the present ruling will be excommunicated, so that the name of God will not be blasphemed.[179]

Of special interest to us is St. Basil's rule of prayer. While he encouraged monastics to practice ceaseless prayer (I Thess. 5:17) in private (this is not a reference to the 'Jesus Prayer'),[180] he promoted communal prayer and increased the number of services of the daily office. Personal prayer was practiced in solitude and in silence, while the daily office was practiced in common. The services of the daily office were embellished with ritual, Scripture readings, prayers, and psalmody and were led by an ordained member of the community. The daily office consisted of seven prayer intervals: at dawn; at the third, sixth, and ninth hours; at evening (sunset); at the beginning of the night; and at midnight.[181] The daily office with its seven prayer-hours as articulated by St. Basil would become, in time, the common inheritance of Eastern monasticism through the Typika of the Lavra of St. Savas and of the Monastery of Stoudios in Constantinople.[182]

The *Lavra* of St. Savas

The monastic liturgical tradition of the Orthodox East has come down to us through the *Typikon of the Church Service of the Holy Lavra at Jerusalem of our Righteous and God-bearing Father Savas – (Τυπικόν τῆς Ἐκκλησιαστικῆς Ἀκλολουθίας τῆς ἐν Ἱεροσολύμοις Ἁγίας Λαύρας τοῦ Ὁσίου καί Θεοφόρου Πατρός ἡμῶν Σάβα* – which is popularly known as the *Typikon of St. Savas* (also spelled Sabas or Sabbas).

As the title indicates, this Typikon originated at the Lavra (a colony of anchorites – ἀναχωρηταί) founded by St. Savas (+532) in the Judean desert southeast of Jerusalem in the year 484.[183] This monastic community grew in prestige and came to be known as the Great Lavra – Μεγίστη Λαύρα.[184]

As is the case with all monastic communities, the Great Lavra was governed by certain rules that were codified in the community's Typikon. The Typikon of a monastery usually includes three parts: the community's rule of life (both personal and communal); its rule of governance (administrative structures); and its rule of prayer (the order and type – τύπος – of its divine services).[185] In the early monastic Typika the rule of prayer was fairly simple, reflecting the sober contemplative ethos of early monastic prayer. However, as the daily office became more elaborate the later Typika contained a greater amount of liturgical detail.

The reputation of the Great Lavra of St. Savas grew steadily among the monastic communities of the East. By virtue of its prominence, its administrative regulations and, more especially, its liturgical usages became widely accepted. Its Typikon became the authoritative model for large segments of Eastern monasticism.

St. Savas, an ordained presbyter and monk, was from Asia Minor. He was familiar with the monastic practices of Cappadocia that were formulated by St. Basil the Great. Traveling into the deserts of Egypt, Syria, and Palestine, he began to familiarize himself with the traditions of desert monasticism in these places. He also spent time in Jerusalem and was exposed to cathedral office of the city before he established the Lavra in the Judean desert. The liturgical practices and customs of the desert monastic communities of Egypt, Syria, Palestine, and Asia Minor and the cathedral office of Jerusalem that helped to shape and form St. Savas were reflected in the Rule that he established for the Great Lavra that bears his name.

The early versions of the monastic office, as noted above, were more contemplative than liturgical in nature. Though there was some hymnody, stronger emphasis was placed on the continuous recitation of the Psalms, on silent prayer, and on the meditation and study of the Scriptures. This was especially true of the monastic communities of the desert.[186] At the Great Lavra the anchorites (monastics who live in seclusion) continued with the familiar practices of the desert in their personal devotions. The daily office at the Lavra, however, drew its form and shape from the Rule of St. Basil. With its seven prayer-hours and eight services,[187] the daily office would develop gradually, especially with the infusion of ecclesiastical poetry. Three celebrated monks of the Lavra contributed significantly to these developments: St. Andrew (+ca. 720), who became bishop of Crete, St. John of Damascus (+ca. 749), and St. Cosmas the Melodist (+ca. 750), who became bishop of Maiouma near Gaza. All three were master hymnographers.

The customs and practices of the Great Lavra came to Constantinople in the latter part of the eighth century through the Monastery of Studios, where the Typikon of St. Savas was re-worked. It was embellished with additional hymnody and synthesized with elements of the cathedral office of the city.

The Monastery of Studios

Monasticism came to Constantinople sometime between the fourth and fifth centuries. Jerusalem, which had developed into an important pilgrim center during the course of the fourth century, was already hosting a number of monastic communities within its walls. For a variety of reasons – influenced perhaps by St. Basil – many monastics no longer sought the solitude of the desert but formed communities in the cities and towns. Organized urban monasticism provided for scores of monastics an attractive alternative to the desert; and so the early anchorite spirit – the departure from the world – made a kind of 'u-turn.' Urban monasticism competed with the desert and began to flourish. By the middle of the sixth century Constantinople and Chalcedon between them had about one hundred and ten monasteries.[188] Urban monasticism would eventually play a significant role in the development of the style and structures of ecclesial governance and on the shape of the Church's liturgy.

Among the early monastic communities of Constantinople was the Monastery of St. John the Forerunner, known popularly as the Monastery of Studios after its founder and benefactor, a Roman consul named Studios, who founded the monastery in 454, or perhaps as early as 450. By 460, Studios populated the monastery with a group of monks dedicated to the practice of perpetual prayer.[189] Through a method of rotation the monks of Studios maintained constant vigil before God, offering him ceaseless prayer. As a result, they were called the ἀκοίμητοι – the sleepless ones. The monastery continued to prosper until 765 but fell thereafter into decline after many iconodule monastics were expelled from Constantinople.

However, the fortunes of Studios would soon be reversed with the arrival in Constantinople some thirty years later of a charismatic monastic named Theodore, who was born in the Imperial City in 759. Although he was educated and trained for service in the imperial bureaucracy, Theodore chose instead the monastic life and retired to Bithynia in Asia Minor. There he became the abbot of the monastery of Sakkoudion, which was established as a private family foundation by his uncle Plato.

In 798 or 799 Theodore (who was to be called the Studite) arrived in Constantinople from Asia Minor with a company (συνοδεία) of monks at the invitation of the iconodule Empress Irene and took up residence at Studios, where he laid the foundations for a new cenobitic community. From this community, a sustained revival of cenobitic monasticism would emanate over the next few centuries, especially with the establishment of satellite or federated communities.[190] For his saintly life and for his many contributions to monasticism, theology, and the liturgical life of the Church, Theodore was canonized sometime after his death in 826.

St. Theodore the Studite was influenced by the ideals of monasticism as expounded by St. Basil and especially by St. Dorotheos of Gaza (ca. 6th century).[191] He was inspired also by the magnificent achievements in hymnography of the monks of the Great Lavra of St. Savas. Like others before him, he recognized the great value of hymnody as a powerful tool for teaching the faith, enlivening the interior life, and inspiring godly actions. To bolster and invigorate the life and mission of his newly founded community at Studios, St. Theodore invited monks from the Lavra of St. Savas to join him and his company as he began a program of reforms that would influence greatly the development of Orthodox monasticism and have a lasting affect on Orthodox liturgy.

One can trace the influence of St. Theodore on the administrative structures and rules of monastic life in Byzantium through two documents, his *Testament* and *Rule,* that comprise his 'ktetorikon' or founder's Typikon,[192] and his influence on the liturgical life of the Church through the Studite liturgical Typikon. A founder's Typikon generally contains administrative and disciplinary regulations, dietary instructions, clothing requirements, manual labor practices, liturgical duties, and sacramental rules. The liturgical Typikon of the monastery, on the other hand, contains the liturgical regulations that pertain to the daily cycle of worship, the fixed calendar and movable feasts, the lectionary, and other pertinent liturgical matters. The liturgical Typikon may also contain the dietary prescriptions of the monastery as they relate to feasts and fasts. Of special interest to us is the liturgical Typikon that the Studites would create under the influence, guidance, and supervision of St. Theodore and his successors.

At Studios, St. Theodore created a new order of services, often referred to as the Studite synthesis, which, in effect, was a fusion of elements from the monastic office of St. Savas and the Sung Office of Constantinople. He grafted the prayers and litanies of the Euchologion of the Great Church – Hagia Sophia – to the Palestinian Daily Office with its hymns and psalmody. The synthesis created by the Studites would weather the uncertainties of history and put its seal upon the essential structures, content, and ethos of the Byzantine Rite, which is in effect a hybrid rite whose Daily Office derives mostly from the monastic tradition, while its Divine Liturgies, sacramental rites, and other services from the cathedral tradition.

The monks of Studios, including Theodore himself and his brother Joseph, were dedicated to the cultivation of hymnography and together they increased the received Palestinian repertoire of hymns. Gradually, the ecclesial poetry produced by the Palestinian and Studite monks and by other eminent hymnographers was codified between the eighth and tenth centuries in the collection of books that we now know as the *Horologion, Oktoechos* (or *Paraklitike*), *Triodion, Pentecostarion,* and *Menaia* that contain both the fixed and variable elements of the daily office. The formation of these books continued in the ensuing centuries with additional material contributed by clerics, monastics, emperors, and lay people from various centers of the Byzantine Empire. In fact, though the printed editions of these books curtailed to a great degree the continued development of their contents, they are technically always open to new material once authorized and approved by the Church.

In addition to the new hymns and the new order of services, the Studite synthesis introduced two other items. First, the Palestinian Monastic Psalter (Ψαλτήριον) replaced the Constantinopolitan Cathedral Psalter; and second, the characteristic Palestinian Vigil for Sundays and for the major feast days was replaced with a modified series of services made up of cathedral and monastic elements: the Compline, the Midnight Service (Mesonyktikon – Μεσονυκτικόν), and the Orthros. This elaboration of the rites at Studios continued even after the death of St. Theodore, carried on by the monks who assisted him over the years and by their successors.

The Studite administrative and liturgical Typikon rapidly became a model for others to emulate. From the monastic communities of Constantinople it spread to other monastic centers. In fact, Studite monasticism – in all of its expressions – would come to dominate the monastic scene of the empire through the twelfth century. It formed the basis of the foundational hagiorite rule (ἁγιορειτικόν τυπικόν) on Mt. Athos (the first monastery, the Great Lavra, was founded by St. Athanasios in 962-963) and of the rule of monastic communities in Ukraine, Russia, Georgia, and Magna Graecia in Southern Italy and Sicily.[193] Eventually, it found its way to Palestine and the Great Lavra of St. Savas, where it would undergo yet another transformation that would be identified as the new Sabaitic synthesis, which in essence constitutes and represents the extant Byzantine Rite.

Surprisingly, no Greek originals of the Studite liturgical Typikon – in any of its variations – would survive, only six Slavonic manuscripts. The closest version in Greek of the Studite synthesis is the twelfth century liturgical Typikon, also known as the Synaxarion of the Monastery of the Theotokos Evergetis in Constantinople,[194] an edition of which (with commentary) has been prepared by Drs. Robert Jordan and John Klentos.[195] However, the liturgical Typikon of the great Monastery of the Theotokos Evergetis shows the strong influence of the neo-Sabaitic synthesis, which gradually prevailed over and replaced the Studite Typikon.

The Neo-Sabaitic Synthesis

Following the Islamic incursions and the destructive iconoclastic controversy, the Great Lavra of St. Savas fell into gradual decline. However, by the late tenth century it began to experience a renaissance. During the eleventh century, as we noted above, the Studite liturgical Typikon – a revised version of the Sabaitic tradition – found its way to Palestine where it was adopted by the monks of the Great Lavra. However, the monks of the Lavra were not content with simply receiving the liturgical Typikon of the Studites. They set about modifying it to suit their more austere needs and characteristic rule, which included the all-night vigil or ἀγρυπνία.

The monks of the Great Lavra, as we mentioned above, were accustomed to holding a vigil in preparation for Sunday and the major feast days. Thus, they reintroduced the all-night vigil, which the Studites had eliminated. The vigil became once again the centerpiece, or the essential element of the monastic system of services. As a result, the monks of the Lavra celebrated two Vespers on the eve of Sunday and major feasts: the 'Small' Vespers at the customary time, i.e. at twilight and the Great Vespers after supper as part of the all-night vigil. This system is reflected in the liturgical books and is readily recognized in the Octoechos, Triodion, and Pentecostarion (Saturday night Vespers) and in the Menaia (for the major feasts).

The monks' penchant for long services was evidenced in other ways as well. The Palestinian monks introduced a system by which the Psalter was read in its entirety each week. The Psalter was divided into twenty sections called kathismata (καθίσματα), each of which consists of three staseis (στάσεις) or subsections. Each day one section or kathisma (κάθισμα) was assigned to the Vespers and two to the Orthros.

The Orthros was also expanded. The canon, a series of

hymns divided into nine odes based on the canticles of the Scriptures, formed a major part of the Orthros.[196] While the Studite liturgical Typikon assigned only three odes (τριώδια) of the canon to each day, the Palestinians included all nine. The reforms of the Palestinian monks were not limited to the expansion of the services; they also contributed to the growing collection of liturgical hymns that would be incorporated into the appropriate liturgical books.

The Studite Typikon, reworked and modified by the Lavra monks, came to be known as the neo-Sabaitic synthesis, the name given by the eminent liturgical scholar Robert Taft. Eventually during the course of the twelfth century, the new revised Sabaitic Typikon – with its intense rule of prayer and strict fasting discipline – began to find its way back to the monasteries of Constantinople and from there to Mt. Athos,[197] which from its founding in the tenth century as a monastic center had evolved within a period of two centuries into a "major meeting point of cultures, from where ideas traveled throughout the Orthodox world, and where major figures... had received their spiritual and intellectual training."[198]

Through an extended network of monastic contacts the neo-Sabaitic usages would spread from Mt. Athos to the entire Orthodox world, gradually replacing both the Sung Office and the Studite synthesis. By the fifteenth century the Sung Office and the Studite synthesis would fall into disuse and the neo-Sabaitic Typikon would become the rite of the Orthodox Church worldwide.[199] The takeover of the Patriarchate of Constantinople by the Athonite monastic party after 1347 helped to insure both the position of the new Sabaitic Typikon and the spread of liturgical art dependent on the Constantinopolitan tradition.[200]

The ascendancy of the new Typikon was further solidified in the sixteenth century when it was published in 1545 under the title *Typikon of the Ecclesiastical Service of the Holy Lavra in Jerusalem of our Righteous Father Savas* – Τυπικόν τῆς Ἐκκλησιαστικῆς Ἀκολουθίας τῆς ἐν Ἱεροσολύμοις Ἁγίας Λαύρας τοῦ Ὁσίου Πατρός ἡμῶν Σάββα. This first printed edition of the new Typikon was, in fact, the fourteenth-century Athonite codification of the new Sabaitic usage, which was authorized and sanctioned by Philotheos Kokkinos, the celebrated Hesychast (ἡσυχαστής) abbot of the Great Lavra of Mt. Athos and later Patriarch of Constantinople (1353 – 1355 and 1364 – 1376).

Philotheos, while abbot of the Great Lavra, composed two important manuals of directives or rubrics (Diataxeis – Διατάξεις) for the Daily Office and for the Divine Liturgy.[201] These rubrics were incorporated into the new Sabaitic Typikon and into the respective liturgical books, initially as a single text in the form of a prologue or introduction and later as individual rubrics at the appropriate places within the text of the divine services. These rubrics with local variations continue to regulate, for the most part, the current liturgical practice of the Orthodox Church.

The several revisions and modifications of the new Sabaitic Typikon represent the evolution which the daily office underwent over the course of many centuries. This long process resulted in the formation of the liturgical books that are currently in use by the Orthodox Church. We can say, therefore, that the liturgical books related to the daily office essentially reflect monastic practices and traditions. However, it is also important to remember that the neo-Sabaitic Typikon is a revised version of the Studite synthesis, a blend of monastic and cathedral office elements.

From the fifteenth century until 1838 – except for minor local variations and rubrical details – the Orthodox Churches throughout the world followed the same Typikon, the neo-Sabaitic synthesis.

The Typikon of the Great Church of Christ
By the beginning of the nineteenth century it had become obvious to many leaders of the Greek Church that the daily office with its long and complex monastic services could not be sustained in the parishes. Already, numerous abbreviations and omissions were taking place. To forestall further arbitrary changes and also sanction new practices that had taken hold, the Ecumenical Patriarchate took an

enormous first step towards revising the monastic Typikon in order to accommodate it to better parish usage.

In 1838 the Ecumenical Patriarchate authorized the publication of a new Typikon prepared and edited by Konstantinos the Protopsaltis (precentor) under the title *The Ecclesiastical Typikon According to the Style of the Great Church of Christ* – *Τυπικόν Εκκλησιαστικόν κατά τό Ύφος τῆς τοῦ Χριστοῦ Μεγάλης Εκκλησίας*. The title 'The Great Church of Christ,' refers to the Ecumenical Patriarchate of Constantinople. The Typikon of Konstantinos was intended for the use of the parish churches under the supervision of the Patriarchate. Monastic communities, however, were expected to retain and use the Typikon of St. Savas. A second, revised edition of the Typikon of Konstantinos appeared in 1868.

Ten years later in 1878, the Ecumenical Patriarchate initiated another review of the Typikon. It established two committees, one under Patriarch Joachim III (1878–1884) and another under Patriarch Dionysios V (1887–1891), to the study the Typikon in detail and to make recommendations for further revisions. These efforts resulted in the creation of yet another Typikon that was destined to survive into our own times.

In 1888 the Ecumenical Patriarchate authorized the publication of the *Typikon of the Great Church of Christ* – *Τυπικόν τῆς τοῦ Χριστοῦ Μεγάλης Ἐκκλησίας*, edited by the Protopsaltis Georgios Violakis.[202] Violakis and the members of the Committee[203] with which he was associated worked from the Typikon of Konstantinos and sought to accomplish two things. First, the Committee set about correcting the errors and the inaccuracies (τά λάθη καί τάς ἀνακριβείας) in the texts of the Typikon of Konstantinos. Second and more importantly, the Committee, building on the work of Konstantinos, introduced additional revisions based on the received oral and written traditions of the Ecumenical Patriarchate and on the established liturgical practice of the times.

Like its immediate forerunner, the new *Typikon of the Great*

Church of Christ did not create a new body of material. The services of the daily office remain essentially the same and bear their monastic origins and identity. The Typikon of 1888 did, however, create a new liturgical practice, which may be described as an abbreviated form of the monastic office adapted to parochial usage.

For example, the Typikon of 1888 modified the Vespers and the Orthros,[204] abbreviated the burial service, abolished the all-night vigil for Sundays and major feast days,[205] and sanctioned several new rituals for the services of Holy Week and Pascha.[206]

Some have suggested that the revisions of the Typikon of 1888 were ill-advised.[207] Yet in spite of any shortcomings that the Typikon may have, the decision of the Ecumenical Patriarchate to authorize its publication and use must be applauded as a necessary response of the Church to emerging needs and circumstances. We should not overlook the fact that even the Churches that have retained the Typikon of St. Savas do not follow it in its exactness in parish practice. Inevitably, abbreviations and modifications are made to fit local conditions and needs. The decision of the Ecumenical Patriarchate to study and revise the Typikon is, I believe, especially significant for our times. It constitutes the basis as well as the supporting argument for the continued comprehensive study and evaluation of the Church's liturgical practice.

The *Typikon of the Great Church of Christ* was adopted by all the local churches under the immediate jurisdiction of the Ecumenical Patriarchate and gradually by other Greek-speaking Churches. Other autocephalous Churches also adopted it in varying degrees. However, the Typikon of St. Savas continues to be used by most monastic communities – if not all – and by the Churches of Jerusalem, Russia, Georgia, Serbia, and several jurisdictions in the United States. Thus in effect, we have two Typika that co-exist side by side in the Church today and regulate our liturgical practice. The differences in liturgical usage, however, are chiefly structural and rubrical rather than essential.

The Four Liturgical Schemata

One significant difference between the two Typika pertains to the celebration of the Divine Liturgy. In the Typika we find four distinctive and independent liturgical schemata. The structure of these schemata is determined chiefly by the position accorded to the Divine Liturgy in the cycle of the daily office. This position, in turn, regulates – at least in principle – the time of the celebration of the Divine Liturgy. I have labeled these schemata as follows: the '*Original* or *Archaic schema*,' the '*schema of the Pre-Sanctified Gifts*,' the '*Monastic schema*,' and the '*Morning schema*.'[208]

Two of the schemata – the *Archaic* and the *Pre-Sanctified*, are common to both Typika. These two schemata connect the Divine Liturgy to a Vesper service. The *Archaic*, while appearing infrequently in the Typika, is nevertheless significant because it is associated with the Vigils of the great feasts of the Church: Pascha, Christmas, Theophany, and Holy Thursday. It can be shown that this schema represents – in broad strokes – an early form of a eucharistic liturgy, inasmuch as the Eucharist, during the first century, was celebrated in the context of an evening meal in the pattern of the Mystical or Last Supper. The Divine Liturgy of St. Basil, which was originally the principal Liturgy of the Byzantine Rite, is assigned to these Vigils. The importance of this detail should not be overlooked, since as it points to the fact that the Vigils marked the principal celebration of these great Feasts.[209] The second Liturgy – that of St. John Chrysostom – which is celebrated on the morning of the feasts of Pascha, Christmas, and Theophany, is duplication, added for pastoral reasons. With the passage of time the significance of the Vigil, and most especially the Paschal Vigil, has been lost and needs to be recovered.

The schema of the *Pre-Sanctified* is limited in both Typika to the Lenten season and to the first three days of Holy Week. There is evidence, however, that in former times the Liturgy of the Pre-Sanctified Gifts was used more widely and more frequently.[210] The Pre-Sanctified Liturgy – like the other services – has a long and complex history. It is sufficient for us at this point simply to mention that its origins can be traced to the practice of self-communion and the rules regulating the practice of fasting. It was customary in the early Church for many Christians – clerics, laity, and ascetics alike – to receive Holy Communion daily in their homes. The consecrated Eucharistic Gifts were distributed for this purpose at the Sunday Eucharist to those who desired them. Though this practice was discontinued, it provided the impetus for the creation of a new form of Communion, i.e., the distribution and the communion of the Reserved Sacrament in the context of a communal worship service. With regard to the rules of fasting, two practices are of special significance in the development of the Pre-Sanctified schema. In the early Church Wednesdays and Fridays were observed with a total fast, which meant complete abstinence from food and drink until the late afternoon. This practice was especially true for Great Lent. Secondly, from early times it was considered inappropriate to celebrate the Divine Liturgy on fast days, because the Eucharist constitutes a feast and therefore is incompatible with the spirit of the fast. While fasting signifies anticipation and the way toward the fullness, the Eucharist is the manifestation of that fullness. The combination of these factors resulted in the development of the Liturgy of the Pre-Sanctified, which can be defined succinctly as the distribution and communion of the pre-sanctified Holy Gifts at the end of a fast day in the context of a communal worship service, consisting mainly of Vespers and Communion elements of the Divine Liturgy.

The other two schemata are peculiar to one or the other of the Typika. They vary significantly in their structure, even though both connect the Divine Liturgy to daytime services. The *Monastic schema* is a characteristic feature of the Typikon of St. Savas about which we have already spoken. For Sundays and certain feast days this Typikon requires an all-night vigil, after which the Divine Liturgy is celebrated. While this model and pattern may be possible in monastic settings, it is hardly an option for parishes. The vigil is kept after a fashion. In the parishes of the Churches that have retained the Typikon of St. Savas the 'vigil' is observed in an abbreviated form. The Great Vespers and the Orthros are conducted on Saturday night as a type of mini-vigil, while the Divine Liturgy is celebrated on Sunday morning after the services of the Third and Sixth Hours.

The *Morning schema* is peculiar to the *Typikon of the Great Church*. As noted above, the Divine Liturgy according to this schema is celebrated after the Orthros. Though the *Morning schema* is found in the newest Typikon, it is not an innovation but rather a return to an earlier practice that can be traced to Christian antiquity. In fact, it represents the second oldest of the four schemata. It developed sometime between the end of the first and the beginning of the second centuries, when for various reasons the original evening Eucharistic synaxis – represented by the *Archaic schema* – was transferred first to the predawn hours of Sunday and later to the third hour of the day (mid-morning – around 9 a.m.). Significantly, the *Morning schema* constituted the normal order in the now defunct Cathedral Office of Constantinople.

Another noteworthy difference pertains to the first part of the Divine Liturgy. According to both Typika – that of St. Savas and of the Great Church – Antiphons are sung only on the feasts of the Lord, the Theotokos, and certain saints. The so-called Typika are assigned for Sundays. The Antiphons consist of verses from three different Psalms that are deemed suitable to the feast and brief ecclesial poems that are used as a refrain between the verses of the Psalms. The Typika, on the other hand, which are also sung in three parts, consist of two fixed Psalms (102/103 and 145/146) whose verses are sung one after the other, and the Beatitudes (from the Gospel of Matthew) with several short hymns. These hymns are found at the end of each Orthros service in the Octoechos or Parakletike. However, according to current Greek practice the Typika are rarely sung on Sundays, having been replaced by the Antiphons. Most other Churches continue to sing the Typika, in part or in full, on Sundays and the Antiphons on the designated feast days.

Contents of the Typikon of the Great Church of Christ

The *Typikon of the Great Church of Christ*, authorized and published in 1888 by the Ecumenical Patriarchate, continues to govern the liturgical praxis of the Greek Church. It is a collection of liturgical rules divided into several sections. It begins with a brief statement, "Instructions and comments on the previously published Typika – Ὁδηγίαι καί παρατηρήσεις ἐπί τῶν προηγουμένων ἐκδόσεων τοῦ Τυπικοῦ" – that explains the changes introduced by the new Typikon. These revisions included corrections and additions in the rubrics as well as modifications in the order of some services, especially the Orthros. The statement also lists seven unresolved issues that require the attention and the decision of the Holy Synod. These issues deal with certain rubrical details, such as the appropriate Entrance Hymn for the Divine Liturgy during the Paschal season and the appropriate hymns for the rites of ordination. The response of the Holy Synod to each of the questions is recorded by way of a summation in a footnote at the conclusion of the statement. The statement also mentions that the new Typikon includes in the appropriate places the Antiphons and Megalynaria that are proper to the feasts of the Lord and the Theotokos, so that they may be readily available to chanters and choir directors.

A second introductory section quotes canon 75 of the Penthekte Synod together with the commentaries of the medieval canonists Zonaras, Balsamon, and Aristenos. This canon deals with the ministry of the Psaltis or Singer and serves as a reminder to singers and clergy alike to conduct the divine services with propriety and decorum.

The main body of the Typikon is preceded by an extensive Preface (Προθεωρία τοῦ Τυπικοῦ) that contains a detailed account of the directives and ceremonials (διατάξεις) for every conceivable circumstance and instance (περίπτωσις) for each of the components that make up the divine services of the Vespers, Orthros, and the variable parts of the Divine Liturgy. These are dealt with in fifty paragraphs, each appropriately titled with the name of the component being addressed, as for example: the Introductory Psalm of Vespers (Προοιμιακός Ψαλμός), the Hexapsalmos (Ἑξάψαλμος), the Canon and the Katavasiai of the Orthros, and the Trisagion and Communion Hymns of the Divine Liturgy.

The section entitled, Manual of Rubrics – Τυπική Διάταξις, follows the Preface. The rubrics in this section deal with the Vespers, Orthros, and the Divine Liturgy both for ordinary and festal days. In this section we also find the Antiphons and the Typika that are chanted at the Divine Liturgy on weekdays and on Sundays; the appropriate places for the interpolation of hymns at the stichera and aposticha of the Vespers and the Orthros; and an outline of the 'audible' parts of the Divine Liturgy. Much of this material has been incorporated into the *Reader's Manual* –Ἐγκόλπιον τοῦ Ἀναγνώστου, a book designed to help the Reader and Psaltis or Chanter.

Three additional groups of rubrics or directives follow, those which are related to the calendar (μηνολόγιον). The first group addresses the fixed feasts and is by far the largest section in the Typikon. It contains the directives for the Vespers, Orthros, and Divine Liturgy of the major feasts beginning with the month of September, which marks the start of the new ecclesiastical year. The next two sections deal with the same services but in the movable cycle of feasts and are entitled respectively 'Rubrical Directives for the Services of the Triodion' and 'Rubrical Directives for the Services of the Pentekostarion.' The former refers to the services included in the Pre-Lenten and Lenten season and Holy Week. The latter refers to the services of the Paschal season beginning with the Orthros of Pascha and ending with the Feast of All Saints, the Sunday after Pentecost.

The *Typikon of the Great Church of Christ* ends with a large addendum that contains descriptions and rubrical directives for several services and ceremonies in accordance with the protocol of the Ecumenical Patriarchate. These include: the Service of the Akathist Hymn, the Orthros of Holy Friday (Ἀκολουθία τῶν Ἁγίων Παθῶν), the Consecration of a Church, the Ceremony on the Elevation of a Patriarch to the Ecumenical Throne, and the Ceremony on the Feast of the Indiction on September 1. The addendum also includes several other items: the time of day the divine services are to be celebrated at the Patriarchate, the divine services at which the Patriarch presides, the hymns used at the ordination of a bishop, directives for concelebrations, the revised order of the burial rite, and a note on memorial services. Finally, the Typikon contains several tables that summarize the rubrics for eighteen major feasts that in a given year may fall within the period of the Triodion and the Pentecostarion. Of course, it should be noted that this table was devised before the Ecumenical Patriarchate adopted the new calendar in 1923.

Digests of the Typikon

To assist those responsible to execute and perform the sacred rites – clergy, chanters, readers, choirs, and others – many local Churches issue annually a digest of the Typikon. These digests appear in many forms with varied contents. Most especially, the digests contain to a greater or lesser degree a summation of the directives and rubrics of the Typikon as they apply to the ordinary and festal days of a given year. A digest may reflect a particular liturgical usage or custom that is peculiar to the local Church. The following are examples of such digests:

* The Hemerologion (Calendar or Almanac) of the Ecumenical Patriarchate – Ἡμερολόγιον τοῦ Οἰκουμενικοῦ Πατριαρχείου. In addition to the comprehensive summary of the Typikon for the given year, the Hemerologion contains general information about the Patriarchate, its diocese, eparchies, and institutions throughout the world and information on the other Autocephalous and Autonomous Orthodox Churches. The Hemerologion also contains a learned study each year on a subject of common interest related to the history, life, and mission of the Church in the modern world. In its liturgical practice the Greek Orthodox Archdiocese of America, as an eparchy or province of the Ecumenical Patriarchate, follows – to the degree possible – the liturgical tradition and usages of the Patriarchate as indicated in the Hemerologion. The Church of Greece under the title, The Diptychs of the Church of

Greece – Δίπτυχα τῆς Ἐκκλησίας τῆς Ἑλλάδος, publishes a similar digest annually. In these and other digests the directives of the Typikon constitute the first section of the book.

* *The Kanonion –* Τό Κανόνιον (short rule). The *Kanonion* is issued annually by the Holy Synod of the Ecumenical Patriarchate and is the briefest form of a digest of the Typikon. It provides on one sheet the following entries for each Sunday of a given year: the tone of the week, the Gospel Lesson of the Orthros (Ἑωθινόν), and the Epistle and Gospel Lessons for the Divine Liturgy. The *Kanonion* also lists other pertinent information related to the periods of the Fast and to the Paschalia or Paschal Tables. Thus with one glance the clergy, readers, and chanters have at their disposal the most essential data for the celebration of the divine services.

* *Similar digests* are prepared and published by individuals, groups and publishing houses with our without formal ecclesiastical approval. For example, the National Forum of Greek Orthodox Musicians, which is under the auspices of the Greek Orthodox Archdiocese of America, publishes annually a helpful and informative guide for chanters and choirs.

The Diataxeis or Manuals of Rubrics and the function of the Typikon

The Diataxeis (Διατάξεις, singular – Διάταξις) were manuals of rubrics that listed the order and the directives for the performance of the various ceremonials and rituals of the divine services. These directives, called rubrics in English from the Latin word *rubrica*, meaning red, were all written in red ink to distinguish them from the text of the prayers and the litanies. This practice continues to the present time.

The Diataxeis began to appear after the tenth century. Earlier directives were conveyed, for the most part, orally. Even now, when the rubrics of a given ritual are spelled out, an oral tradition is still presupposed because no rubric in itself is complete or capable of transmitting all the nuances of a particular liturgical act, ceremony, gesture, or movement.

The Diataxis as a separate liturgical book fell into disuse

many centuries ago. The need for Diataxeis was obviated when the ceremonial directives were placed initially at the beginning of the service books and later when the rubrics were interpolated at the appropriate places within the texts.

Of the many Diataxeis that appeared between the twelfth and fourteenth centuries, none proved to be more influential than the two written by Philotheos Kokkinos, twice Patriarch of Constantinople (1353-1355 and 1364-1376). He composed these works while he was Hegoumenos or abbot of the Great Lavra on Mt. Athos. The two Diataxeis of Philotheos, the Diataxis of the Diaconate (Διάταξις τῆς Ἱεροδιακονίας) and the Diataxis of the Divine Liturgy (Διά ταξις τῆς Θείας Λειτουργίας), gained universal recognition as part of the liturgical reforms that took place in the wake of the Hysechastic controversy.[211] The rubrics of Philotheos were gradually incorporated into the divine services of the Greek Church. To this day they retain, for the most part, their vitality though changes have been made through the centuries.

In his classical study, *Αἱ Τρεῖς Λειτουργίαι*, Panagiotis Trempelas includes two Diataxeis for the Divine Liturgy. One is of an anonymous author from a 12-13th century manuscript entitled Διάταξις τῆς Θείας Ἱερουργίας. The other is the Diataxis of Philotheos Kokkinos from a 14th century manuscript.

Rubrics are not meant to stifle the dynamism of authentic worship. Rather, their essential function is to prevent liturgical chaos by securing for the Church recognizable standards of usage and a healthy balance and tension between historical tradition and present-day life. For these reasons, the Typikon is essential to the Church if she is to preserve and foster the fundamental characteristics and the ethos of her liturgy. Having said this, it is also important to note that the rubrics are not an end unto themselves, to be used blindly, arbitrarily, or in isolation. They are best understood in terms of language and grammatical rules, a metaphor as suggested by a noted liturgical scholar. "The adequacy of liturgical celebration rests upon [rubrics] as adequacy of language rests upon rules of grammar. And while grammatical rules alone will not produce a great speech any more than liturgical rubrics alone will result in a great act of celebration, neither great speech nor great liturgy can afford to ignore the rules basic to each without risking the collapse of both."[212]

In a similar vein, it is important to emphasize again that the Typikon does not create the liturgy. The sacred rites – the Church's rule of prayer – preceded the Typikon in all of its manifestations and versions. The function of the rubrics is to adapt the liturgy to this or that need in a given time and place. Father Alexander Schmemann underscored this point when he wrote:

> The relationship of the written rubrics to worship is analogous to the relationship of the canons to the structure of the Church. The canons did not create the Church or determine her structure; they arose for the defense, clarification, and definition of that structure, which already existed and is essential to the very nature of the Church. The written ordo does not so much determine the law of worship as it adapts this law to this or that need. And this means that it presupposes the existence of this law or general element.[213]

Understanding the purpose and function of the Typikon properly is essential if we are to avoid two extreme views. There are people in the Church – clergy and laity – who hold a legalistic or formalistic view of the Typikon. They believe that all liturgical regulations form "an absolute and immutable law, and to touch or change this material in any way whatever is tantamount to the subversion of Orthodoxy."[214] Such a view, however, denies historical facts and realities and robs the liturgy of its dynamism, filling it with ceremonial excess and rendering it lifeless. On the other hand, there are people – clergy and laity – who are indifferent to the rule of prayer and the structures of worship. They ignore the Typikon altogether and are absorbed with subjective and arbitrary experiments removed from the real life of people. Inevitably they make liturgy unrecognizable and trivial. The one extreme view leads to liturgical pompousness, the other to liturgical minimalism. Neither one upholds the solemn simplicity, clarity, and grandeur of genuine spiritual worship; they only tend to obscure it.

The Typikon helps to support and define the communal character of Orthodox worship, the dynamic coordination of liturgical orders and ministries, and the complex mode of divine and human communication. Although the rubrics and ceremonials are not always universally observed and although by nature they are alterable, they are nonetheless indispensable. Without them Orthodox liturgy would lose its objectivity, integrity, continuity, and coherency. Neither an antiquarian approach nor a revolutionary approach will help people discover authentic liturgy and find in it an inexhaustible source for the cultivation and advancement of the interior life.

The Typikon makes clear that authentic worship requires faithfulness and constancy – "Stand fast and hold the traditions which you were taught" (2 Thess. 2:15). Hence, a repertoire of authoritative texts, music, and ceremonies as well as intelligent rules, directives, and rubrics are essential characteristics of authentic liturgy. Authoritative texts, structures, and rules provide order, authenticity, diversity in unity, and creative continuity. Indeed, authentic liturgy requires that worship be expressive without losing its dignity, simplicity, or beauty; be relevant without breaking with tradition; and be intelligible, while preserving doctrinal depth and mystical wonder.[215]

Authentic Orthodox liturgy is characterized by a balanced wholeness that makes it, in the words of Robert Taft, "transcendent but not distant, hieratic but not clericalized, communal but not impersonal, traditional but not formalistic."[216]

5

The Euchologion: A Brief History

A brief history of the Euchologion *

The *Euchologion* – *Εὐχολόγιον* (Book of Prayers – *Trebnik* in Slavonic)[217] is the official service book of the Orthodox Church. It contains the priestly prayers, the diaconal litanies, and the rubrics and ceremonials of the holy sacraments and other divine services, together with many prayers and blessings for special needs and circumstances.

The Euchologion was formed over the course of many centuries, its content varying according to time and place. With the appearance of the first printed editions in the sixteenth century its contents and arrangement were more or less standardized. The comprehensive form of the Euchologion came to be known as the Great Euchologion (Μέγα Εὐχολόγιον).

The divine services and prayers that would eventually form the Euchologion were the product of a long evolutionary process. For this and other reasons it is difficult to trace its origins and development. Nonetheless, we can say with certainty that from the beginning the Church had a rule of prayer that was both oral and written.

The New Testament and many early Christian documents, including Church Orders and writings of the Fathers, contain important information on the state of the liturgy in the ancient Church. In addition to descriptions and explanations of liturgical practices, these documents contain ancient formulas of liturgical prayers, hymns, doxologies, and blessings.[218]

As liturgical rites and texts evolved, the multiform practices and customs of the earlier centuries developed into unified and standardized forms. The movement towards unification of rite and text began as early as the second century and gathered momentum in the fourth. This trend towards the unification of rites into liturgical families coincided with the development of new ecclesial forms of government centered on major political and ecclesial centers.[219] As noted above, the Byzantine Rite constitutes the final unification of liturgical usage in the Orthodox Church.[220]

Over the course of time, the prayer of the Church was augmented and refined to assure and to reflect doctrinal accuracy. Composed by many persons, both known and unknown, the prayers and hymns of the Church were collected to form distinct volumes. These collections of formularies (prescribed forms of prayers) always differed in content since they were intended for the use of particular order in the Church. These collections were generally called Euchologia – Prayer Books or Service Books. When an Euchologion was designed for a particular ministerial order, it usually bore the name of the order, as for example the *Archieratikon* – Ἀρχιερατικόν , which contains the prayers and ceremonials of the rites performed by a bishop.

The earliest extant collection of priestly prayers, thirty in all, is the Prayer Book of Serapion, Bishop of Thmuis in Egypt, compiled or composed by him around 350.[221] Other ancient forms of prayer books include: *The Apostolic Tradition*, a Church Order ascribed to Hippolytos of Rome, which contains several prayers and a description of rites and practices in use at Rome and elsewhere in the early third century;[222] *The Apostolic Constitutions*, another Church Order which has an extensive collection of liturgical prayers and canonical material and is of Syrian and Constantinopolitan origins (ca 380);[223] and *The Euchologion of Der Balyzeh*, which is a collection of papyrus fragments dating from the sixth century found in the ruins of a Greek monastery in Upper Egypt.[224]

The earliest extant manuscript of a Constantinopolitan Euchologion is the eighth century *Barberini Codex* – S. Marci III. 55, which is now referred to as Barberini 336 or Vat. gr. 336.[225] The codex was discovered among the famous collection of manuscripts in the library of the noble Barberini family of Rome. Before passing to the Barberini family, the manuscript belonged to the monastic order of St. Mark in Florence. The manuscripts of the Barberini Library were incorporated into the Vatican Library at the beginning of the twentieth century.

Remembering that the Byzantine Rite constitutes the final unification of the Orthodox liturgical tradition and practice, we cannot emphasize enough the importance of the *Barberini Codex* for our knowledge of the actual liturgical practice of the Constantinopolitan Church in the eighth century. Remarkably, when we compare the essential elements of the *Great Euchologion* currently in use and the contents of the *Barberini Codex*, we see clearly that significant portions of the divine services – prayers and litanies – are substantially the same. At its core the Byzantine Rite is a synthesis of the monastic ordo of Palestine and the Euchologion of the Great Church (Patriarchate of Constantinople – Hagia Sophia), the oldest surviving version of which is the *Barberini Codex 336*.

The first printed edition of the Greek Euchologion appeared in 1526. Two additional editions were also published in the sixteenth century. In 1647 Jacques Goar, a Dominican monk, published his now famous *Εὐχολόγιον Sive Rituale Graecorum*, which he based on ancient manuscripts and the early printed editions of the Euchologion. The Euchologion of Goar contains valuable variant readings (including the *Barberini Codex 336*),[226] a Latin translation of the services, and extensive notes on the divine services. An improved second edition of Goar's Euchologion appeared in 1730 and a facsimile of this edition in 1960. It should not escape notice, however, that Goar's endeavors were directed toward proselytism.[227]

The first printed edition of the Euchologion in 1526 was preceded by some months by the first printed Greek edition of the three Divine Liturgies of St. John Chrysostom, St. Basil, and the Pre-Sanctified Gifts – *Αἱ Θεῖαι Λειτουργίαι τοῦ Ἁγίου Ἰωάννου τοῦ Χρυσοστόμου, Βασιλείου τοῦ Μεγάλου καί ἡ τῶν Προηγιασμένων* . This *editio princeps* was published in Rome by Demetrios Doukas. Significantly, the rubrics in this first edition were printed in red ink to distinguish them from the text of the prayers and were inserted in the appropriate places within the text, a practice that was to become routine.

In 1901 Aleksej Dmitrievskij published in Kiev a collection of Euchologia, *Opisanie Liturgitseskich Rukopsej*, vol. II – Εὐχολόγια. The collection contains transcriptions, extracts or summaries of one hundred and sixty-two manuscripts, beginning with a ninth-tenth century manuscript from the library of Mt. Sinai and ending with eighteenth and nineteenth century manuscripts. The volume also contains a valuable index of subjects.

In 1935, Panayiotes Trempelas began publishing several critical studies treating portions of the Euchologion based chiefly on manuscripts in the National Library in Athens. Trempelas undertook this work soon after his appointment as secretary of the Liturgical Committee, which the Ecumenical Patriarchate established in 1932. The Committee was commissioned to examine the liturgical books and to produce, in time, two types of material: critical editions for scholarly endeavors and revised texts for liturgical use. Historical circumstances – chiefly World War II – prevented the Committee from completing its mission. Yet Trempelas continued his research and produced three important volumes: Αἱ Τρεῖς Λειτουργίαι (Athens 1935) which contains the three Divine Liturgies of the Constantinopolitan Rite and the Service of the Proskomide and the Diataxeis; Μικρόν Εὐχολόγιον, Α (Athens 1950) which contains the sacraments of Marriage, Holy Unction, Ordination, Baptism, and Chrismation; Μικρόν Εὐχολόγιον, Β (Athens 1955) which has the divine services of the Hagiasmos, the Consecration of Churches, the Orthros, and the Vespers.

The more recent publications of the Greek *Great Euchologion* are based chiefly on two editions. The first is the *Great Euchologion* edited by the priest Spyridon Zervos, an Archimandrite of the Ecumenical Patriarchate, which was first published in Venice in 1851. A second edition appeared in 1862. The other is the *Great Euchologion* edited by the priest Nikolaos Papadopoulos, which was published in Athens in

1927. The Papadopoulos edition was an improvement over the earlier published works. He corrected mistakes and added forty new prayers for special needs as well as variant readings, brief notes, comments, and references.

Each autocephalous Church has its own official version of the Euchologion in the liturgical language of the local Church. These Euchologia are based mainly on ancient manuscripts and on the early printed editions of the Greek Euchologion. They also reflect the liturgical traditions, usages, practices, ceremonials, and reforms of the local Church. The differences in the practices of the Churches, however, are minimal.

English translations of the Euchologion

The first English translation of major parts of the Euchologion was produced and published in the late eighteenth century by John Glen King under the title *The Rites and Ceremonies of the Greek Church in Russia; Containing an Account of its Doctrine, Worship, and Discipline* (London 1772). The book was reproduced in 1970 by the AMS Press of New York. King was a Fellow of the Royal and Antiquarian Societies and Chaplain to the British Factory at St. Petersburg. In addition to his own religious and literary interests, King was moved to write his book and translate the Orthodox liturgy out of his concern to correct certain misapprehensions and distortions that were circulating at the time about the faith and practice of the Orthodox Church. He wrote the following in the Preface of his book:

> The Greek Church, as it is at present established in Russia, may be considered in respect of its service as a model of the highest antiquity now extant... I imagined therefore it might be a good step towards illustrating the antiquities of the Christian church at large, to give an account of the ceremonies of this: and I resolved to study them in the Slavonian language, the language in which they are performed, that my materials being taken from the books of the services might be authentic, and that the veracity and exactness might compensate for the defects, which may be found in the execution... The many falsehoods and ridiculous stories reported of this Church, and spread over all countries, persuades me that this is a subject hitherto little

known... The consequence has been that (the) mistakes, for want of being contradicted and cut off at first, have grown and multiplied, by being copied and translated from one language to another (p. vii).

King's own description of the faith and practice of the Orthodox Church, although fair and helpful, is deficient in certain instances. His work reflects essentially the practices of the Russian Church of his time and is colored inevitably by that experience. Nonetheless, his comments and notes are valuable and his translation of the divine services into English was a significant literary contribution.

Numerous English translations of the sacramental rites and other services in the Euchologion have appeared here and abroad, especially in the last several decades. These translations have been executed by Orthodox as well as non-Orthodox clergy, scholars, and litterateurs.[228] However, only a few of these translations have received the official approval of Church authorities. And even then, the approval is usually limited to the particular jurisdiction that has authorized its use.

In 1992 The Standing Conference of Canonical Orthodox Bishops in America (SCOBA) established a Liturgical Commission composed of representatives from the several jurisdictions, in order to address the issue of translations and to provide the Church with an authoritative common English translation of the divine services. The Commission began its work in the autumn of 1992 and completed the first phase of its initial project, a translation of the Divine Liturgy of St. John Chrysostom, using the translation of the Faculty of Holy Cross Greek Orthodox School of Theology as the base, in the summer of 1994. Due to several unfortunate circumstances, the work of the Commission came to a halt soon after and has not been resumed, officially or unofficially. The draft of the translation, however, was circulated for private use and evaluation among a large group of hierarchs, priests, musicians, and scholars.

The contents of the Great Euchologion

The arrangement and contents of the *Great Euchologion* have varied according to time and place. Typically, the arrangement is according to subject matter. The *Great Euchologion* edited by Spyridon Zervos, for example has the following order:

(a) The Diataxis of the diaconate concerning the celebration of the Daily Office (or Divine Office); and the order of the Vespers and the Orthros together with the presbyteral prayers and diaconal litanies appropriate to these services.

(b) The Diataxis for the celebration of the Divine Liturgy, which includes the Preparatory Service known as the 'Kairos – Καιρός,' the order of Vesting and the Washing of the hands, and the Service of the Proskomide (the Preparation of the Eucharistic Gifts – Προσκομιδή), which is performed at the Prothesis (Table of Preparation – Πρόθεσις). The text of the three Divine Liturgies of St. John Chrysostom, St. Basil the Great, and the Pre-Sanctified Gifts follow these services.

(c) The three pre-baptismal services (First – Eighth – Fortieth Day Rites) for newborn infants and women who have given birth, followed by the Sacrament of Baptism and Chrismation and related services.

(d) A series of prayers of exorcism for persons possessed or who are suffering from various kinds of maladies and afflictions.

(e) The Service of the Holy Myron (the consecration of the holy oils of Chrism), which is celebrated in accordance with the protocol of each Autocephalous Church on Great and Holy Thursday.

(f) The rites of Ordination (χειροτονία) for deacon,[229] presbyter, and bishop; and the rites of appointment (χειροθεσία) to ecclesiastical offices (eg. protopresbyter, oikonomos) and to 'minor' orders, such as sub-deacon, reader, psaltis (chanter).

(g) The rites of monastic profession known as the Small and Great Schema.

(h) The sacramental rites of Penance, Holy Matrimony, and Holy Unction.

(i) The Services of: Consecration of a Church, the Small and Great Blessing of Water (Hagiasmos), the Washing of Feet on Holy Thursday (rarely used), and the Great Vespers of Pentecost known as the Service of Kneeling.

(j) Burial rites for clergy, adults, and children and related services.

(k) Numerous other prayers of blessing and intercession for various human needs and circumstances, from natural disasters and calamities to sicknesses, wars, invasions, famines, plagues, and agricultural necessities; for adoptions, the reception of converts, the re-establishment of the lapsed, and various other supplicatory canons and prayers.

(l) The Epistle and Gospel lessons for major feasts, the Eleven Morning Gospel lessons for the Sunday Orthros ('Εωθινά Εὐαγγέλια), and the special apolysis (dismissal) assigned to each feast of the Lord. Also included is a list and a description of the several ecclesiastical and honorific titles ('Οφφίκια) bestowed upon clergy and lay people by the Ecumenical Patriarchate.

The abridged versions of the Great Euchologion

There are several abridged versions of the Great Euchologion that are intended for particular orders of the clergy. The practice of providing separate books for the different liturgical ministries is quite old. Among those currently in use by the clergy are the *Small Euchologion* (Μικρόν Εὐχολόγιον), *Archieratikon* (Ἀρχιερατικόν), *Ieratikon* (Ἱερατικόν), *Diakonikon* (Διακονικόν), and *Sylleitourgikon* (Συλλειτουργικόν).

(a) The *Small Euchologion* is specifically designed to meet the needs of the parish clergy. The initial service in most editions of the Small Euchologion of the Greek Church is the Small Agiasmos or Lesser Blessing of the Water (Μικρός Ἁγιασμός). Hence, the Small Euchologion is sometimes called the Hagiasmatarion – Ἁγιασματάριον.

Generally, the Small Supplicatory Canon to the Theotokos (Μικρός Παρακλητικός Κανών εἰς τήν Ὑπεραγίαν Θεοτόκου) follows the initial service, which in turn is followed by a series of services. These include: the pre-baptismal rites for infants and women who have just given birth; the Baptismal rites; the rites of Matrimony, Penance (Confession), and Holy Unction; and the Funeral rites and memorial services. The Small Euchologion also contains a supplicatory canon for the sick; a service for those who are at the point of death (εἰς ψυχορραγοῦντα); prayers of exorcism; and numerous prayers of blessing for various needs and circumstances.

In addition, the Small Euchologion includes a menologion

(μηνολόγιον), a calendar of the fixed feasts beginning with the month of September (which marked the beginning of the civil year in the Byzantine empire); and an alphabetical list of Saints with the date on which they are commemorated in the calendar.

Some older editions of the Small Euchologion include the priestly prayers and diaconal litanies of the Vespers, the Orthros, and the Divine Liturgy of St. John Chrysostom. Others also contain the Eleven Morning Gospel Lessons, and the Katavasiai of the Feasts of Pascha, and the Exaltation of the Cross, which are usually sung at the baptismal service.

The editions of the Small Euchologion published in the last several decades by the Apostolike Diakonia of the Church of Greece have several useful occasional offices of the Hagiasmos (Blessing of Water). These offices were created to serve special pastoral needs and constitute a variation of the Small Hagiasmos. Shorter in length than the Small Hagiasmos, these services contain, among other things, Epistle and Gospel lessons, petitions and a prayer that are suitable to the occasion for which they are being performed. These occasions include: the laying of foundations for a church or school building, the beginning or end of a school year, the establishment of a commercial enterprise, the dedication of a philanthropic institution, and others.

In the United States each Orthodox jurisdiction has its own version of the Small Euchologion. These often differ from one another in form, content, and rubrical details. These differences, however, do not affect the essentials of the divine services. In fact, each jurisdiction has two types of the Small Euchologion: the principal edition representing the liturgical tradition of the 'mother' Church in the liturgical language of that Church; and a more or less complete English version(s), some of which have been approved officially by the respective ecclesial authorities while others circulate with the tacit consent of the hierarchy.[230]

In the last few decades a new trend has developed. Many of the services in the Euchologion, and especially those of the sacraments and the burial rites, are being published under separate volumes, each of which bears the name of the individual office.[231] The Apostolike Diakonia, the publishing house of the Church of Greece, initiated this practice in Greece. It has been imitated by other local Churches and by some private publishing houses. Also in recent times, numerous monolingual and bilingual versions of the Divine Liturgies have been published exclusively for the laity and are used extensively in the parishes.

(b) *The Archieratikon* is the special book of prayers and blessings which, as the name indicates, is used by the bishop. It contains the order of the services as celebrated by a bishop and includes rubrics, ceremonials, and prayers for the following services. (i) The text and rubrics of the three Divine Liturgies together with the Entrance hymns and the special dismissals (ἀπολύσεις); (ii) the rites of Ordination (χειροτονί α) for deacon, presbyter, and bishop; the rites of Appointment (χειροθεσία) to minor orders and ecclesial offices; (iii) the rites of Betrothal and Marriage (some of the more recent editions include a marriage rite within the context of a Divine Liturgy); (iv) burial rites and memorial services; and (v) the service of the Artoclasia (Blessing of the Loaves) and other prayers for special needs, occasions, and circumstances.

(c) *The Ieratikon*, as the title indicates, is the altar book of the priest (ἱερεύς) or presbyter. It is also known by other names such as the *Leiturgikon* (Λειτουργικόν), *Phyllada* (Φυλλάδα), *The Divine Liturgy* (Θεία Λειτουργία), *and Sluzhebnick* (in Slavonic).

The *Ieratikon* contains the order, rubrics, ceremonials, diaconal petitions, and priestly prayers for the following divine services. (i) The several forms of the Vespers, Mesonyktikon (Midnight service), and Orthros; (ii) the Preparatory rites for the celebration of the Divine Liturgy (Kairos, Vesting, Washing of the hands, Proskomide), the text of the three Divine Liturgies, the Office of Preparation for Holy Communion, and the rubrics for a concelebration (συλλείτουργον); (iii) the services for the Veneration and the Elevation of the Cross, the Great Blessing of the Waters, and the Great Vespers or Kneeling Service of Pentecost; and (iv) doxologies, prayers of blessing and forgiveness, and prayers for the dead.

The *Ieratikon* also contains the following material. (i) The office of the Artoklasia; (ii) the Entrance hymns (called Eisodika – Εἰσοδικά, and the special prologues for the dismissals of the feasts of the Lord; (iii) a menologion or calendar; and (iv) the text of the Symmartyria (Συμμαρτυρί α), the document which the Father Confessor gives to a candidate for Holy Orders. Some editions also include the festal kontakia and the eight resurrectional apolytikia.

As in the case of the *Euchologion*, the contents and the arrangement of the *Ieratikon* may vary from one edition to another and from one local Church to another. These differences, however, are minor.

The earliest printed version of an *Ieratikon* was the *edition principes* of the three Divine Liturgies published by Demetrios Doukas in 1526. Earlier, the monk Pachomios published in Venice in 1519 a Slavonic *Sluzhebnik*, commissioned by the Serbian Duke Bozidar Vuckovic. Although many printed editions of the Greek *Ieratikon* began to appear in the subsequent centuries, the first one to receive the official approval of the Church appeared only in 1895. It was edited and published by the priest Makarios Tantalides with the consent and approval of the Ecumenical Patriarchate.

Later editions include the *Divine Liturgy – Θεία Λειτουργία* edited by the priest Nikolaos Papadopoulos (1927). The book enjoyed wide use among the Greek clergy until it was displaced by the *Ieratikon* of the Apostolike Diakonia, which was first published in 1956 with many subsequent printings. Today, the *Ieratikon* of the Apostolike Diakonia is the preferred edition of the Greek clergy both here and abroad.

Abridged Greek versions of the *Ieratikon* and the *Small Euchologion* were edited and published in 1943 by Bishop Athenagoras Kavadas, then Dean of Holy Cross School of Theology. Printed in limited numbers, these books began to fall into disuse after the Second World War. In part, these books reflected the attempt of the editor to initiate and establish both rubrical as well as substantive reforms in the divine services.[232]

The first English edition of a more or less complete *Ieratikon* is the *Liturgikon – The Book of Divine Services for the Priest and Deacon* published in 1989 by the Antiochian Archdiocese of North America. The text was prepared using various Greek and Arabic *Ieratika, Archieratika* and *Horologia* that were published by the Churches of Constantinople, Antioch, Jerusalem, and Greece.

Abbreviated monolingual and bilingual forms of the *Ieratikon* have been published by most Orthodox jurisdictions in the Americas and elsewhere.[233] Today, the bilingual editions of the three Divine Liturgies published by the Holy Cross Orthodox Press have gained considerable popularity among the clergy and the parishes of the Greek Orthodox Archdiocese of America. However, these editions do not contain the entire authoritative text of the Divine Liturgies. Certain elements that have fallen into disuse have been omitted from the published text. More recently, the liturgical books produced by the Narthex Press are also enjoying wide use.

The Monks of New Skete, a monastic community located in Cambridge, New York serving under the supervision of the Orthodox Church in America (OCA), have produced several handsome volumes that are abridged versions of some of the liturgical books, including the *Ieratikon*. These books, however, reflect the liturgical practices that are unique to New Skete.

(d) *The Diakonikon*, as the name indicates, is the book of directives, petitions, and ceremonials used by the deacon. The Diakonikon is now rarely published as a separate volume, since the material assigned to the deacon is contained in *Ieratikon* and the *Small Euchologion*. In recent years, the Monastery of Simonos Petra at Mt. Athos has published a volume of the Diakonikon. However, as one would expect, the rubrics and ceremonials reflect monastic usages.

(e) *The Sylleitourgikon* (the Book of Concelebration – Συλλειτουργικόν, ἤτοι ἡ τάξις τοῦ Ἀναγνώστου καί Ψάλτου) is designed to meet the needs of Readers and Chanters. At the start of the twentieth century, if not earlier, this book began to be published under a different name, (Compendium or Manual of the Reader – Ἐγκόλπιον τοῦ Ἀναγνώστου). The book contains the fixed portions or elements of the Vespers,

Orthros, and Divine Liturgy, for which the Reader and Chanter are responsible. The Apostolike Diakonia has published the Ἐγκόλπιον numerous times. In 1996 the Monastery of Simonos Petra published the book under its earlier title, *Sylleitourgikon*. The two versions differ little in content. Most of the material of this book is collected from the Horologion, which is essentially the liturgical book of the Reader and Chanter and of the laity in general.

The emerging ecclesial realities in America and the Euchologion

As the Orthodox Churches in America move to accomplish their organic unity, as is required of them by the holy canons and Orthodox ecclesiology, matters pertaining to legal and organizational structures but also to liturgical practices, customs, and usages, are of special significance. To avoid acrimony between the jurisdictions in these matters, especially in the initial steps of the process towards unity, the Churches must be sensitive to and patient with one another's particularities regarding statutes and regulations but also language, culture, liturgical customs, and pastoral practices.[234]

An organically unified Church, however, cannot function indefinitely with diverse practices in polity, liturgy, and pastoral praxis. That is why, I believe, the Standing Conference of Canonical Orthodox Bishops (SCOBA), which brings together the canonical hierarchs of the Orthodox jurisdictions (an unfortunate but unavoidable term) in America, ought to begin in earnest the arduous and complex process of canonical normalization by setting in motion the mechanisms through which the diverse legal documents and practices of the jurisdictions will be properly studied, evaluated, and resolved. One method of addressing the issues is the establishment of special commissions, one of which would be the Commission on the Liturgy to deal with all liturgical matters. Of course, the success of these Commissions will depend in large measure on the commitment of the hierarchy, the clergy, and the people to the goal of unity and on the good will, the generosity of spirit, the openness of mind, and competence of the members of each Commission.

The task of the Commission on the Liturgy – composed of pastors, liturgists, theologians, linguists, and musicians – would be to conduct a systematic analysis and a comprehensive study of the received ritual data, followed by a number of recommendations for the renewal of the liturgy in response to the emerging needs and realities of the Church in America.

One could argue that the *Euchologion*, for two simple reasons, should be the top priority of the Commission's work, the first object of inquiry. To begin with, the *Euchologion* is the official service book of the Church. Therefore any attempt at evaluating, integrating, and renewing the liturgical practice of the Church in America must start with the divine services and that, in essence, means the *Euchologion*. However, while the *Euchologion* is substantially the same for each jurisdiction, it is not identical in every detail, especially when it comes to content, rubrics, and regulations. These differences have to be resolved eventually, which leads us to the second reason why the *Euchologion* has to be the starting point of all liturgical discussions. An organically united Orthodox Church of America will be obliged, in due course, to authorize the publication of its own official version of the *Euchologion* adapted to the requirements and realities of our times, culture, and society. Over time, the Church in America will reflect in her *Euchologion* a rich liturgical praxis that is consistent and relevant with her needs, basically uniform, based on the most authentic traditions, and marked by the very best of the customs and practices of the jurisdictions.

Obviously, the comprehensive examination of the *Euchologion* is both a difficult and complex task, and therefore a long-term project. In fact, the task can only be accomplished little by little over a long period of time through a series of studies and publications, starting with the texts of the Eucharistic Liturgies, followed by the other sacraments, the burial rites, and the daily office.

To help guarantee the rapid acceptance of the texts produced by the Commission and sanctioned by the proper ecclesial authorities, it will be necessary to annotate them, providing the clergy and the laity with a study guide. The critical explanatory notes, based on solid liturgical scholarship and sound theological reflection, will help to answer legitimate questions and concerns and assure everyone that intelligent and creative responses to the changing cultural conditions of our times neither betray the ancient forms of worship nor alter the Church's authentic living tradition. Indeed, while the Orthodox liturgy does not need radical reform or transformation, we have to admit that it is burdened by some irrelevant cultic rituals; lifeless remnants of another time and place that carry little, if any, meaning for the modern worshipper.

As the Church is something given historically but also constantly realized through the divine action of the Holy Spirit, so also is the Church's liturgy, constant and traditional but also alive and dynamic. Its basic structures and contents, as is well known, were shaped in times past. While its core – remarkably rich and precious – remains constant, its forms and expressions are inescapably conditioned by the realities of history and culture. Authentic liturgy is changeless and changing, ageless but also adaptable, traditional yet relevant.

For this reason we must dare to hope that the Church in America in response to her mission in this land will have the wisdom, resolve, and fortitude to produce one day in the not too distant future a modern version of the *Euchologion* with liturgical formularies that are faithful to the tradition, theologically precise, scientifically accurate, and liturgically correct, but also linguistically elegant, lucid, and intelligible, and above all relevant to the real life of the people who live and worship now. Let us remember that "living tradition involves that kind of change and adaptability which preserves its continuous relevance; otherwise the Church becomes a museum of pomposity and ritualism, quite acceptable in the framework of a pluralistic and basically superficial society but actually unfaithful to Orthodoxy itself."[235]

6

The Spirit and Ethos of Orthodox Prayer as Reflected in the Euchologion

*The Euchologion – a glimpse into the mind of the Church** *

The *Euchologion* (Book of Prayers or Εὐχολόγιον) is the official service book of the Orthodox Church. It contains the priestly prayers, the diaconal litanies, and the rubrics and ceremonials of the holy sacraments and other divine services, together with many prayers and blessings for special needs and circumstances.

The Euchologion brings us into the sphere of the Church's prayer and worship. Through the many services and prayers in the Euchologion we gain an understanding of the mystery of our salvation. Through it we experience the Church's extraordinarily rich, varied, and highly ritualized liturgical tradition and perceive the spirit and ethos of her liturgical prayer.[236]

The many prayers contained therein, replete with biblical imagery and expressions, set forth the Church's authentic and living tradition in doxological form. They reflect the fundamental truths of the faith and convey the vision of the new life in Christ. As a window on God and the created order, the prayers contain in precise and concise form the Orthodox teaching about the Triune God, about creation and salvation, and about the purpose and destiny of the cosmos and human life. They deal with the unfathomable depths of the human person and reveal the meaning of the sacred sacraments. Simply put, the Euchologion is a glimpse into the mind of the Church, a significant source for theological reflection and teaching.[237]

Apophatic and cataphatic language in the prayers

The prayers in the Euchologion convey a deep sense of God's holiness and his loving presence in the life of the world. God is the absolute Other, who is inaccessible in himself while at the very same time he is always near, revealing himself voluntarily in his uncreated energies or actions in his love for the world. This simultaneous otherness and nearness of God is expressed in the prayers of the Euchologion. The prayers are filled with apophatic (negative) as well as cataphatic (positive) language.

Apophatic language is used especially to highlight the transcendence of God, as for example in the Anaphora of the St. John Chrysostom:

> It is proper to sing to you, to bless you, to praise you, to thank you, and to worship you in all places of your dominion; for you are God *ineffable, inconceivable, invisible, incomprehensible*, existing forever and ever the same, you and your only begotten Son and your Holy Spirit.

Cataphatic language, on the other hand, is used especially to reflect the nearness of God, his loving providence and judgment. This is seen, for example, in the anamnestic (recalling to mind) character of the priestly prayers. God's promises and mighty acts in history are not only remembered, they become the point of departure for every petition. As one liturgical scholar put it, "the remembrance or memorial of salvation that is offered to God along with our requests, as a genuine sacrifice, expresses the certainty that God's saving intervention in the past retains all it dynamic power in the present."[238] The prayer for the blessing of the font at the Service of Baptism is an example of cataphatic language. It reads, in part, as follows:

> You are great, O Lord, and your works are marvelous and no word can suffice to praise your wonders! For you, Lord, willed to bring all things out of nothing into being. You uphold all creation by your might. You govern the world by your providence... Because of your compassionate love and mercy, bearing not to see humankind oppressed by the devil, you came and

saved us. We confess your grace, we proclaim your mercy, we conceal not your beneficence.

Prayer is an act of adoration and supplication

The prayer of the Church is an act of adoration and thanksgiving as well as an act of confession, petition, and supplication. In prayer we come to recognize the inexpressible might and holiness of God and we call to mind the many wonders of his immeasurable love. Thus, we are empowered to call upon him with praise and thanksgiving and to bring before him in filial trust and confidence various petitions for the most sublime as well as the most humble of needs.

The prayers and services in the Euchologion underscore the loving care and concern of the Church for the human being in every circumstance and condition. Time and again the prayers make reference to the practical, everyday things with their many limitations, anxieties, and fears as well as their untold possibilities for growth and development both in life and in faith. As Bishop Kallistos Ware tells it, "In prayer we do not think only in vertical terms about the Church in glory and the communion of the saints, but we also think horizontally about our involvement with the rest of humankind."[239]

Most of the divine services contain several sets of petitions, such the Great Litany, the Fervent Litany, and the Dismissal Litany. The basic series of petitions in the Great and Fervent Litanies are often augmented with special petitions to fit a given circumstance, as for example at the rites of baptism and marriage. Also, petitions and supplications of one kind or another for spiritual and material needs are included in the priestly prayers and in the prayers of the people. One such prayer, said by both the clergy and the laity, is the Prayer of the Hours (Ὁ ἐν παντί καιρῷ καί πάση ὥρα). It includes expressions of praise and adoration as well as supplications and petitions:

Christ our God, who at all times and at every hour, both in

heaven and on earth, is worshiped and glorified, long-suffering and plenteous in mercy and compassion; who loves the just and is merciful to sinners; who calls all to salvation through the promise of the blessings to come; receive also our supplications at this present time, O Lord, and direct our lives toward your commandments. Sanctify our souls; purify our bodies; set our minds aright; cleanse our thoughts; and deliver us from all afflictions, evils and distress. Encompass us with your holy Angels, so that guided and guarded by their host, we may attain to the unity of the faith and the comprehension of your ineffable glory. For you are blessed until the ages of ages. Amen.

The communal character of Orthodox worship

The complex ritual splendor of the divine services contained in the Euchologion points to the communal character of Orthodox worship and to the dynamic coordination of orders: bishops, presbyters, deacons, baptized faithful, readers, chanters, servers, and others. The whole Church – clergy and laity – enacts the divine services in faith.

The liturgical rites bring to the fore both the particularity of the various orders and the unity of the faith community. In the enactment of these roles, we discover the dynamic complementarity of the institutional and charismatic aspects of Church life. We also discover what it means to be a community of persons. In other words, the liturgy through its many expressions and forms reveals the meaning of the hierarchical and synodal nature and structure of the Church as well as the requirements that are essential for the building up of authentic community. However, as Susan White has observed, community formation is not easy:

> It takes many competencies that the workaday world rarely teaches or rewards: humility, cooperation, forgiveness, imagination, interdependence, and vulnerability. Throughout the liturgical tradition there is the deep conviction that not only does the liturgy help us to develop these traits necessary for the formation of true human community, but is also, in the relationships it fosters and models, a sign to the world of how that community is intended by God to look and behave.[240]

The Church as community, however, is not limited to the faithful who constitute her membership in any given time and place. The Church catholic is present at every liturgical assembly, as is the choir of saints and every righteous spirit who has completed this life in faith.[241] The Church on either side of death joins together to adore, praise, and supplicate the living God. Moreover, the richness of the Church's ritual is intended to reflect the splendor of the heavenly liturgy. In worship, the angelic hosts become our co-celebrants.

The icons of the Lord and of his saints that cover the iconostasis and the walls of our Churches, surrounding us in worship, make us especially aware of the glorious expanse of the communal character of Orthodox worship. The wondrous mystery of revelation – part of which concerns the unity of the Church in heaven and on earth – proclaimed in the Gospel, told in the hymns of the Church, and depicted on icons is also echoed in the prayers of the liturgy. We read for example, in the prologue of the prayer for the blessing of the waters on the feast of Theophany, "For today the time of the feast is at hand for us: the choir of saints assembles with us and angels join with men in keeping festival... Today the whole creation shines with light from on high... Today things above keep feast with things below, and things below commune with things above."[242]

The services and prayers manifest a vision of life

Through the many services and prayers contained in the Euchologion we come to recognize that we are members of a faith community that is graced with a particular vision of life. This community – the Church – affirms and defines our Christian identity and reminds us of our ultimate vocation. Through its rules of faith, prayer, and practice the community calls us to abjure the false values of the fallen world and inspires us to seek and struggle for all that is noble, good, natural, lovely, just, holy, and sinless. Put succinctly, the liturgy encourages us to struggle against all forms of oppression and unjust conditions that devalue and diminish human life; to do more for the life of others in the world; and to work for the fulfillment of the Church's vocation and mission in the world.

Eschatology, solidarity, and catholicity

Finally, the prayers and services in the Euchologion emphasize three additional things: the eschatological orientation of the Church's life, the solidarity between humankind and creation, and the catholicity of the Church.

Eschatology. The Church at prayer above all else reflects the future, the final stage of things. Thus, Orthodox worship celebrates the Kingdom of God already come and already given as the very pledge of salvation through the incarnation, death, resurrection, and ascension of Jesus Christ. Formed continuously into the Body of Christ, the faithful are called to a mission: to transform themselves and the world by furthering the Kingdom of God within themselves and within the world. The Kingdom of God is the life of the Holy Trinity in the world. It is the Kingdom of holiness, goodness, truth, beauty, love, peace, and joy. These qualities, however, do not derive from the works of the human spirit. They proceed from the life of God and reveal God. The Kingdom is Christ himself, the God-Man, who brought God down to earth (Jn. 1:1, 14). The Kingdom does not lie at some point or place in the distant future. It is not only at hand (Mt. 3:2 and 4:7), it is also within us (Lk. 17:21). It is both a present reality and a future realization (Mt. 6:10).

Solidarity. In the age to come the world and we will not be restored simply to the present state. All of creation will be brought into a new mode of existence, into something better and more perfect. The life we once lived will be raised up, in order to be clothed in immortality. We will inherit not only Paradise from where we fell, but the heaven of heavens. All of creation will also share in the freedom "from its bondage to decay and obtain the glorious liberty of the children of God" (Rom 8:21).

Through his resurrection Christ has disclosed the ultimate value and worth of creation and affirmed its fundamental goodness. Christ created the cosmos. It belongs to him. It is his gift of life to us. Therefore, it also belongs to us as coheirs of Christ. We are called to be the stewards of creation. Through our creative activity we are called to liberate the world from its limitations.

Catholicity. Nothing remains outside the scope of the Church's prayer. She embraces everyone and everything, in order to bring all within the realm of salvation. As Bishop Kallistos Ware says:

> As Christians we are necessarily materialists; ours is an incarnate faith, earthy, rooted in this world. Thus our Orthodox service books contain prayers for sowing, threshing and winemaking, for diseased sheep or cattle, for blessings of cars, tractors and fishing nets... Jesus Christ at his human birth took upon him our whole nature – body, soul and spirit – and so he is rightly involved in everything we do. We meet him everywhere.[243]

Nothing and no one escapes the concern of the Church at prayer because she is God's eternal witness, the sacrament of his love for everyone and everything, the sign and herald of his Kingdom in the midst of the contradictions and anomalies of the fallen world. The Church is the house of all, the universal community. She welcomes all and prays for all – as intercessor in the image of her Lord, the unique Mediator – in order to heal the brokenness of all and to bring about everyone's return from estrangement of their own authenticity. All this is especially evident in the Anaphora of the Divine Liturgy of St. Basil, which contains one of the most beautiful and harmonious formulas of intercession. It reads in part as follows:

> Remember also all who have fallen asleep in the hope of the resurrection to eternal life... Again, we pray to You, be mindful of your holy, catholic and apostolic Church, which is from one end of the inhabited earth to the other. Grant peace to her, which You have obtained with the precious blood of Your Christ. Strengthen also this holy house to the end of the ages. Remember, Lord, those who have brought you these gifts, and for whom and through whom and the intentions for which they were of-

fered. Remember, Lord, those who bear fruit and do good works in Your holy churches, and those who remember the poor... Remember, Lord, those who are in the deserts, on mountains, in caverns, and in the chambers of the earth. Remember, Lord, those living in chastity and godliness, in asceticism and holiness of life. Remember, Lord, this country and all those in public service... Sustain the good in their goodness; make the wicked good through Your goodness. Remember, Lord, the people here present and those who are absent with good cause... Fill their treasuries with every good thing; preserve their marriages in peace and harmony; nurture the infants; instruct the young; strengthen the aged; give courage to the faint-hearted; reunite those separated; bring back those in error and unite them to Your holy, catholic and apostolic Church. Free those who are held captive by unclean spirits; sail with those who sail, travel with those who travel; defend the widows; protect the orphans; liberate the captives; heal the sick. Remember, Lord, those who are in mines, in exile, in harsh labor, and those in every kind of affliction, necessity, or distress; those who entreat Your loving kindness; those who love us and those who hate us; those who have asked us to pray for them...

The image of the Church as intercessor is with us continually, reminding us of the invisible community of saints surrounding us. As we join our individual prayers to those of the community, we strengthen not only ourselves but the community as well.

7

Analyzing the History and Content
of Liturgical Texts: Risks and Challenges

I. THE PROBLEM OF RITUAL FORMALISM

Risks, challenges, and opportunities

The essential elements that constitute the shape and content of worship include liturgical texts,[244] sacramental matter,[245] prayer times, ceremonials, iconography, music, and architecture,[246] as well as a calendar of feasts and fasts and such other things as liturgical symbols, gestures, postures, vessels, and vestments. These things define the way the community stands before God and provide it with its most distinguishing characteristics. They also help to form the identity of the community and to shape its tasks and activities and its mission to the world. Hence, it is necessary that we know the history and the meaning of each essential component of the liturgy.

The invitation to examine the history and the inner meanings of worship, however, entails a certain risk as well as a challenge. Some of our favored ideas, widely-accepted notions and explanations, and familiar customs do not now or may not in the future stand up well under the scrutiny of historical research and sound theological reflection.

What should we do, for example, when the facts reveal that a particular liturgical praxis, text, or custom is obscure, ambiguous, or inadequate? Do we do nothing, simply because it is safer not to offend those few vocal adherents who are rigidly attached to and fiercely defend the 'unalterableness' of the inherited structures of worship? Or, do we allow the facts to become the catalyst for the release of new power and energy in the body of the Church? To neglect the facts may be 'safe' in the short term, but disastrous in the long term. When the facts are flagrantly ignored or depreciated and when liturgical deficiencies are neglected or concealed, liturgy is robbed of its vitality. It declines steadily into the deadening malaise of ritual formalism and decadent piety.

A sad and disturbing commentary

More than twenty years ago Father Alexander Schmemann issued a harsh critique, which forces us once again to ask ourselves if his critical observations were correct then and if they continue to be true now? And if they are, are we ready to repair the problem with the necessary bold theological, liturgical, and pastoral initiatives? This was Father Schmemann's sad and disturbing commentary: "A decadent liturgy supported by a decadent theology and leading to a decadent piety: such is the sad situation in which we find ourselves today and which must be corrected if we love the Church and want her to become again the power which transforms the life of man."[247]

Father Schmemann's stern critique – whether one accepts it or not as a valid evaluation of contemporary ecclesial realities – is a strong reminder of the serious dangers that face the Church whenever her theology is robbed of vigor and meaning and whenever her liturgy becomes opaque, burdened with ritual formalism, and turned into superstition or into a purely intellectual system divorced from real life. Both theology and liturgy are devitalized when theology is unwittingly allowed to decline into uncritical, repetitive, and sterile pietistic formulations and when the liturgy is unwittingly allowed to deteriorate into empty actions and words that have little meaning and have no appeal to the heart and mind of the contemporary worshipper.

When liturgical rituals, symbols, and words are emptied of their real meaning and content, the liturgy not only loses its vitality and authenticity, it also becomes easy prey to those who would apply subjective antiquarianisms or arbitrary experimentations, both of which trivialize it. Hence, whatever one thinks of Father Schmemann's critique, it must be taken, at least, as a warning that we should spare no effort to arrest and reverse any and all tendencies that would compromise the vitality and the beauty of the Orthodox liturgy.

The liturgical life of the Church must be vibrant and relevant

The Christian mystery, said Louis Bouyer, "is neither an ancient rite, nor the interpretation of an ancient rite: it is only the revelation of a divine design. In that revelation our history is recapitulated short of sin and consummated in the very life of God."[248] Nevertheless, as Bouyer also said, the same Christian mystery was from the start clothed in ritual expression. Christ himself at the Mystical (Last) Supper recast the material of ancient natural rites, already purified by Judaism, to express the divine meaning of his cross by changing bread and wine into his Body and Blood.[249] The liturgical rites are, no more and no less than, the faith of the Church in action. Through them the Church transacts her life of faith for the life of the world and satisfies our endless longing for the sacred that is utterly real, liberating, and transforming.

The great Fathers of the Church were passionately interested in the liturgy and were keenly aware of its pivotal role in the life of the people. That is why, in their times, they strove to make the liturgical life of the Church vibrant and relevant to life.

In like manner, we too must be ready to provide the substantive responses to the emerging needs of the Church in our own times. We must provide the necessary, carefully researched, judiciously considered, and well-planned liturgical reforms that will allow us to be in creative continuity with the past and true to the dynamic nature of the Church and the liturgy.

However, an earnest and unhindered search for truth may put into question many of our liturgical assumptions and challenge the appropriateness of many of the things we now do in worship. This raises the question about our readiness to accept the challenges that the liturgical inquiry may generate. Clearly, we have no choice but to accept and to work through the challenges, if we are to avoid the dangers of religious formalism and the 'decadent liturgy and piety' that it produces. Rather than obstructing or stifling the Spirit, we must discern and follow His stirrings, eager and ready to shape our tomorrows. However, we must not be fooled. The task is both difficult and complex. But the benefits that can accrue are enormous.

II. ARE LITURGICAL TEXTS ABSOLUTE AND IMMUTABLE?

The role and the authority of liturgical texts

To understand better the inner meanings of Orthodox worship we must begin with an analysis of the liturgical books. Liturgical texts are of special significance to the faith community. They form the core of the liturgy and play a central role in maintaining the identity of the community and its members. The liturgical texts are made up of prayers, blessings, petitions, hymns and rubrics. The corpus also includes a lectionary system, the Psalter, and several odes or canticles of the Bible.

As we have mentioned in some of the preceding essays, liturgical texts express the faith of the Church in doxological, poetical, and rhetorical language. They present and interpret the central truths of the faith in a given solemnity and celebration. At the same time they proclaim the promise of salvation and evoke devotional responses of the mind and heart. The liturgical texts also provide direction for continued edification in the life of faith as they prompt the faithful toward godly action in the circumstances and uncertainties of everyday life.

Worship is by nature open to legitimate progress and adaptation. The structures and the content of rituals have expanded, contracted, and changed through the centuries. That is why the authority of the liturgical books, though mighty and weighty, is not absolute.[250] The authority of a liturgical text is not derived from the text itself, but from the Church, which authorizes it and uses it for her prayer. Liturgical texts are neither permanent nor unchangeable. In fact, they became fixed and received their definitive form in large measure as a result of the invention of printing.

The printing of liturgical texts and some initiatives at reform

The first printed editions of the liturgical books now in use by the Greek Orthodox Church were based mainly on Greek manuscripts collected from throughout the Mediterranean world and published first in Italy between the years 1486 and 1587.[251] The editors of these books were usually Greeks working for Italian publishing houses.[252] The subject matter of each book was selected and arranged in accordance with the judgment of its editors and publishers. This monumental task, however, was accomplished largely without the benefit of critical research and, above all, without the approbation of the Church.[253] After a time and at various stages, each autocephalous Church authorized the publication of liturgical books in the language of the local church. These publications were based mostly on the early printed editions.

From time to time the Church has recognized the need to review the liturgical books. However, not all of the efforts were carefully thought out or successful. One calls to mind, for example, the arbitrary reforms of the liturgical books and of other practices that were initiated by the Russian Church under Tsar Alexis and Patriarch Nikon in the seventeenth century.[254]

In his excellent study, *Russia, Ritual, and Reform*, Paul Meyendorff presents us with a fascinating, penetrating, and thorough analysis of the events and personages, and of the nature, purpose, and content of the reforms that Tsar Alexis and Patriarch Nikon initiated. These notorious reforms were intended to bring the liturgical practices of the Russian Church into agreement with those of the Greek Churches. The proponents of the changes claimed that the reforms constituted a return to primitive Russian and Greek practice. In fact, they conformed to contemporary Greek practice and were based chiefly on the 1602 Greek *Euchologion* printed in

Venice and on the so-called Lithuanian books, published in areas under Polish, and therefore Latin, influence. In addition to the stylistic and grammatical changes in the liturgical texts, the reforms included such other changes as the three-fingered sign of the Cross, the number and form of prostrations during Lent, the number of alleluias, monastic headgear, and the attire of bishops. The actual changes in the liturgy were minimal and chiefly rubrical rather than textual in nature. Nevertheless, the reforms provoked a grave crisis that resulted in the Old-Believers schism that continues to the present day. The liturgical books issued by the Nikonian reforms remain essentially unchanged to the present day in the Russian Church.

The reform of the Typikon, on the other hand, that the Ecumenical Patriarchate initiated in the 19th century, as noted in a previous essay, proved to be a necessary and, albeit limited, successful response to the emerging needs and requirements of parochial worship.[255]

More recently, as mentioned in a previous essay, in 1932 the Ecumenical Patriarchate established a Patriarchal Committee composed of hierarchs and scholars to make a thorough study of the liturgical books.[256] One of the tasks of the Committee was to encourage scholars to produce critical studies of the divine services. Unfortunately, historical circumstances – and most especially the outbreak of World War II and the ruinous events that followed – prevented the committee from fulfilling its important mission. However, the noted theologian and scholar Panayiotis Trempelas of the Theological School of the University of Athens, who was the secretary of the Patriarchal Committee, worked single-handedly to bring to fruition one of the important tasks of the Committee. In 1935 Trempelas began to publish critical editions of the divine services. He based his studies on the Barberini Codex, some forty-six manuscripts of Euchologia in the National Library in Athens, six liturgical scrolls of the Byzantine Museum in Athens, and over thirty published Euchologia from Mt. Sinai, Patmos, Mt. Athos, and elsewhere.[257]

A related topic of great significance is the matter of adequate translations of the received texts especially in the languages of the people living in the so-called diaspora, i.e., in lands outside the traditional Orthodox countries. For example, after these many years of organized ecclesial life in America we still lack an officially sanctioned English translation of the entire corpus of the official liturgical books of the Church. I recognize with gratitude the efforts of those institutions and persons who have spent countless hours researching and translating various portions of the liturgical books. While much of this work is rich and valuable, it lacks cohesion because the translators have not worked, for example, from one recognized and approved set of principles.

It is, therefore, the duty of the Standing Conference of Canonical Orthodox Bishops (SCOBA) to assume a leadership role in this regard by appointing a Liturgical Commission of qualified persons to conduct critical studies of the received texts and to lay the ground rules for and supervise the actual work of translations. The challenge is formidable but the rewards will be inestimable. To be true to her history and to her mission in this land, the Church is responsible to make the riches of our liturgical tradition available to the faithful in the best possible form and in the language they understand best.

However, as important as the work of preparing excellent translations is, the task of probing the liturgical texts in order to grasp their meaning and to ascertain their ability to speak meaningfully to the worshipper of today is of greater significance.

III. THE SEARCH FOR MEANINGS IN TEXTS AND RITUALS

Investigating the received liturgical tradition – A necessary but difficult task

The investigation of the received liturgical tradition – and especially of those elements that form the essential core and content of Orthodox worship – must be unfettered and as complete as possible, if it is to be true to its purposes. Because liturgical texts express the mind and faith of the Church, we are obliged to respect them. But we must also examine them thoroughly, if we are to fully comprehend and properly appreciate their rich spiritual, doctrinal, and devotional treasures.

To begin, we must acknowledge the fact that the language, style, references, metaphors, and theological emphases of the received formularies – the prayers, blessings, petitions, hymns, and rubrics – are drawn from another era and from a cultural milieu different from our own. Therefore, in order to ascertain their ability to engage – consciously and intelligibly – the minds and the hearts of people today in the mystery of salvation, we are obliged to probe them carefully and to critique them prayerfully.

The critique of such time-honored and venerable liturgical texts is both an enormous responsibility and a difficult task. In fact, in the execution of this task we must expect to encounter hesitation and even resistance, especially from some quarters of the Church. However, an unencumbered search for meanings – which is essential to authentic liturgical renewal – requires that we conduct analytical studies of the liturgical formularies comparable to those carried out by biblical and patristic scholars.

When critiquing liturgical texts, we are obliged to ask several questions, some of which follow: Is the vision of faith embodied in a particular text conveyed fully and adequately? Is it congruent to the experiences, understandings, sensibilities, and needs of the people today? How does the text fare against the emerging data in biblical, patristic, and liturgical scholarship? If found wanting, could or should the text be corrected, amended, improved, modified, revised, or deleted? Who would authorize these procedures and make these decisions, and by what process?

Texts and rituals convey layers of meaning

In conjunction with these important questions, we also have to think about, analyze, and understand the several senses in which texts and rituals are received by the faithful and have meaning for them. In an informative essay on ritual meaning, Lawrence Hoffman warns us against depending only on what he calls the *official* meaning of a rite.[258] In fact, like all things, liturgical texts and rituals convey more than a single meaning. Hoffman defines four levels of ritual meanings, namely, *private, official, public, and normative,* all of which are present at the same time.[259] When investigating the received liturgical texts and the rituals with which they are connected, we would be served well to keep these four layers of meanings in mind if we are to measure with some degree of accuracy the ability of texts and rituals to speak meaningfully to the modern worshipper.

People have a way of supplying rituals and texts with private interpretations and emphases that Hoffman defines as the *private* meaning, the "idiosyncratic interpretations people find in things."[260] Some of the more insightful and challenging allegorical and representational interpretations that the medieval authors of the liturgical commentaries[261] attached to the sacred rituals of the Church are, in fact, a product of private but theologically informed devotional interpretations. The Church, which is the sole arbiter of truth and of religious creativity, received these allegorical interpretations because she recognized their value to convey knowledge at a certain level and used them to teach people the mysteries of the faith.

People form private meanings through thoughtful reflection or by borrowing from others. Sometimes people concoct private meanings in response to personal needs and feelings, especially when the official teaching of the Church appears to be obscure, incomprehensible, or perhaps irrelevant. Of course, not all private meanings are theologically sound, valid, or edifying. They are especially unprofitable when they are arbitrary, based on erroneous assumptions, false ideas, or irrational superstition. In fact bad meanings, like bad food, can produce ill effects.

When private meanings are deficient they need to be remedied; when erroneous they need to be corrected. An incident in the Gospel illustrates the point. Shortly before the passion Jesus placed a crucial question before his disciples concerning his messianic identity and divinity. He asked them, "Who do men say that I, the Son of Man, am?' So they said, 'Some say John the Baptist, some Elijah, and others Jeremiah or one of the prophets.' He said to them, 'But who do you say that I am?' Simon Peter answered and said, 'You are the Christ, the Son of the living God.' Jesus answered and said to him, 'Blessed are you, Simon Bar-Jonah, for flesh and blood has not revealed this to you, but my Father who is in heaven" (Mt. 16:13-17). This passage tells us clearly that private meanings must always be tested against the Church's authoritative teaching to avoid trivializing the religious experience. Hence, liturgical preaching and catechesis and especially liturgical texts, as bearers of the Church's official teachings, must always be clear and unambiguous, if they are to help people form appropriate private meanings.

Indeed, people are thirsty for and seek after *official* meanings,[262] those promulgated by the Church through her doctrinal formulations, liturgical expressions, and canonical regulations, as taught by her pastors and theologians, whose responsibility it is to illumine, instruct, edify, guide, and nurture the faithful through the right explanation of the contents of the Orthodox faith, "which was once delivered to the saints" (Jude 3). Official meanings are absolutely essential because their function is to transform the way we see things. They fill life with purpose, import, and significance. They are a message of salvation, hope, and joy.

We must recognize the fact, however, that pastors and theologians, as well as the Church they serve, are culturally conditioned. Therefore every theological statement is inextricably bound to particular historical and socio-cultural life-contexts. Thus, yesterday's issues, explanations, emphases, or meanings may prove unappealing today and, therefore, "unable to accomplish what they are supposed to do."[263] To be compelling and attractive official meanings – the Church's teachings and liturgy – must be relevant to life, capable of engaging each generation in its own search for meanings.

Pastors and theologians must be ever mindful of the fact

that authentic theology – through which official meanings are conveyed – is dynamic. True theology is not only a protective and conserving principle but also a principle of regeneration and growth. It is supposed to reinterpret the dogmatic definitions, the liturgical expressions, and the canonical formulations of the Church in relation to the Church's present needs and the perennial human quest for meanings. It does this while remaining faithful to the uninterrupted historical and theological life of the Church.[264]

Theology is always a means, the ultimate end of which is union with God or deification, the theosis (θέωσις) of the Greek Fathers. All official teaching, therefore, in all of its expressions and formulations is intended to glorify God, to confer union with God, and to bring about the transfiguration of the human being. To accomplish these things properly in every generation pastors and theologians, who convey the Church's official meanings, are obliged, as Father Theodore Stylianopoulos says, to "take into account a greater balance between faith and reason, mystical cognition and scholarship, individual and community faith, Church and culture, according to the testimonies of the Fathers."[265] To do otherwise would doom the theological enterprise to uncritical, repetitive, and sterile pietistic formulations. Such a failure would rob the Church of the vigor necessary to evangelize the world, to reveal to men and women in every circumstance of life the beauty and the power of life renewed in Christ.

There is a third and fourth layer of meanings that Hoffman defines as *public* and *normative*. Public meanings, he says, are the "agreed-on meanings shared by a number of ritual participants, even though they are not officially preached by the experts."[266] In other words, such meanings are vaguely related to matters of faith and the official meanings of the Church. They are based on secondary and tertiary matters; influenced more by familial, social, and cultural reasons than by religious and theological truths. For example, some people attend baptisms, marriages, and funerals more out of familial obligations and social customs than out of deeply held personal beliefs.

Public meanings are formed more by a sense of familial solidarity and social etiquette than by religious faith, even though much of what they value most about family traditions and friendships has been conditioned by the Orthodox faith, a faith that remains latent in the heart. This is especially obvious during the Great and Holy Week. Take, for example, the many hundreds in every parish who flock to the Paschal Vigil service. For some, attendance at the Paschal Vigil is more of a response to the customs, traditions, and rites of one's people rather than a conscious expression of personal faith in the cosmic significance of Christ's resurrection and a celebration of the newness of life that he has bestowed upon the world and upon all who heed his call. Nonetheless, a dormant faith – however weak, uncertain, and ambiguous – drives them to the Church to share in the festival that constitutes so much of one's cultural and religious identity.

Public meanings disclose the fact that where there is little or no insight into the mysteries of the faith, cultural distortions creep in and shape meanings. However, we must not be quick to dismiss public meanings, deficient as they may be. Generally speaking, public meanings are related to matters of intimacy and the search for identity. They are points of departure and points of reference. They are moments to seize, opportunities to present people with the blazing and liberating message of the Gospel that illumines all relationships and perfects all identities.

The Church delivers the message of faith through various forms, but most especially through the liturgy. Therefore, liturgical homilies must be thoughtful and persuasive, liturgical rituals dignified and inspiring, and liturgical texts elegant – especially clear and unambiguous, given that they transmit official meanings. Lucid and intelligible texts invite attention. They allow the truths of the faith to nestle in people's hearts and in their ways of thinking, thereby challenging their outlook on life, so that sluggish faith may be rekindled and active faith may be strengthened.

Finally, ritual conveys what Hoffman calls *normative* meaning, which, in my own mind is as important as official meanings. Normative meaning, he says, is "a structure of signification that ritual affixes upon the non-ritualized world the ritual participants re-enter when the rite has been concluded."[267] In other words, normative meanings have the capacity "to form values and guide activity outside the context of the rite itself."[268] Normative meanings are transmitted at every liturgical assembly through word, song, and ritual. They are especially important, inasmuch as they constitute a call to action. Hence, liturgical texts must help people form normative meanings, which is to say the desire to apply official meanings – the truths of the faith – to everyday life.

The power of a given liturgical text or ritual can be fully understood and measured when it places us completely within the mystery of God's salvation. This power enables us – both in and outside of the liturgical assembly – to comprehend correctly the message of the Gospel; experience joyfully the limitless expanse of the new life in Christ; engage the potentialities and blessings of life with gladness and thanksgiving and its trials, vicissitudes, and uncertainties with courage and hope; and embrace the world and its people – especially the oppressed, the alienated, the outcasts, the loveless, the lonely, the marginalized, and the disadvantaged – with compassion and love.

8

Why Textual Reform Is Necessary – A Case Study

Dealing with problems in liturgical texts – The pre-baptismal rites for infants

In the previous essay we discussed the need for a thoughtful, studied review and prayerful critique of the received liturgical tradition, especially since many of its elements – prayers, rituals, rubrics – were shaped in years long past and in cultural contexts very different from our own. To avoid the pitfalls of liturgical formalism and the dangers of misguided piety, liturgy must pulsate with life, be relevant to the lives of people, and responsive to their deepest needs and aspirations. In other words, we are obliged to probe the tradition to see how convincingly it speaks to the hearts and minds of the people of today.

A number of liturgical texts, at least in the opinion of some, are open to question and debate. Let me illustrate this point by making reference to the series of rites for a mother and her newborn infant on the first, the eighth, and the fortieth day after birth.[269] The rite of the first day concentrates on the mother and on her newborn child. Through this rite the Church thanks God for the safe delivery of the mother and celebrates joyously the birth of a new human being. The rite of the eighth day is for the naming of the infant, while the rite of the fortieth day is for the 'churching' of the child and the mother.

Although these rites have significant spiritual and pastoral value, they are seldom used today in parochial worship except for the rite of the fortieth day, which still has currency among a large segment of the people. The slow decline of these rites may be attributed to several factors. The gradual disappearance of the neighborhood Church in the so-called diaspora, changing family customs and social habits, and the marked improvements in pre- and post-natal care are but some of the factors that have contributed to their decline. One may certainly applaud the efforts of the many priests who are trying to revive these rites in their parishes. However, more is required of the Church than simply promoting their use among young parents who are spiritually aware and who desire spiritual nourishment and the blessings of the Church upon the birth of their child.

To be fully responsive to today's needs, we must first take a good hard look at the contents of these rites. There are people today – clergy, theologians, and laypeople – who feel that the received texts express concepts that are ambiguous and, some would even say offensive to the modern worshipper and most especially to women. We are bound, therefore, to examine the appropriateness of the prayers in these rites and to evaluate their ability to convey clearly the purpose for which they are intended.

Father Alexander Schmemann, writing on this subject years ago, chided those who claimed that these prayers express an antiquated worldview. "One must be not only in error but, above all, small and petty to find offense in these prayers, so full of divine love and concern for man, so full of the only genuine – because truly divine – respect for the human person. And rather than blindly following 'this world' in its cheap rebellions – in the name of empty 'rights,' meaningless 'dignity' and futile 'happiness' – we ought to recover and make ours again the Church's vision of life."[270]

The rebuke of Father Schmemann notwithstanding, the lengthy explanations he uses to defend the texts indicate, I believe, that the prayers are, at the very least, ambiguous, lending themselves to narrow and negative interpretations of human sexuality, female nature, conception, and childbirth. Professor Ioannis Fountoulis, for example, points to two significant shortcomings that overshadow the positive aspects of the prayers. First, the Rites totally ignore the father of the newborn infant. And second, the joyous event of the birth is drowned out by ancient concepts regarding female nature and childbirth that have been abolished by the law of grace.[271]

While I agree with Father Schmemann that these rites are inherently positive, some of the prayers, nevertheless – as we shall see below – contain phrases that are vague and seem to imply that sexual intercourse, pregnancy, parturition, and menstruation are unclean and are occasions for sacramental proscriptions and ritual purification.[272] Such ideas, however, are not only incompatible with modern sensibilities; they are also inconsistent with the Gospel and are doctrinally and morally untenable. Therefore, as Father Schmemann himself suggests, it is essential for us "to recover and make ours again the vision of the Church." To do this, I believe we must revisit these rites and reformulate the prayers in order to erase any and all misconceptions regarding human sexuality and the natural functions of the human body. [273]

The reason for having raised these issues is to make a point, which is simply this. When a liturgical prayer is found wanting for any legitimate reason, the Church should not hesitate to revise it, so that the ambiguities are corrected and the faith of the Church is stated as clearly and precisely as possible.[274]

The search for meanings and theological precision require textual changes

A brief look at one of the prayers in the Rite of the First Day will serve as an example of the ambiguities and difficulties we have been discussing. I have highlighted these features of the prayer using italics. The prayer reads as follows.

Lord our God, You graciously consented to descend from heaven and to be born of the holy Theotokos and ever-virgin Mary for the salvation of us sinners. *Knowing the frailty of human nature, according to the multitude of your mercies forgive your servant (N.) who today has given birth.* For you, O Lord, said, 'Increase and multiply, and replenish the earth and have dominion over it.' On account of this we your servants pray to you, and encouraged by your forbearing love invoke in fear the holy name of your Kingdom. *Look down from heaven and have regard for our weakness, as we are under judgment, and forgive your servant (N.) and the entire household in which the child was born. As a good and loving God forgive also all those who have touched her and all those who are here present.* For you alone have the power to forgive sins, through the intercessions of the holy Theotokos and of all your saints. Amen.

The images the prayer conjures up are foreign to present-day realities and experiences. For one thing, in western societies births almost always occur in hospitals with medical professionals in attendance and not in houses under the care of midwives and relatives. More importantly, however, the petitions that implore God to forgive the mother, her entire household, and all who have touched her are especially perplexing, strange sounding, and almost embarrassing. They are, at the very least, confusing, if not provocative and offensive.

Why, one might ask, is the mother blameworthy? Of what sin is she, the members of her household, and all who have touched her guilty? What offences did they commit to warrant the intercessions of the Church for their forgiveness?[275] Is not marriage a sacrament and childbirth a great blessing? Why then is there need for penitential language at a time of great joy, when a pregnant woman has been safely delivered and a new human being has come into the world? To answer these questions we must look first to the Old Testament and especially to the Book of Leviticus because the concepts and ideas expressed in this and other similar prayers are based on the ceremonial laws of the Old Testament.

Ceremonial laws of the Old Testament

According to the Book of Leviticus (12:1-8), a woman at childbirth is considered to be in a state of temporary uncleanness. Her impurity is caused not from the act of conception or from her delivery, but from the loss of blood. The loss of blood in parturition, according to the beliefs of numerous ancient peoples, including the Jews, caused the mother's vitality to weaken and diminish. The decrease in vigor, according to the beliefs of the Israelites, resulted in her separation from Yahweh (God), the source of life. The separation was healed once her integrity was restored. A woman in

childbed was required to undergo ritual purification for another reason as well. Giving birth set her apart. It brought
her into contact with the creative power of God. She touched
the sacred. To return to her everyday activity, after this awesome experience, the Levitical Law required of her to be
purified through a ritual offering when the days of her purification were fulfilled. At the end of the designated period,
the woman affected her own purification through the offering of atoning sacrifices.[276]

These regulations, however, have long since ceased to pertain, not only because of the changed cultural and societal
realities and the advances we have made in the medical sciences and in human hygiene, but especially because the law
of grace has superseded the Mosaic Law and its ceremonial
requirements. If this is the case, one might well ask why the
Church, as Joanne Pierce has noted, revived and kept the
purification rituals of women after childbirth, when other
regulations and ceremonials also rooted in the Law, such as
circumcision, the Sabbath, and dietary regulations, were
dropped and never revived.[277] The answer, as we shall see
below, may well lie in cultural factors and in the widespread
superstitious beliefs about menstruating women among the
people of ancient societies and civilizations.

While we clearly and absolutely acknowledge the continuity between the two Covenants – the Old and the New –
we also affirm the radical uniqueness of the New Covenant.
The self-communication of God has been historically revealed
in Jesus Christ and this revelation is present and active in his
mystical body, the Church. In Christ the Law has been fulfilled and returned to its essential foundation and center (Mt.
5:17-20 and 22:34-40; Rom. 8:3-5). As a result, the ceremonial
law is abrogated and cancelled (Gal. 5:2-6). Christ has freed
us from the ceremonial law and its material observances. The
regulations on legal purity are neither relevant nor valid. Yet,
the canonical tradition, at least on one level, confronts us
with a different reality.

Ancient attitudes towards menstruating women

Deep-rooted ideas are hard to overcome. People in antiquity believed that menstruating women and women in childbirth were especially susceptible to demonic influences so that even the work they might do could bring ruin.[278] Besides, the limited sanitary conditions and the lack of adequate means of hygiene in the ancient world, as among people today in primitive societies, made menstruating women 'unsociable.' The concept of female impurity, in part, arose from this fact. The Old Testament tended to reinforce these ideas. As mentioned above, Levitical law considered childbirth, menstrual and all other bloody vaginal discharges, and abnormal penile discharges as physical impurities. Although these things did not constitute a moral wrong, women or men whose bodies were so affected had nevertheless to undergo purifying ablutions through which the physical impurities were removed (Lev. 12 and 15). Eventually, these negative cultural and religious attitudes towards menstruating women and women in childbirth found their way into the Church.

The canonical tradition and menstruating women

Three canonical letters, those of Dionysios of Alexandria (ca. 265), Timothy of Alexandria (ca. 372), and St. John the Faster, Patriarch of Constantinople (+619), were especially influential in this regard. The three were men of their times and echoed in their writings the prevailing attitudes of their day. They lent credence to and helped propagate the popular beliefs of the ancients about the inferiority of bodily functions and the impurity of women during their monthly cycle and in childbirth. Eventually, these ideas led to the creation of purification or 'churching' rites after a designated period of time after delivery. The teachings of the Church, however, do not ascribe any moral wrong to menstruating women and women in childbirth. Nevertheless, the ancient negative attitudes towards menstruating women have prevailed among the general populace to this day, due in large measure to the ideas expressed in the three canonical letters of Dionysios, Timothy, and John the Faster.

These letters were eventually incorporated into the collection of canons that regulate the praxis of the Church. The second canon of Dionysios,[279] upon which the canons of Timothy[280] and John the Faster[281] are based, reads as follows.

> Concerning women in menstruation, whether they ought to enter the temple of God while in such a state... There is no objection to one's praying no matter how he may be or to one's remembering the Lord at any time and in any state whatever, and petitioning to receive help; but if one is not wholly clean both in soul and in body, he shall be prevented from coming to the Holy of Holies.

Based on this and the two subsequent canons, women were gradually inhibited from receiving Holy Communion and from entering the nave during their monthly cycle and by extension after childbirth until their day of purification was completed and their return to the community was accomplished through the rite of 'churching.'[282] While most women have long since abandoned the prohibition against entering the nave and participating in the divine services, or kissing the icons and receiving antidoron during their monthly cycle, most continue to refrain from Holy Communion during menstruation and from participating in church services after childbirth until their days of 'purification' are completed.

One of the earliest sources to make direct mention of the purification of women after childbirth is the document known as *The Canons of Hippolytus* (ca. 500).[283] This document and the canonical letters mentioned above were clearly influenced by the Old Testament laws and by a variety of cultural attitudes – mostly negative – towards sex, menstruating women, and women in childbirth. Although *The Canons of Hippolytus* were never incorporated into the collection of canons of the Orthodox Church, they were well known and highly influential in the East, having been originally compiled in Greek.[284] The thoughts expressed in these canons were perpetuated by others, including the author(s) of the prayer of the Rite of the First Day that we have been discussing. For example, *The Canons*, as the prayer in question, consider impure not only new mothers but also midwives. According to the *Canons of Hippolytus*, the midwife, like the new mother, was also prohibited from receiving Communion, although for a shorter period than the mother, after assisting at the birth.[285]

Another perspective

However, negative ideas about human sexuality and bodily functions were not the only ones in circulation in the early Church. Other views, more balanced, less severe and less ascetical were also advocated. For example, the *Apostolic Constitutions*, a late fourth century Church Order, has this to say about such matters.

> For neither lawful mixture [intercourse], nor childbearing, nor the menstrual purgation, nor nocturnal pollution can defile the nature of man, or separate the Holy Spirit from him. Nothing but impiety and unlawful practice can do that. For the Holy Spirit always abides with those that are possessed of it, so long as they are worthy.[286]

The attitudes expressed by the author(s) of the *Apostolic Constitutions* appear to be more in harmony with the spirit of the Gospel than the canonical admonitions, which were highly influenced by the popular beliefs of the times and especially by the proscriptions of the Levitical laws on 'cleanness' and 'uncleanness.'

Pope Gregory the Great (590-604), known in the East as Pope Gregory the Dialogos, expressed similar liberating views. In response to an inquiry by Augustine of Canterbury about issues pertaining to the 'churching' of women, Pope Gregory observed that menstruating women could receive Holy Communion, though they may also choose to refrain out of a deep sense of reverence. "If ... no food is unclean to one pure in mind," he said, "how can a woman who endures the laws of nature with a pure mind be considered impure?"[287] The words of Pope Gregory – who is counted among the saints of the Church – are full of wisdom and compassion.[288] Yet, the prohibitions of the past – imposed by the religious customs and the social attitudes of ancient societies – linger on and continue to influence many people of our day, clergy and laity alike.

The liturgical tradition and the rites of 'churching'

John Klentos reminds us "canons dictate abstract principles while liturgical texts testify to actual practices."[289] It would be helpful, therefore, to look at the early liturgical texts to see the actual practice of the Church as it relates to childbirth and the 'churching' of mothers.

The earliest extant *Euchologion* of the Byzantine Rite is the *Barberini gr. 336*, a manuscript of the late eighth century. It contains only two pre-baptismal prayers, both of which are for newly-born infants. The first prayer is entitled, "A prayer for the sealing [blessing] of a child receiving a name on the eighth day of his birth," through which the name of the child, as chosen by the parents, is confirmed. The content of the prayer, however, reveals a more important dimension. It is not so much the given name of the child that is being confirmed, as the name of God in whose Name the child is being received and sealed by the Church. "Lord our God, we pray and beseech You, let the light of your countenance shine upon your servant (N) and let the Cross of your Only-begotten Son be sealed in his heart and thoughts... And grant, Lord, that your holy Name shall remain indelible upon him, so that in due time he may be joined to your holy Church and be perfected through the awesome mysteries of your Christ..."[290] In other words, together with a personal name, the infant is sealed with, bears, and is called by the grandest of all names, Christian. The infant born to Christian parents is received by the Church as a catechumen, as a peripheral member of the community, awaiting and preparing for baptism, by which he/she will be incorporated into the Body of Christ, the Church, to share fully in the blessings and privileges of the new life.

The second prayer is entitled, *"A prayer at the time when a child enters the church on the fortieth day of his birth."* The prayer likens the churching of the child to the presentation of our

Lord Jesus Christ to the Temple on the fortieth day after his birth by Mary, his holy Mother, in fulfillment of the Law (Lk. 2:22-38); and supplicates God for the child's safekeeping until the day of baptism when he/she will become a partaker of the blessings reserved for God's elect.

The *Barberini* codex presents us with two important facts that are pertinent to our discussion. The first is that in the eighth century the Church had not yet established a rite for the First Day or a rite for the "purification and churching of the mother." Also, in the two prayers for newborn infants there is no mention – whether negative or positive – of the mother. Hence, we may safely assume that the prevailing popular social practices related to women in childbirth had not yet influenced the liturgy.

In fact, according to the evidence in the manuscript tradition, the Rite of the First Day was introduced only in the fourteenth century and the Prayers for the 'Churching' of the mother forty days after birth were introduced in the eleventh and twelfth century, at a time when severe ascetical attitudes were in vogue and the Levitical regulations were revived and kept.[291]

The original form of these rites was very simple, consisting of a single prayer. Gradually, the two simple rites (of the First Day and the Fortieth Day) were transformed into services (ἀκολουθίαι) through the addition of hymns, ceremonial actions, and additional prayers, most of which reflect the purity codes of the Old Testament. With the addition of these elements, the essential theme of the First Day rite – joyous thanksgiving for the safe delivery of the mother and the birth of a new human being – was eclipsed by the themes of physical impurity and forgiveness. The same occurred with the rites of 'churching.'

In the printed *Euchologia* the service of 'churching' is called, "The Service for the Churching of a Woman – Ἀκολουθία εἰς τό Σαραντίσαι Γυναῖκα." In the original Greek the term for 'churching' is 'σαραντίσαι' (or σαραντισμός). It is derived from the word σαράντα, which means forty. It is used to indicate the time when the woman's menstrual flow and confinement are completed and her 'churching' is at hand. The service, as we noted above, was established in the eleventh and twelfth century and was built around the third prayer in the present rite, which is a variation of the prayer for the 'churching' of an infant found in the *Barberini* codex, which, as we saw above, was a prayer of blessing for the infant. The service of the 'churching' of the mother, like that of the 'churching' of an infant, was established in imitation of Mary's entrance into the temple with the infant Jesus; and was meant to mark the reentry of the new mother into the regular routines of daily life, into the church, and into the ecclesial community from which she was excluded – by social and religious custom – for forty days, the period of her confinement and 'purification.'

The second prayer in the present rite was added in the twelfth century and shortly thereafter the first prayer of the present rite was also introduced into the service. Both the second prayer and the first part of the first prayer ask for the purification of the mother from physical and spiritual impurities. The second part of the first prayer asks for blessings upon the newborn child. Finally, a fourth prayer was added to the service, which, like the earliest prayer in the rite – the third in the present rite – is a prayer of blessing and thanksgiving. It recalls the presentation by Mary and Joseph of the infant Jesus into the temple and his meeting with St. Symeon the Elder and invokes God's blessings upon the child, the parents, and the Godparent.

The value of the Pre-baptismal Rites

I believe there is great value in the three pre-baptismal rites. They signify the importance and the great worth the Church places upon marriage, children, and the family. The rites serve many purposes. In the case of the Rite of the First Day, the Church acts – through the priest – to share in the joy of the parents and relatives of the newborn and to give thanks to God for the miracle of birth and the safe delivery of the mother. Praying for the well-being of the infant and the mother, the Church also lays claim to the child in the Name of Christ, and offers felicitations, encouragement, and assistance to the parents.

In the case of the Rite of the Eighth Day, the Church emphasizes the worth of the human being – as person and as nature – by confirming a personal identity through the name chosen by the parents with which he/she will be baptized and with which at every stage and circumstance of life will receive the sacraments and all other blessings of the Church. Moreover, the infant is sealed with the Name of Christ so that he/she may be identified with him and become both in name and in essence a Christian.

The "churching" of the mother and the child is also an important communal event, especially when the service is conducted in the presence of the liturgical assembly. Through the churching service the community not only recalls one of the mysteries of the faith, Christ's meeting with St. Symeon in the temple, but also welcomes the mother and the child into its midst and rejoices with the family offering prayers of thanksgiving for the mother's safe delivery and for the creation of a new life.

Lessons from the Feast of the Meeting

It would be helpful at this point to view the rite of 'churching' from the perspective of the Feast of the Meeting or Presentation of our Lord (Ὑπαπαντή), inasmuch as the rite of churching of mother and child was established in imitation of Mary's entrance into the temple with the infant Jesus. The Feast of the Meeting (Ὑπαπαντή) is celebrated on February 2, forty days after Christmas. In the west the Feast is known as the Feast of the Presentation or of the Purification of Mary. It is significant, however, that in the east neither the name of the Feast nor the hymnology of the Feast make mention of the purification of Mary. On the contrary, the Feast is centered on the infant Christ; and the Theotokos is addressed only in the most positive terms: "the undefiled Maiden," "the Theotokos full of grace," "the pure Mother," "the heavenly gate and cloud of light," and other such epithets. In fact, as the Kontakion – a central hymn of the Orthros – tells it, our

Lady did not need purification because her virginal womb was already sanctified by the fact that she bore the Son of God, "[Lord], You have sanctified by your birth a virgin womb..." The Feast of the Meeting ends the Nativity sequence that began with the fore- feast of Christmas. Together with Christmas it highlights the self-emptying of Christ, the eternal word of God who became flesh for our salvation:

> Today He who once gave the Law to Moses on Sinai submits himself to the ordinance of the Law, in his compassion becoming for our sakes as we are. Now the God of purity as a holy child has opened a pure womb, and as God He is brought as an offering to Himself, setting us free from the curse of the Law and granting light to our souls.[292]

The Feast is called "The Meeting of the Lord," because the infant Christ met his chosen people in the person of St. Symeon the Elder and Anna the Prophetess (Lk 2:25-38) who recognized him as the expected Messiah and proclaimed him "a light to bring revelation to the Gentiles, and the glory of [God's] people Israel" (Lk. 2:32). The Feast is meant to emphasize the passionate love of God for the world, the light of revelation that he has granted us through the incarnation of his Son, our Lord Jesus Christ, and the salvation that he came to bestow upon us.

The focus of the Feast, like the whole of the Nativity cycle, is on the uniqueness of Jesus Christ and the continuity between God's promises and fulfillment. It is a feast of joy for the redemption that Christ has brought us. In like manner, the service of "churching" should focus on the joyous event of parturition and the period of confinement that precedes the service should embody the joy of childbirth and not be burdened with the ancient concepts of physical impurity. St. Paul has assured us that, "If anyone is in Christ, he is a new creation; old things have passed away; behold, all things have become new" (2 Cor. 5:17).

Hence, the time of a woman's confinement after birth ought to be seen in more positive terms; released from the proscriptions of the Levitical law and the limiting social attitudes of the past that have turned it into a period of unsociableness and exclusion from domestic duties and social and ecclesial activities for reasons of blood pollution and uncleanness. The attitudes and the practices of the past are a distraction.

The Church should encourage the faithful to welcome the period of confinement as a time of special joy, when the household contemplates the gift of life and offers thanks for the wonders of God's grace and the abundance of his mani-fold blessings – both seen and unseen – amidst the contradictions and the anomalies of the fallen world. It is a period for family bonding, a time to experience anew the joys of marriage, and a time to reflect upon the privilege of childbearing and the gift of parenthood. It is a time also for the mother to rest and recuperate – physically, mentally, and spiritually – from the stresses of pregnancy and the pains of labor; and for the husband to assume and learn the joys and the responsibilities of fatherhood. From the perspective of the child, it is a time to grow in strength and vigor, a time to limit possibly unhealthy exposure to large numbers of people.

For these reasons, I believe, the prayers of the pre-baptis-mal rites should be reviewed so that their language may reflect more accurately modern sensibilities about bodily functions and express better the Christian understanding of human sexuality, conception, birth, and the blessings of fam-ily life, especially because we honor marriage as a sacrament, revere motherhood as a blessing, and value children as a gift, joy, and privilege.

In the following paragraphs I should like to address some related subjects which require the Church's prayerful atten-tion.

The Rite of Churching and entrance into the sanctuary

The Rite of Churching presents us with another trouble-some problem that rightly irritates some people who view it as discriminatory. At the conclusion of the service, accord-ing to current liturgical practice, male infants only are brought into the sanctuary while female infants are brought before the holy doors. This practice is, in fact, a late development.

St. Symeon of Thessalonike (+1429), for example, tells us that in his time, due to the dangers of infant mortality, most children were baptized by the fortieth day after their birth. Hence, at the time of 'churching' all baptized infants, regardless of sex, were admitted into the sanctuary, while infants who were yet to be baptized were brought before the holy doors of the sanctuary. Thus, baptism and not the gender of the infant determined entrance into the sanctuary.

Today, most infants are baptized well after the fortieth day. The current practice, which distinguishes between male and female infants and excludes girl babies from the sanctuary, is untenable. After all, as St. Paul tells us, there is neither male nor female, for all are one in Christ (Gal. 3:28). Hence, gender should not be counted as an obstacle, inasmuch as boys and girls are equal in honor and grace; both have been created in the image of God, and both are endowed with the same Holy Spirit. Either all infants, regardless of gender, are brought into the sanctuary at the end of the 'churching' service, or all should be excluded.[293]

Infertility, stillbirth, and miscarriage

Thus far, our discussion has centered on motherhood and parturition. But what of women, as Karen Westerfield Tucker asks, who have not yet become joyous mothers for some unfortunate circumstance such as infertility or a failed pregnancy that ends in miscarriage or a stillbirth?[294] What sort of rites does the Church have for such sad events? Sadly, there is no rite for infertility and the prayers for miscarriage and stillbirth (the birth of a dead fetus) are, to say the least, woefully deficient and vexing.

In the case of stillbirth or of the death of an infant before the fortieth day, current practice requires that we 'church' the mother using the first and second prayer of the Rite of Churching. Clearly, this is an inadequate, if not an insensitive, approach to the pain and the deep sense of loss experienced by the grieving mother and father.

The Prayer for Miscarriage in the printed *Euchologia* is equally inadequate. It is replete with language that is strident and accusatory, when, in fact, a miscarriage is a natural phenomenon, an uncontrolled spontaneous expulsion of the fetus before it is viable. The prayer reads in part as follows. "Have regard for this your servant who this day is in sin, having fallen even into voluntary or involuntary sin, and has aborted that which was conceived in her. Be gracious unto her willing and unwilling iniquities, preserving her from every wile of the devil; cleanse her of her sin; heal her suffering, granting to her, Loving Lord, health and strength of body and soul." Whatever positive elements may be contained in the prayer, they are overshadowed and drowned out by the harsh and judgmental language.

A miscarriage, like stillbirth, produces physical pain, emotional stress, mental anguish, and spiritual suffering. A woman who has experienced a miscarriage (and for that matter stillbirth or the death of a newborn child) ought to be comforted, strengthened, and encouraged by the Church; not chided. A miscarriage should not be confused with an abortion, which is a willful act to terminate an unwanted pregnancy and which is rightly condemned by the Church. The current prayer for miscarriage is need of revision and new prayers for infertility and stillbirth should be formulated.

Some attempts at reforming the Pre-baptismal Rites

The Church is obliged to review carefully the prayers and rubrics of the Pre-baptismal Rites and to take the necessary steps to eliminate any and all ambiguities from the received texts using appropriate language to reflect clearly the wondrous mystery and the many blessings of marriage, children, and family.

Father Konstantinos Papayiannis, the author of several learned studies on the liturgy and a priest of the Church of Greece, for example, has made several concrete proposals for the reform of the pre-baptismal rites.[295] Unfortunately, the call by many for the necessary reform of the Pre-Baptismal Rites for Infants has gone unheeded. However, when the Church hesitates to act through indifference or fear and remains unresponsive to the emerging needs, then individuals, for good or for ill, seize the initiative. Let me cite two examples of this from two recently published bilingual (Greek – English) liturgical books that contain the sacramental rites and other services of the Greek *Euchologion*, including, of course, the Rite of the First Day. Many clergymen of the Greek Orthodox Archdiocese in the United States use one or the other of these publications.

The first example comes from the volume *Sacraments and Services – Book Two*, published by the Narthex Press.[296] Here, the prayer we discussed above from the Rite of the First Day is presented in two forms. On one side is the Greek text, faithful to the original found in the Greek *Euchologion*. On the other side is the English translation, in which the penitential language of the original is missing. The translator has replaced the word 'forgive' with the words 'be gracious' and 'bless,' thus changing the intent, tone, and meaning of the prayer. This, to say the least, is disingenuous. Nonetheless, with the stroke of the pen the translator has, in fact, clearly and absolutely revised the prayer, at least in its English version. The English text reads in part as follows. "Lord our God... Knowing the frailty of human nature, *be gracious to Your handmaid (N.)* who today has given birth, in the abundance of Your mercies... Look down from heaven... *and bless this Your handmaid (N.), and all her household and all here present, for You are a good and loving and merciful God.*" By comparing this English version of the prayer from the one given above, which is an exact translation of the Greek original, the reader can see how liturgical reforms are sometimes quietly introduced and accomplished.

The second example comes from the volume *The Priest's Service Book*, compiled and edited by Father Evagoras Constantinides. Here, the editor has taken the process one step further by altering both the original Greek text and of course, in turn, the English translation thereby producing, in effect, a new prayer.[297] Both of these publications have also changed the prayer for miscarriage, removing the vexing language in both Greek and English texts.

Who has the authority to change liturgical texts?

As commendable as the efforts of these two publishers may be, in fact, they raise some very serious questions. Is an individual editor or translator, however well intentioned and informed, at liberty to alter a received text without proper authorization? And who, in the end, has the authority to initiate alterations in the received texts and the liturgical praxis?

The answer, I believe, is obvious. While many qualified persons may propose changes and work diligently to achieve them, when all is said and done, the local Church acting judiciously and not an individual clergyman is the final arbiter and the responsible agent of liturgical change. Were it to be otherwise, chaos would prevail and the liturgy of the Church would loose its authenticity and its catholicity and be robbed of its dignity and vitality.

Hence, every local Church – diocese or archdiocese – is obliged to regulate and guard the liturgy, but it is also equally obliged to continuously evaluate its effectiveness and to develop its shape and expression to meet the needs and demands of the times without betraying the essential traditions and the faith of the Church. The problem is that the Church is reticent to act purposefully and decisively, especially when it comes to matters of liturgical reform. It is easier and safer to maintain the status quo than to recognize and conform to the dynamic character of Orthodox worship. It is far more difficult – if not daring – to tackle the issues of the day thoughtfully and to act responsibly in response to the needs of the people who live and worship in the modern world. We have to admit that not every single rite of the Church, formed and shaped by the needs and ideas of another time and place, can speak with the same adequacy and force – well and completely – to the people of the cultures in which it is celebrated today.

Another example from the Baptismal Rite

On a different note, let me cite another example which also highlights the need for substantial revisions in the received texts. The Prayer for the blessing of the font at the baptismal rite, "You are great, O Lord – Μέγας εἶ, Κύριε," is a classic example of a beautiful doxological prayer. Admittedly, the prayer has a lovely poetic tone, but the cosmology it sets forth is based on an antiquated worldview according to which the universe is arranged in four tiers, the heavens and what is above the heavens, the earth and that which is below the earth. In addition, the prayer contains archaic imagery, which is incomprehensible to the modern mind. It contains, for example, such phrases as: "You have joined together the universe out of four elements... You did crush the heads of the dragons,[298] which lurked there (i.e. in the streams of the Jordan)... Let every aerial and obscure phantom withdraw itself from us."

With some revisions this lovely prayer can retain its poetic beauty and at the same time convey more clearly the truths of the faith through the use of images and language that are comprehensible to the people of today. The three phrases mentioned above could, for example, be re-worked to read: "You created the universe out of nothing and from many elements You made it good and beautiful ... You crushed the monstrous dragons, the fearsome and menacing powers of rebellion and death that haunt us and lurk in us and around us... Let every persistent dread and incomprehensible fear withdraw from us."

Another example from the Burial Rite

The reform of the liturgy sometimes requires of us to re-discover older useful elements that were once part of a given rite but disappeared over the course of time for one reason or another. The rites of burial, for example, present us with just such a case.

As Elena Velkovska has shown in her excellent study on the development of the funeral services of the Byzantine Rite, the burial rites as they appear in the manuscripts consist essentially of an ancient repertory of prayers that were later inserted into a ritual framework modeled after a monastic Orthros of the Studite type.[299] Indeed, the hymnody of the rites is derived mostly from the funereal hymns (νεκρώσιμα τροπάρια) of the Octoechos or Parakletike, which contains the variable portions for the daily office throughout the week in a series of eight offices, one for each of the eight tones. The Octoechos is of monastic origin, formed especially by the hymnographers of the Lavra of St. Savas and of Studion.[300] The funereal hymns are assigned to the Vespers and Orthros services for Saturdays, which is dedicated to the martyrs, the ascetics, and the dead.

The motifs of the funeral prayers in the manuscripts, as Velkovska reminds us, represent ancient Christian ideas revolving around the concepts of life, resurrection, light, peace, rest, refreshment, forgiveness, divine love and mercy, and particularly repose in the "bosom of Abraham," based on Luke 16:22-23 and Hebrews 4:10-11. The hymnography, on the other hand, addresses the stark realities of death and the vanity of human endeavors.

In addition to the prayers and the hymnody, the funeral rites also contain two Scripture lessons, one from the *Apostolos* (the liturgical book that contains the lections from the Book of Acts and the Epistles) and another from the *Evangelion* (the liturgical book of the four Gospels arranged in pericopes or lections). In the printed editions of the *Euchologion* and in the *Typikon of the Great Church of Christ* the Epistle and Gospel readings assigned to the service are 1 Thess. 4:14-17 and John 5:24-30 respectively. The *Apostolos* and the *Evangelion* also list several alternate readings. The order of the listings in the *Apostolos* is as follows: 1 Cor. 15:47-57; 1 Cor. 15:20-28; and Rom. 14:6-9. The alternate readings in the *Evangelion* are: John 5:17-24; John 6:35-39; John 6:40-44; and John 6:48-54.

These several passages reflect the Church's belief in the reality of Christ's death and resurrection and of the benefits that we derive from them, namely, the resurrection of our body on the last day, incorruption (ἀφθαρσία), and immortality (ἀθανασία). They speak also of Christ's two activities, judging and giving life. On the last day he will judge all. Death and judgment, however, are not the future of those who hear, believe, and do the will of God, but everlasting life. Christ, the Bread of life makes the realities of the Kingdom a present reality for all those who eat his flesh and drink his blood. The realities of the general resurrection are not only anticipated; they are already experienced by those who live by the will of God.

Of the several prayers contained in the ancient manuscripts, one, which is the oldest, "God of spirits and of all flesh," was retained in all the manuscripts and entered into the printed *Euchologia*. However, another prayer of significant value was gradually eliminated from the burial service. It was a prayer of inclination said for the mourners just prior to the conclusion of the service. As a prayer of inclination it was preceded by the diaconal admonition, "Bow your heads to the Lord." The prayer is ancient, as evidenced by its inclusion in the *Barberini Codex*. It reads as follows:

> Lord O Lord, you are the relief of the troubled, and the consolation of those who mourn, and the redeemer of all the afflicted. Comfort those who are seized with pain for the deceased; being merciful, heal the suffering of sadness gripping their hearts, and give rest to your servant reposing in the bosom of Abraham in the hope of the resurrection. For you are the rest of your servants and to you we give the glory.[301]

The usefulness of such a prayer is obvious. The Church prays not only for the deceased but also for the survivors who are in need of God's succor and consolation. The remembrance of the mourners in prayer gives them strength. It brings comfort and healing to their bereaved souls. For this reason, this or some other similar prayer should be restored to the funeral rites of the Church.

It is well known that the Patriarchate of Constantinople established the burial rite currently in use by the Greek Church with the publication of the *Typikon of the Great Church of Christ* in 1888.[302] The 'new' service is an abbreviated form of the longer, more elaborate rite for lay people (Ἀκολουθία Νεκρώσιμος εἰς Κοσμικούς) contained in the *Great Euchologion*.[303] Among the several elements that were eliminated from the longer rite of the *Euchologion* were the Beatitudes (Matt. 5:3-12). In recent times the Church of Greece restored the Beatitudes to the rite, as evidenced by the *Mikron Euchologion* published by the Apostolike Diakonia, the publishing house of the Church of Greece. Most other Greek and bilingual editions of the funeral service, however, follow the order of the *Typikon* of 1888 and omit them from the service.

The significance of the Beatitudes as a source of comfort is unmistakable, as they remind the mourners of the blessings of true discipleship. The Beatitudes are a statement of faith in the resplendent invincible joy of the Christian life. The joy and blessedness of which the Beatitudes speak do not lie in some faraway future world, but are a present reality. While Christian joy will find its completion in God's Kingdom, it is a completely unassailable present possession (John 16:22). Nothing in life or death can take it away. Sorrow, loss, pain, and grief are powerless to touch it. Worldly fortunes change; but Christian joy is permanent. For the hope the Beatitudes bring, they should be restored to the funeral rites that all may recite them prayerfully.

If, at the end of the 19th century, the Greek Church saw fit to reform the funeral service by responding to the pastoral needs of the time, what prevents us from doing the same today? In his article on the Byzantine Funeral Rite, Peter Galadza – with whose conclusions and suggestions I concur wholeheartedly – proposes that the Eastern Churches give special attention to four areas that would enhance the rite and meet present-day pastoral needs. These areas are: the strengthening of paschal themes in the funeral rites; the inclusion of prayers for the bereaved; the restoration of greater diversity in lections, hymnography, and prayers; and the renewal of liturgical elements that would facilitate greater participation by the people.[304]

The need to be responsive

Modern liturgical scholarship has raised and continues to raise a variety of questions that require consideration and has set before us numerous problems that beg for resolution.

If the liturgy of the Church is to remain vibrant and relevant, we are obliged to explore the history, uncover the

meaning, and weigh the effectiveness of each of its components. I recognize that some people would find the latter
pursuit especially troublesome and unsettling. Yet, no less a
personage than Saint Symeon of Thessalonike (+1429), who
certainly was no firebrand liberal and revisionist, made a
significant observation in his treatises on just such a matter.
He remarked that when the Church comes up against a practice that has been properly examined and appropriately
determined to be defective, she is obliged to change it, because ignorance or neglect allowed it to become a practice in
the first place.[305]

It is not enough, however, simply to talk about defective
practices or about recovering lost and displaced elements of
the liturgy. It is more important that the Church be determined to act on these things, to wrestle with the practices,
texts, and rubrics of the divine services that tend to obscure
meanings and mystify the liturgy, rendering it meaningless
to those who celebrate it and to those who participate in it.

No one, however, should construe the call for renewal and
reform of the liturgy as an attempt to undo or to betray the
tradition. Change for the sake of change is not only unwar-
ranted it is also dangerous. Neither a misguided ordering of
the contents of the divine services nor, for that matter, the
maintenance of the status quo is of any consequence, if the
inherent relationship between being a Christian and the liturgy is not the normative principle behind all that we say
and do about the liturgy.

The Church, as we have said often, is primarily a worshipping community; and Christians draw their identity
primarily from the liturgy through which the life of faith is
constantly renewed. Liturgical forms, practices, and expressions grow out of the theological core of a given rite. Therefore
before all else, we are obliged to grasp and comprehend the
theological meanings of liturgy before we can speak of its
performance or of its reform.

The world is always changing. That which remains constant, however, for Christians, is the saving truths of the
Gospel and the theological core of the sacred rites. The forms

and expressions of worship are conditioned by history and culture. That is why some liturgical forms and expressions of one era do not always carry the same force and meaning in another. The problem becomes more acute when, for ambiguous sentimentalities, we perpetuate forms of worship that are heavily encrusted with cultural debris of times past that do not allow their theological core to shine forth as clearly as it should. It is true that liturgical forms and practices must always be consistent with tradition, but they must also be connected with the real lives of real people. Only then does the normative principal of the inherent relationship between being a Christian and the liturgy remain alive and well.

Truly, the liturgy has been both the expression and the guardian of divine revelation. Not only does it express, represent, and communicate the saving events of Christ's life but it is also for the members of the Church the living anticipation of the Kingdom to come. For these very reasons the liturgy must be traditional but also relevant to the lives of worshippers.

9

An Introduction To The Divine Liturgy

I. HISTORY AND OUTLINE *

The phrase 'Divine Liturgy'

The Divine Liturgy is the sacred rite by which the Orthodox Church celebrates the mystery of the Eucharist. This title for the Eucharist is derived from two Greek words *theia* (θεία) and *leitourgia* (λειτουργία). The word *theia* means pertaining to God, hence, divine. The word *leitourgia* comes from two words *leitos* (λέϊτος, λεῖτος, λεώς or λαός), which means people, and *ergon* (ἔργον), which means work, hence the work of the people or a public service, act or function.

The word *leitourgia* was used in Greek antiquity to describe those services and acts that were performed and discharged by the richer citizens either voluntarily or by appointment and in rotation for the benefit and common interest of all, including acts of worship. It was in this latter religious sense that the word found its way into the vocabulary of Scripture and the Church. In the Septuagint (the Greek translation of the Old Testament) the word was applied to the Temple services and the functions of the priests.

In the New Testament, where the word appears infrequently, it describes the saving work of Christ (Heb 8.6) and Christian worship (Acts 13.21). In the Apostolic Fathers and later tradition the word was applied to the worship of the Church, inasmuch as Christian worship is something that the people do or enact together as a community of faith. By the fourth century, the word *leitourgia*, together with the adjective *theia* (i.e. Divine Liturgy), had become the technical term for the mystery of the Eucharist, the central act of worship of the community. The word Eucharist (Εὐχαριστία) in

162

turn means thanksgiving. It takes its name from the central prayer of the Divine Liturgy, the Great Prayer of Thanksgiving (Eucharist) called the Anaphora (᾿Αναφορά), which the presiding presbyter or bishop recites for and on behalf of the People of God, of which he is a part. Significantly, the Anaphora is introduced by the priest's admonition "Let us give thanks to the Lord – Εὐχαριστήσωμεν τῷ Κυρίῳ," after which he begins to recite the Anaphora. "It is proper and right to sing to You, bless You, praise You, thank You, and worship You in all places of Your dominion…"

The origins of the Divine Liturgy

The Divine Liturgy is composed of two parts. The first part is called the Liturgy of the Word, the Synaxis, or the Proanaphora. It is also referred to as the Liturgy of the Catechumens. Each of these names emphasizes a particular aspect of the first part of the Divine Liturgy. It is called the Liturgy of the Word because the central element of the service is the presentation, proclamation, and explication of the Scriptures, the Word of God. It is also called Synaxis (σύναξις, which means a gathering or assembly) because it comprises the coming together of God's People to hear the Word of God and to celebrate the Eucharist. It is called the Proanaphora (προαναφορά) because it precedes the Great Eucharistic Prayer (the Anaphora – ᾿Αναφορά). Finally, it is also called the Liturgy of the Catechumens (τῶν Κατηχουμένων), because the catechumens are the hearers, the unbaptized people who are receiving instruction in doctrine and discipline before baptism. As peripheral members of the Church they could not partake of the Eucharist but were encouraged – indeed required – to participate in the Synaxis to worship with the community through the reading of the Scriptures and to hear the homily that normally followed, after which they were prayed over and dismissed.

The second part of the Divine Liturgy is the Eucharist proper, when the precious Gifts are presented, consecrated, and communed. It is also called the Liturgy of the Faithful (τῶν Πιστῶν) because only baptized Christians may properly celebrate the Eucharist and partake of the holy Gifts. St. Justin the Martyr (ca 150 A.D.) put it best with these words:

> This food we call Eucharist, of which no one is allowed to partake except one who believes that the things we teach are true, and has received the washing [Baptism] for forgiveness of sins and for rebirth, and who lives as Christ handed down to us. For we do not receive these things as common bread or common drink; but as Jesus Christ our Savior being incarnate by God's word took flesh and blood for our salvation, so also we have been taught that the food consecrated by the word of prayer which comes from him, from which our flesh and blood are nourished by transformation, is the flesh and blood of that incarnate Jesus.[306]

While all may hear the word of God and pray, only Orthodox Christians in canonical order with the Church, according to ancient practice and tradition, may rightfully approach the Table and partake of the Eucharist.

The Liturgy of the Word in its basic, classical shape is a Christianized version of the synagogue service focusing on the reading of biblical passages, the homily, and prayer. The Eucharist, on the other hand, is derived from the words and actions of our Lord and Savior Jesus Christ at the Mystical (Last) Supper. The Liturgy of the Word and the Eucharist are intimately related and inseparable. In the Divine Liturgy we encounter, celebrate, and partake of the mystery of Christ both in Word and Sacrament. In fact, the Liturgy of the Word constitutes the most essential and the most proper preparation for the Eucharist, because the Word of God has the power to judge, convert, purify, heal, and transform the lives of people. "You are already clean because of the word which I have spoken to you. Abide in Me, and I in you... He who abides in Me, and I in him, bears much fruit; for without Me you can do nothing... If you abide in Me, and My words abide in you, you will ask what you desire, and it shall be done for you... These things I have spoken to you, that My joy may remain in you, and that your joy may be full ... This is My commandment, that you love one another as I have loved you" (John 15:3-5, 7, 11-12).

The connection of the Divine Liturgy to the prayer service of the synagogue and to a Jewish household or fraternal ritual meal must be understood against the backdrop of the nascent Christian community. The Lord, His Apostles, and the first Christians were Jews. It is clear that the Church is characterized forever by its Semitic origins. It is equally clear that the Church has close connections with Hellenism. The Church was born in Jerusalem, but grew up within the Hellenistic civilization. The fundamental contents of her faith and liturgy were essentially shaped within the historical and cultural contexts of her beginnings. Her liturgy, art, and theology are radiant with the imperishable traces of this perennial double experience. Louis Bouyer observes: "It is true that the Christian liturgy, and the Eucharist especially, is one of the most original creations of Christianity. But however original it is, it is not a sort of an *ex nihilo* creation. To think so is to condemn ourselves to a minimal understanding of it."[307] The Church's identity is always clear, precise, and unambiguous, never abstract. While she is not to be identified with any single race, society, or culture, she is nevertheless incarnated, embodied into various cultures. She implants and unites herself with the traditions and cultures of people, imparting to them the truths of the Gospel. Yet, even as she does this, she bears always the marks of her origins, her Semitic and Hellenic roots. It must be remembered that the Church, though founded in Palestine, for the most part, flourished in a Greek-speaking and a Greek-thinking world. Historical Orthodoxy has always remained truly biblical in its content. But her doctrinal and liturgical formularies are unintelligible without reference to her Jewish and Hellenic upbringing and education.

Christ our Lord instituted the Eucharist at the Supper he shared with his disciples just prior to his Passion on the evening of what we now call Great and Holy Thursday to perpetuate the remembrance *(anamnesis – ἀνάμνησις)* of His redemptive work and to establish a continuous intimate communion *(koinonia–κοινωνία)* between himself and those who believe in him. In establishing the Eucharist during the course

of a Jewish ritual meal, Christ conformed to a familiar practice already filled with human and sacred values. Jewish
custom required that a blessing be pronounced over the bread
at the beginning of every solemn meal and over the cup of
wine mixed with water at the end of the meal. At the Last or
Mystical Supper (Μυστικός Δεῖπνος) Jesus gave a radically
new meaning to the food and drink of the sacred meal. He
identified himself with the bread and wine. He gave his flesh
as food, "Take, eat; this is my Body… Drink of it, all of you;
for this is my Blood of the covenant, which is poured out for
many for the forgiveness of sins"(Matt. 26:26-28).

The actions and words of the Lord concerning the bread
and wine formed the basis for the Eucharist, the central act
and chief recurrent liturgical rite of the Church. The nucleus
of every eucharistic rite consists in four actions: the preparation, transfer, and placing of bread and wine mixed with
water on the holy Table; the *Anaphora* or Great Eucharist
prayer, which includes the remembrance of God's mighty
acts in history and especially the economy of the Son of God
(the Christ event), the words of institution at the Last Supper, and the invocation to the Father to send down the Holy
Spirit upon the assembly and gifts for their consecration; the
breaking of the consecrated Bread (an act called the fraction-
κλάσις τοῦ ἄρτου); and the communion of the consecrated
sacramental gifts by the people of God.

In the beginning the Eucharist was celebrated within the
context of an evening community meal, referred to as the
agape or love feast. By the end of the first or at the beginning
of the second century, the celebration of the Eucharist was
separated from the community meal and transposed to the
early morning hours. From that time forward, every Eucharistic celebration is preceded by a fast, called the Eucharistic
fast.

The Eucharist is Christ himself. It is his sacrificed, risen,
and glorified body, which is given to the faithful "for the
forgiveness of sins and life eternal."[308] As such, it is the most
precious of gifts, through which the life of God continually
becomes the life of those who believe in him, receive him in

faith, and abide in him. That is why the Eucharistic fast has become a fixed prerequisite for Holy Communion. It is meant to place the faithful in a state of readiness, vigilance, expectation, and anticipation for an encounter with the living God who calls his people to communion and holiness.

Participation in the Divine Liturgy, therefore, requires prayerful preparation, for we stand on holy ground in the presence of the Triune God (Ex. 3:4-7). Hence, in preparation for this profound experience, we are called to quietness, abstinence, and forbearance, to a quickening of body and soul that we may receive the King of all. Fasted from the night before, as a sign of spiritual vigilance and awareness, we approach the Holy Table "with the fear of God, with faith, and with love,"[309] to receive the Holy Gifts as the first meal of the day and as the essential food of life.

The development of the Divine Liturgy

The Divine Liturgy is a complex act of movement, sound, and sights characterized by a deep sense of harmony, beauty, dignity, and mystery. It is structured around two solemn entrances, which today are abbreviated forms of earlier more elaborate ceremonies; the reading and the exposition of Holy Scripture; the great Eucharistic Prayer (the Anaphora); and the distribution of Holy Communion. Elaborate opening rites *(enarxis)* and a series of dismissal rites *(apolysis)* embrace the whole action.

The first or Little Entrance, the entry of the clergy and the people into the Church, once marked the beginning of the Liturgy of the Word. The Little Entrance is a solemn procession with the Gospel accompanied with entrance hymns.

The second or Great Entrance once marked the beginning of the second part of the Divine Liturgy, the Eucharist. It is a solemn procession with the gifts of the bread and wine that are to be offered and consecrated. The gifts are brought to the Church by the people and are prepared by the clergy before the Divine Liturgy begins, usually during the Orthros. The service of preparation is called the Proskomide (Προσκομιδή). It is performed at the Table of Preparation called the Prothesis (Πρόθεσις). The portion of the bread to be offered for consecration is called the Lamb – Ἀμνός (John 1:29; Rev. 5:6-14), the name or title given to Jesus by John the Baptist, because he is the Messiah, the Anointed of God, the Suffering Servant, who bore our infirmities and our sufferings and gave his life as an offering to take away the sins of the world (Is. 53:1-12).

The priest excises the Lamb from a loaf of leavened bread, called prosphoron or prosphora (πρόσφορον, προσφορά), which means 'offering,' and places it on the discos or diskarion (paten, plate). When the Lamb is properly prepared, the priest fills the cup or chalice (ἅγιον Ποτήριον) ceremoniously with wine and water. Then, he begins a series of commemorations with particles of bread that are arranged on the paten to the right and left of the Lamb. The first of the commemorations is in honor of the Theotokos, with a particle placed to the right of the Lamb. Nine additional particles arranged in three vertical rows of three particles each are placed to the left of the Lamb in honor of the angels and the saints. The commemorations end when the priest places smaller particles of bread in front of the Lamb for the living and the dead, whom he remembers by name. The service concludes with the veiling and the censing of the gifts and a prayer.

Let me cite at this point a lovely passage from St. Symeon of Thessalonike on the meaning of the Church and the Kingdom of God, drawn from the image of the particles on the paten. He writes:

In the divine figure and action of the holy Proskomide we see Jesus himself and we contemplate the one Church. Through him, who is the true light, she acquires eternal life, and is illumined and constituted. On the one hand, he is in the center through the Bread; on the other, his Mother is at his right through the particle, while the saints and the angels are at the left. And, below him is the entire devout assemblage (ἄθροισμα) of those who have believed in him. There is a great mystery here: God in men and

God among gods (Θεός ἐν ἀνθρώποις καί ἐν μέσῳ θεῶν), who have received deification from him, who is the true God by nature, and who was made flesh for their sake. The future Kingdom is here, too, and the revelation of eternal life: God with us, both seen and partaken (Θεός μεθ᾽ ἡμῶν ὁρώμενός τε καί μεταλαμβανόμενος).[310]

The verbal and non-verbal elements of the Divine Liturgy are fitted together harmoniously, so as to weave a pattern of prayer that addresses and inspires the whole person, body and soul. The principle behind the development of the Liturgy's ceremonial splendor rests upon the notion that our earthly worship reflects the joy and majesty of heavenly worship.

On the verbal side of the Liturgy we hear eloquent prayers of praise, thanksgiving, intercession, and confession; litanies, petitions, acclamations, greetings, and invitations; hymns, chants, psalmody, and creedal statements; and scriptural readings and a homily. On the non-verbal side, we are involved with solemn processions and an assortment of liturgical gestures. The eyes are filled with the actions of the servers, as well as with the sights of the Lord and His saints gazing at us from the icons. The nostrils are filled with the fragrance of incense and the heart is grasped by the profound silence of the divine presence. People touch hands gently, saying, "Christ is in our midst,"[311] when called upon to love one another before the offering of the Gifts as a sign of mutual forgiveness and love. With one voice and heart they recite the Creed and the Lord's Prayer, and recommit themselves to the fullness of the truth of the Orthodox faith and life. Participating in Holy Communion, the faithful "taste and see that the Lord is good" (Ps. 33/34:8).

The basic outline of the Divine Liturgy goes back to the New Testament. Ritual and text evolved gradually. The several elements of the Divine Liturgy developed unevenly and at different stages. Its structures were expanded, augmented and adorned with chants, prayers, and various ceremonials. By the tenth century, the Eucharistic rites of Constantinople, the chief see of the Orthodox East, had become more or less crystallized. The process of growth, modification, and adaptation has been relatively slow ever since.

By virtue of its prestige, the rites of Constantinople, the great imperial city, first influenced and finally replaced all other rites in the Orthodox East. Since the end of the twelfth century, with minor variations that reflect local customs, the liturgy of Constantinople – usually referred to as the Byzantine Rite – has become the common rite of all Orthodox Churches.

The Three Liturgies

Constantinople was the magnificent crucible in which several liturgical traditions converged. Out of this synthesis came three Liturgies, which were distinctly Constantinopolitan. Firmly rooted in God's written word and strongly influenced by the patristic experience, these Liturgies take us to the heart of God's ineffable glory and boundless philanthropy. They also expose us to the fundamental doctrines of the faith and to the essential requirements of the new life in Christ, which we acquired through Baptism and Chrismation. Indeed, the new life is constantly renewed and advanced through the Eucharist. "Our manner of thinking is conformed to the Eucharist and the Eucharist confirms our manner of thinking," said St. Irenaeus.[312]

The Liturgy of Saint Basil was, until the twelfth century, the chief liturgy of Constantinople. Its anaphora is probably the most eloquent of all Liturgies, east and west. Powerful in its unity of thought, theological depth, and rich biblical imagery, it was celebrated every Sunday and great feast day. Now it is used only ten times during the year: on the five Sundays of the Great Fast (or Lent); on the vigils of Pascha, Christmas, and Epiphany; on Holy Thursday; and on the Feast of Saint Basil, January 1.

The Liturgy of Saint John Chrysostom is shorter and less rhetorical than that of Saint Basil. It is distinguished by its simplicity, directness, and clarity. Originally it was probably used as the weekday Eucharistic rite of Constantinople. Gradually, around the twelfth century, it superseded and replaced the Liturgy of Saint Basil to become the main Liturgy of the Orthodox East. It is now celebrated at every Eucharistic assembly, unless the Liturgy of Saint Basil or the Liturgy of the Pre-Sanctified Gifts is to be celebrated.

The Liturgy of the Pre-Sanctified Gifts is not a full Divine Liturgy in that it does not contain the Anaphora. This liturgy is now used on Wednesdays and Fridays of the Great Fast (or Lent) and on the first three days of Holy Week. It is comprised of Vespers, the solemn transfer to the holy Table of the pre-sanctified Holy Gifts consecrated at the Divine Liturgy the previous Sunday or Saturday, and the order of the distribution of Holy Communion as in the other Liturgies.

According to local custom, three other ancient Liturgies are also used by Orthodox Churches on the occasion of the feast day of the saints, to which their authorship is traditionally attributed. These are the Liturgies of Saint James (Iakovos), the ancient Liturgy of Jerusalem; Saint Mark, the ancient Liturgy of Alexandria; and Saint Gregory the Theologian, an ancient Liturgy of Cappadocia and Alexandria.

The celebrants of the Divine Liturgy

The Divine Liturgy is a corporate action of the whole people of God. The clergy and the laity together constitute the one, living, divine-human organism, the Body of Christ, the Church. The eucharistic assembly presupposes the presence and active participation of clergy and laity, each with their own essential and distinctive ministry, role, and function. Together they enter into the depths of the divine light, in accordance to the measure of the faith given them by God and the purity of their heart.

The chief celebrant of the Eucharist is the bishop or, in his absence, the presbyter, without whom there can be no Eucharist. The bishop or priest (presbyter) acts in the place of Christ who is the true priest and celebrant of the Eucharistic mystery.

Christ Himself is the one "Who offers and is offered, the

one who receives and distributes" (prayer of the Liturgy). Through His perfect self-offering, as the unique High Priest and mediator of the New Covenant, Christ continues to unite redeemed humanity to God (Heb 9.11-15; 10.10).

Reception of Holy Communion

The Eucharist belongs to and is shared by those who have been baptized into the Church and who hold a common faith in the bond of love. Thus, only those Orthodox Christians in full communion with the Church may partake of the Holy Gifts. For the Orthodox, the Eucharist is not an instrument or means for achieving Christian unity, but the very sign and crowning of that union based on doctrinal truths and canonical harmony already held and possessed in common. The Eucharist is both a celebration and a confession of the faith of the Church. Hence it is not possible to approach Holy Communion by way of hospitality.

It is expected that every baptized and chrismated Orthodox adult, child, and infant be regular and frequent recipients of the Divine Mysteries. It is presupposed that adult and children communicants have fasted from the evening meal prior to receiving Holy Communion at the morning Eucharist. However, care must be exercised never to consider Holy Communion a reward for pious feelings and actions, but as a gift of the Lord to the members who comprise his Body, the Church.

Thus, it is necessary that one approaches Holy Communion with spiritual discernment. Saint Nicholas Cabasilas teaches: "Let not everyone come to receive it, but only those who are worthy, 'for the holy gifts are for the holy people of God.' Those whom the priest calls holy are *not only* those who have attained perfection, *but also* those who are striving for it without having yet obtained it . . . That is why Christians, if they have not committed such sins (mortal sins) as would cut them off from Christ and bring death, are in no way prevented, when partaking of the holy mysteries, from receiving sanctification . . . For no one has holiness of himself; it is not the consequence of human virtue, but comes for all from Him and through Him."[313]

In the Eucharist we are called to repentance and to share in what is divine

For the faithful the Divine Liturgy is experienced at one and the same time as judgment, forgiveness, healing, fullness, and true life. In every Divine Liturgy people hear the good news of Christ and enter into a process of conversion or repentance. Repentance is offered as a way of life, a continuous journey toward God the Father. We learn to live in communion with Christ not only in the moments of the Liturgy, but also in the experiences of daily life. Repentance should never be experienced as a gloomy, guilt-ridden existence but as a joyful on-going conversion of the heart and as a constant remembrance of the true God, who shines within our hearts the pure light of his divine knowledge, opens our minds to comprehend the message of his Gospel, and instills in us reverence for his blessed commandments so that we may conquer sinful desires and pursue a spiritual life thinking doing all those things that are pleasing to Him (Prayer of the Divine Liturgy). Walking thusly in the Spirit as children of God, life is experienced as an ascent, as a humble, peaceful, and joyous journey toward God the Father, who embraces us through the boundless love of his Son, our Lord Jesus Christ.

In the Divine Liturgy we share in the power of Christ's resurrection, which alone liberates and transfigures all of life and makes possible the reconstruction of all order, personal and social. The resurrection of Jesus Christ is the fundamental truth and the absolute fact of the Christian faith. It is the guarantee of our salvation. Although the consequences of Christ's resurrection will be disclosed fully at the Parousia (Παρουσία) or Second Coming, participation in these eternal blessings begins here in this life, especially through the sacraments. Through the Eucharist, Christ calls us to share in what is divine, namely immortality and incorruptibility. He sends us the Holy Spirit, who vivifies our souls and actualizes within us the hidden mysteries of God's Kingdom, joining us to the Triune God in a personal union.

Every worship service – and especially the Divine Liturgy

– is an opportunity for a new dynamic encounter with the Holy Trinity for the renewal and sanctification of human persons and creation.

II. THEOLOGICAL MEANING

The Eucharist and the parish

The mystery of the Church as the Body of Christ is fully realized in the Divine Liturgy, for the Eucharist is Christ crucified and risen, in His personal presence. Every parish, living in full the sacramental life, according to John Meyendorff, is the miracle of the new life in Christ lived in community and built upon and around the Table of the Lord. "Whenever and wherever the Divine Liturgy is celebrated, in the context of doctrinal unity and canonical norms, the local church possesses the marks of the true Church of God: unity, holiness, catholicity, and apostolicity. These marks cannot belong to any human gathering; they are the eschatological signs given to a community through the Spirit of God."[314]

The whole life of the local community is centered essentially on the weekly celebration of the Eucharist, for it is there that the faithful experience the mystery of God's presence and the new reality in the world which God has wrought through the incarnation of his Son. It is at the Divine Liturgy that we confess our common faith, express our indissoluble unity in love, find another life, new, true, and eternal, receive the seeds of sanctity to bear fruit commensurate to the gift, and experience the transfiguration of our being by communicating in the Lord and becoming members of his Body, the Church.

The parish, in canonical union with the local bishop, is the essential eucharistic cell, without which there is no Church, for the Eucharist constitutes the Church and it is never celebrated in the abstract but always at a particular time in some concrete place, the parish or any legitimate and canonical extension of it.

Christ is wholly present at every Eucharist. Hence, the Divine Liturgy is the same wherever and whenever it is celebrated, for there is Christ and his Church. Thus, every other activity of the parish – social, educational, philanthropic, or cultural – is informed by and serves the purposes of the eucharistic assembly for which the parish exists.[315]

The Eucharist at the center of the Church's life

The Eucharist is at the center of the Church's life because it "completes all the other sacraments"[316] and "recapitulates the entire economy of salvation."[317] The Eucharist, being truly Christ, is the focus and content of both liturgy and faith. Thus, as St. Irenaeus writes, "our manner of thinking is conformed to the Eucharist and the Eucharist confirms our manner of thinking."[318]

Literary documents on the lives of saints often contain important information on Christian life, liturgy, and doctrine. One such document, which dates to AD 304, at the height of the fierce persecutions initiated by the Emperors Diocletian and Maximian, is an eyewitness account describing the trial of a group of Christians in a town of North Africa. Of particular interest is the brief testimony of two of those martyrs. Their words concerning the Eucharist provide us with a succinct statement that sums up the Church's understanding of the Eucharist as the center of her life.

Then Saturninus, the priest, was arraigned for combat.

The proconsul asked, "Did you, contrary to the orders of the emperors, arrange for these persons to hold an assembly?"

Saturninus replied, "Certainly. We celebrated the Eucharist."

"Why?"

"Because the Eucharist cannot be abandoned."

As soon as he said this, the proconsul ordered him to be put immediately on the rack...

Then Felix, a son of Saturninus and a reader in the Church, came forward to the contest. Wherupon the proconsul inquired of him, "I am not asking you if you are a Christian. You can hold your peace about that! But were you one of the assembly; and do you possess any copies of the Scriptures?"

"As if a Christian could exist without the Eucharist, or the Eucharist be celebrated without a Christian!" answered Felix.

"Don't you know that a Christian is constituted by the Eucharist, and the Eucharist by a Christian? Neither avails without the other. We celebrated our assembly right gloriously. We always convene at the Eucharist for the reading of the Lord's Scriptures."
 Enraged by the confession, Anulinus ordered Felix to be beaten with clubs...[318a]

The testimony of these two ancient martyrs serves to highlight the significance and the uniqueness of the Eucharist in the life of the Church and in the life of each of her members. The weekly celebration of the Eucharist on the Lord's Day is an indispensable activity of the Church.

Our weekly participation in the Divine Liturgy is not meant to fulfill a vague religious obligation but to give evidence to our voluntary kenosis, which is to say, the emptying of our sin-scarred and moribund self, so that we may pass from death to life, or put another way, to exchange life for life. Participation in the Eucharistic is the necessary remedy for our weakness, inasmuch as through it Christ continuously changes and transforms us into himself. We come to the Eucharist in faith to enter into union with the divine nature, to become by grace flesh of Christ's Flesh. United with Christ, our humanity becomes consubstantial with the deified and glorified humanity of Christ, not as a result of human virtue but of God's immeasurable love and boundless goodness. When we eat and drink worthily at the Eucharist, we are no longer clay but of the Body of Christ.

The Eucharist is the source and summit of the Church's life

The Eucharist or Divine Liturgy is the central mystery of the Church. It is not simply one sacrament among many. It is at once both the source and the summit of the Church's life. It is "an event constitutive of the being of the Church, enabling the Church to be."[319] It is the condition of growth and of the very existence of the Church. In it the Church is continuously changed from a human community to the Body of Christ, the temple of the Holy Spirit, and the holy people of God.

The Eucharist, according to Saint Nicholas Cabasilas, is the final and greatest of the mysteries "since it is not possible to go beyond it or add anything to it... After the Eucharist there is nowhere further to go. There we must stand, and try to examine the means by which we may preserve the treasure to the end... For in it we obtain God Himself, and God is united with us in the most perfect union."[320]

Every sacred mystery makes its partakers into members of Christ. But the Eucharist accomplishes this perfectly. To quote Saint Gregory of Nyssa: "By dispensation of His grace, He (Christ) disseminates Himself in every believer through that flesh whose substance comes from bread and wine, blending Himself with the bodies of believers, to secure by this union with the Immortal that man, too, may be a sharer in incorruption. He gives these gifts by virtue of the benediction through which He transelements (μεταστοιχείωσας) the natural quality of these visible things to that immortal thing."[321]

Through the Eucharist, divine life flows into us and penetrates the fabric of our humanity. The future life is infused into the present one and is blended with it, so that our fallen humanity may be transformed into the glorified humanity of the new Adam, Christ. The Eucharist, as Saint Ignatios of Antioch says, is the "medicine of immortality and the antidote against death, enabling us to live forever in Jesus Christ."[322] Through the sacred mysteries of baptism and the Eucharist Christ "unites us to himself, and makes us each, according to our individual merit and purity, sharers through him in those graces which are his own."[323]

The Eucharist as memorial-anamnesis

In worship and particularly in the Divine Liturgy, the Church remembers and celebrates the mighty acts of God in history. Through this remembrance, or anamnesis, the Church recognizes the positive nature of space, time, and history, in and through which human life exists – called out of nothing into being by the Word and Son of God – and the love and grace of God are made manifest.

For the Church, time is not an endless, meaningless cycle of recurring events. It has both a beginning as well as an end, which is to say a fulfillment. And the miracle of miracles is that the event towards which all time is moving – God's Kingdom – has already entered the world. "When the fullness of time had come, God sent forth his Son, born of a woman, born under the law, to redeem those who were under the law, that we might receive the adoption as sons" (Gal. 4:4-5). When the fullness of time had come, God spoke to us through his Son, our Lord Jesus Christ, through whom all things were made. And although the appearance of Christ is a singular event of the past, his coming ushered in the age to come. In Christ the end times have already occurred; the Kingdom of God – the Kingdom of light, justice, life, joy, peace, love – has come in power and the transfiguration and sanctification of all life has begun: "Go tell John the things you hear and see: The blind see and the lame walk; the lepers are cleansed and the deaf hear; the dead are raised up and the poor have the gospel preached to them" (Matt. 11:4-5).

Although it is yet to come in fullness, the reign of God has already appeared in the person of Jesus Christ. The end times have been disclosed in and through the holy earthly life, the compelling and unique teachings, the extraordinary works, the life-creating death, the glorious resurrection, and the wondrous glorification of Jesus Christ, the Son of God made flesh. Christ and his redemptive work stand at the center of history and fill it with ultimate meaning and purpose.

Through the incarnation, creation has been graced with supreme worth and value. Accordingly, time is filled with untold possibilities and history constitutes the saving and redeeming dialogue between God and man. The Triune God is ever present to his world, constantly acting. Though the world is in a fallen and rebellious state, God has not ceased doing everything for the world and humanity until he has led us to heaven and granted his Kingdom to come (Anaphora of St. John Chrysostom). The Father cares for the work of his hands, providing for and renewing and perfecting man and the cosmos.

Worship – and especially the Divine Liturgy – constitutes the remembrance and the celebration of God's redemptive activity as well as the thanksgiving for all that God has done and continues to do for the world. The remembrance of the Church is not merely a psychological calling to mind of past events but an actual participation in the paschal presence of Christ, who said, "Lo I am with you always, even to the end of the age" (Matt. 28:20), and who promised that "where two or three are gathered together in [his] name, [he] is there in the midst of them" (Matt. 18:20). "The event which is actualized in the Eucharist," wrote Father Alexander Schmemann, "is an event of the past when viewed within the categories of time, but by virtue of its eschatological, determining, completing significance it is also an event which is taking place eternally… The Eucharist is therefore the manifestation of the Church as the new aeon; it is participation in the Kingdom as *parousia*, as the presence of the resurrected and resurrecting Lord."[324]

In Christ the anamnesis or remembrance of his past saving acts and of his future promises does not constitute nostalgia, which is to say a sentimental yearning for an irrecoverable past, nor does it constitute a futuristic longing for an unfulfilled distant coming event. In Christ the past and the future are always present realities, for "Jesus Christ is the same yesterday, today, and forever" (Heb. 13:8). He is the One "who is and who was and who is to come" (Rev. 1:4). In the Divine Liturgy we enact the saving commandment – 'Do this in memory of me' – and remember all that came to pass for our sake (Anaphora of St. John Chrysostom), both the historic time of salvation as well as the exaltation and Second Coming of Christ. In other words, in the anamnesis the efficacy of God's saving work is present to the Church granting us communion with Christ.

At the Divine Liturgy we proclaim Christ's death and confess his resurrection (Anaphora of St. Basil). We are immersed into and participate in the profound mystery of our salvation. We receive Christ, whose presence abolishes the spatial-temporal limitations of the past and the boundaries that lie ahead. We share in the Paschal victory and partake of the Holy Gifts for the "fulfillment of the Kingdom of heaven" (Anaphora of St. John Chrysostom); and we pray earnestly to "find mercy and grace with all the saints who through the ages have pleased [God]: forefathers, fathers, patriarchs, prophets, apostles, preachers, evangelists, martyrs, confessors, teachers, and every righteous spirit made perfect in faith" (Anaphora of St. Basil). In the liturgy time, space, history, and the very people of God encounter and enter into the eternal 'present' of God.

The Eucharist as messianic banquet

In this present age between the two comings of Jesus Christ our Lord, the Divine Liturgy is always the messianic banquet, the meal of the kingdom, the time and place in which the heavenly joins and mingles with the earthly. The Eucharist initiates humankind, nature, and time into the mystery of the uncreated Trinity. The Divine Liturgy is not some sacred drama or a mere representation of past events. It constitutes the very presence of God's embracing love, which purifies, enlightens, perfects, and deifies (2 Pet 1.4) all those who are invited to the marriage supper of the Lamb (Rev 19.9), all who through baptism and chrismation have been incorporated into the Church and have become Christ-bearers and Spirit-bearers.

In the Divine Liturgy we do not commemorate one or another isolated event of sacred history. We celebrate, in joy and thanksgiving, the whole mystery of the divine economy, from creation to the incarnation, especially, in the words of the Divine Liturgy, "the cross, the tomb, the resurrection on the third day, the ascension into heaven, the enthronement at the right hand of the Father, and the second glorious coming." Thus, in experiencing the risen and reigning Christ in the Divine Liturgy, the past, present, and future of the history of salvation are lived as one reality.

Through the Eucharist the messianic Kingdom becomes real to the people of God assembled in faith. Celebrating the Eucharist, we touch eternity. The Eucharist, as Father

Alexander Schmemann observed, "is not the repetition of his advent or coming into the world, but the lifting up of the Church into his *parousia*, the Church's participation in his heavenly glory."[325]

In the Eucharist the Church is always becoming concorporeal (σύσσωμος) with the risen and glorified Christ. This concorporeality – becoming one body – of Christians with Christ begins with baptism and is fully revealed and continuously realized and perfected in the Eucharist. Through the incarnation God joined and bound himself to us in Christ Jesus by sharing our humanity, our flesh and blood (Gal. 4:4-5) and placed himself within our reach. By eating his Body and drinking his Blood we enter into a profound union with Christ. Through this communion Christ assimilates us to himself and gives us his divine and eternal life. United and clothed with him we are deified, we become gods by grace, heavenly and eternal.

At the Eucharist the divine Bridegroom of the Church calls his people to sit together with him in the heavenly places. We are raised to where he is, sitting at the right hand of the Father (Ephes. 2:6; Col. 3:1), that he may grant to us his divine perfections. In the words of Saint Gregory Palamas, "by this flesh [of Christ in the Eucharist] our community is raised to heaven; that is where this Bread truly dwells; and we enter into the Holy of Holies by the pure offering of the Body of Christ."[326] Through the Eucharist we experience in faith the eschatological union of Christ and the Church.

The Eucharist as a continuous Pentecost

The Divine Liturgy celebrates the inrushing of eternal life into our perishable, mortal existence and the abolition of our deaths through the presence of the Holy Spirit, who is ever present in the Church, animating and vivifying the Church, transforming the assembly into the Body of Christ, and liberating, sanctifying, and perfecting the members of the community. Every Divine Liturgy is a renewal and a confirmation of the constant coming of the Holy Spirit, as the prayer of the Liturgy tells it. "Make us worthy to find grace in Your presence so that our sacrifice may be pleasing to You and that Your good and gracious Spirit may abide with us and with the gifts here presented and with all Your people"(Liturgy of St. John Chrysostom – Prayer of the Proskomide).

Each Divine Liturgy becomes a continuation of the mystery of Pentecost as the Church prays to the Father for the gift of the Holy Spirit. "We ask, pray, and entreat You – send down Your Holy Spirit upon us and upon these gifts here presented." The Church also prays that the consecrated gifts may become a "communion of the Holy Spirit and the fulfillment of the Kingdom of heaven"(The Anaphora of Saint John Chrysostom). In the Eucharist we become Spirit-bearers so that we may receive Christ.

The Holy Spirit, to paraphrase St. Irenaeus, prepares us for Christ, by bringing us from oldness to the newness of Christ, who leads us to the Father, who grants us eternal life. At the Divine Liturgy we experience the abolishment of sin, corruption, and death, the divisive and destructive powers of Satan. We receive Holy Communion "for the forgiveness of sins and life eternal," two gifts of divine love, so that we may find mercy and grace with all the saints, who throughout the ages have been pleasing to God. In the Eucharist all things are united with God through the Holy Spirit.

In the changed elements of the bread and wine, creation itself, freed from the bondage of corruption, becomes Spirit-bearing. The incarnation, resurrection, and glorification of Christ as well as the sacramental life of the Church, through which material things come to bear divine perfections, disclose the ultimate worth and the fundamental goodness of God's creation. We are not saved from the material world but with it. While the age to come will reveal the comprehensive renovation, transfiguration, and glorification of man and the cosmos, the radical freedom from the bondage of corruption and all limitations is made known to us through Christ's resurrection and the perfecting grace of the Holy Spirit, which are present to us in the sacraments, and particularly in the Eucharist.

The whole action of the Divine Liturgy depends on the Holy Spirit. He makes the crucified and risen Christ really present to us in the eucharistic elements. Through his transforming and sanctifying power the bread and wine of the Eucharist become, in a real but mysterious way, the Body and Blood of Christ – which is to say, the living Christ present in all his fullness – through which our entire being is nourished and transfigured.

The Eucharist as food and communion

We have learned to equate food with life because food sustains our earthly existence. Our bodies do not possess life but are continuously fed and maintained by nourishment that comes from without. In the womb we are fed by our mother's blood. After birth, we are fed by her milk and by the food and drink that comes from the earth. Our body possesses nothing belonging to itself, but exists to forces and nourishment that are introduced into it.[327] Accordingly, food not only sustains life, it also symbolizes it. Now, the baking of bread and the making of wine, as St. Nicholas Cabasilas notes, is peculiar to man.[328] Hence, we can say that bread and wine are distinctively unique human foods and therefore the very symbols of our mortal life.

It is no accident that bread and wine mixed with water are so central to the Eucharistic mystery. They were not only central to the Last Supper, as we noted above, but they constitute the appropriate symbol for the mystery of life and communion. We speak of life in terms of food but also in terms of 'flesh and blood.' In fact, we cannot conceive of or know life except in terms of flesh and blood. A mother, for example, refers to her children – the fruit of her womb – as her flesh and blood. We recognize immediately the significant correlation between bread and wine and flesh and blood, the language that permeates the Eucharist. Both speak of life. The Holy Spirit changes the holy Gifts – the bread and wine of the Eucharist – the symbols of our life into the Body and Blood of Christ. Jesus Christ gives us his life – his flesh and blood – as food. Communion constitutes an exchange of life for life.

The union of life involves a sharing of life. The act of eating and drinking become the suitable sign of the great mystery of God and the divine-human encounter. God feeds humanity with his own being, while still remaining distinct. "The Logos," says St. Clemet of Alexandria, "becomes everything to his little ones: Father and Mother and Teacher and Nourisher! 'Eat my flesh,' He says, 'and drink my blood.' The Lord supplies these as the foods most appropriate for us."[329]

The Eucharist as sacrifice

The Church has a radically new and different understanding and meaning of sacrifice. In the first place, the initiative for sacrifice is not with man but with God, who continually offers himself to us. In the second place, the sacrifice offered by the Church is not an act of appeasement, but an offering in return, an antiprosphora (ἀντιπροσφορά). As St. Nicholas Cabasilas put it, "The mere remembering of the benefits bestowed upon us rouses us to make some sort of return, and to offer something at least to him who has showered so many graces on us."[330]

The Eucharist brings us before the unutterable mystery of the Father's inscrutable love and initiative: the offering of his Son in the Holy Spirit for the salvation and life of the world. "For God so loved the world that he gave his only begotten Son, that whoever believes in him should not perish but have everlasting life" (John 3:16). The mystery of this once for all offering of the Father is actualized essentially and perfectly time and again at every celebration of the Eucharist. At every Divine Liturgy we experience the self-offering of God. When offering the eucharistic gifts, the Church implores God the Father to send down his Holy Spirit upon the assembled faithful and upon the gifts they have set forth to make them be the Body and Blood of his Son, whom he offers to all for the forgiveness of sins and life eternal (Matt. 26:28; John 6:51).

This does not suggest, however, that the Eucharist attempts to reclaim past events; it does not repeat what is unique and unrepeatable. Christ is not slain anew and repeatedly at every Eucharist, for he died once for all. Ours is a spiritual worship without the shedding of blood (ἀναίμακτος λατρεί α). At each Eucharist the Holy Spirit changes the offering of the Church, the holy Gifts – the bread and the wine – into a reality that remains constant, the Body of Christ that was sacrificed once for all and now lives.

In the Eucharist we experience the eternal priesthood of Christ, the God-Man (Θεάνθρωπος – Theanthropos). His sacrifice, accomplished once for all through his entire earthly ministry and most especially through the Cross of Golgotha, remains operative for all in the Church, which is his Body. The Eucharist, according to Nicholas of Methone, renders present and makes manifest the sacrifice of Christ that is being eternally celebrated upon the altar in heaven.[331] As the great High Priest and Intercessor, Christ, the God-Man, continues in a state of sacrifice before the Father, making intercession on our behalf and uniting our prayers within his own (Heb. 7:24, 9:24). As he relates to us, Christ, the God-Man, continually offers himself to us through his Word and through the consecrated Gifts, giving us his life, his own risen and glorified Body, which died once for our sake and now lives and reigns (Heb. 10:12; Rev. 1:18).

The Eucharist is neither a mere representation nor a simple memorial of the sacrifice of the Cross. The Eucharistic elements are changed concretely and really into the Body and Blood of the Lamb of God, who freely sacrificed Himself and gave Himself as ransom to death in which we were held captive, sold under sin (Anaphora of St. Basil). Through his sacrifice Christ penetrated the deepest abysses of hell to lead the captives to the limitless expanses of true life, drawing us into his own sacrificial action.

At the Eucharist we experience and participate in the mystery of our salvation, the self-offering of God. As St. Nicholas Cabasilas noted, through the incarnation, death, and resurrection of his Son, God has set aside the triple barrier of nature, sin, and death that separates us from him.[332] Human nature, which had been abased by the sin of the progenitors of the race, is exalted by the incarnation of the Son of God. In the words of St. Romanos the Melodist, "The heap of earth is renewed, dust has been deified... [In Christ] man became god, possessing God; he became royal and bore the title of God."[333]

The sin that polluted God's creation from the breaking dawn of human history reached its frightful climax on the hill of Golgotha. However, Christ's death condemned irrevocably the fallen world by revealing its true and abnormal nature. Sin, in all its madness and cruelty, was utterly neutralized and destroyed on the Cross by the enormity of divine love and forgiveness: "Father, forgive them, for they do not know what they do" (Luke 23:34).

Death, the final indignity and the ultimate enemy, casts its cruel shadow over all creation. Its fear shackles us to the appearances of life and makes rebellion and sin erupt in us (Heb. 2:14-15). But Christ destroyed the fortress of death with his resurrection. Deathlessness, a divine attribute, has become a gift for all who cling to the Lamb of God (John 5:24-29). "Through his body," wrote Melito of Sardis, "which was subject to suffering [Christ] put an end to the suffering of the flesh, and through his Spirit who cannot die he slew the death that slays men... It is he who took flesh in the Virgin; he was hung on the tree, he was buried in the earth, he was awakened from among the dead, he was exalted to the heights of heaven... He is the silent Lamb, he is the Lamb slain... It is I, says Christ, I who have destroyed death, and triumphed over the enemy and trodden hell under foot, and chained the strong man [the devil] and brought man to the heights of heaven... [It is] I, your purification, I, your life, I your resurrection, I, your light, I your salvation, I, your King... It is I who shall raise you up [and] show you the eternal Father."[334]

At the Eucharist we commune the Gift of the Father, the incarnate Word and Son of God, "who gave himself for our sins that he might deliver us from this present evil age, according to the will of our God and Father" (Gal. 1:4). In response to this offering, the Church also offers a sacrifice.

However, the sacrifice we offer can only be an offering given in return on account of the riches of God's great goodness, mercy, and love. It is a sacrifice of praise and thanksgiving, "for things that we know and do not know, for blessings seen and unseen that have been bestowed upon us" (Anaphora of St. John Chrysostom).

Our offering has a multiplicity of forms, including commitment to the Gospel, loyalty to the true faith, constant prayer, watchfulness, the struggle against the passions, and works of charity. At its deepest level, however, the offering in return is experienced in the Eucharist, where we experience the self-offering of the Church and each of her members to God and acknowledge our complete dependence on him and offer up our hymns of praise and our life through the bread and wine – the unique human food – in exchange for Christ's life. In the words of St. Nicholas Cabasilas, " It is he who commands us to offer bread and wine; it is he who gives us in return the living Bread and the Chalice of eternal life... So here he commands those to whom he would give eternal life (that is, his life-giving Body and Blood) to offer the food of our fleeting mortal life: so that we may receive life for life, eternity for temporality."[335]

In the Eucharist we experience and enact for ourselves the mystery of Christ's kenosis. He, the eternal Word and Son of God, took on the form of a bondservant and "emptied Himself and became obedient to the point of death, even the death of the cross. Therefore, God also has highly exalted Him... that every tongue should confess that Jesus Christ is Lord, to the glory of God the Father (Phil. 2:7-9, 11). At its deepest level our offering in return must also be an act of kenosis, a willingness to loose our life in order to gain it. "If anyone desires to come after Me, let him deny himself, and take up his cross daily, and follow Me. For whoever desires to save his life will lose it, but whoever loses his life for my sake will save it" (Lk. 9:23-24).

Through the words of the offering of the Divine Liturgy, "We offer to you these gifts from Your own gifts," we enact our kenosis. We acknowledge that nothing of ours is our own, even life itself. And then, through the bread and wine, the appropriate symbols of our life, we offer up to God our life in exchange for his. Archimandrite Vasileios speaks of it in this way. "The more we advance voluntarily towards diminishing, finally becoming so small that we vanish, the more the glory that cannot be approached shines, realizing and bringing from nonbeing into existence endless new creations and joys."[336]

At the Eucharist we come to recognize that what we offer is not something that is ours at all, but that which is his already: the kenosis or sacrifice of God's Only-begotten Son. In the final analysis, our offering in return can only be Christ himself, whose saving work remains constant and immediate for every generation in every place, until he comes again. At the Divine Liturgy "God accepts our bread and wine, and gives us in return his own Son."[337]

At the Eucharist we become partakers of divine nature

Christ abides with his Church (Matt. 28:20), in order to communicate his divine life to the world. This life is constantly present in the Church, especially through the Eucharist. "Christ does not say that he is in us by a relation of an affective kind, but by physical participation (κατά μέ θεξιν φυσικήν)," notes St. Cyril of Alexandria.[338] Christ nourishes us with his own flesh. "I am the living bread which came down from heaven. If anyone eats of this bread, he will live forever; and the bread that I shall give is my flesh, which I shall give for the life of the world" (John 6:51).

Through the power of the Holy Spirit the bread and wine of the Liturgy are changed into the very Body and Blood of Christ. This change is not physical but mystical and sacramental. While the qualities of the bread and wine remain, we partake of the true Body and Blood of Christ, according to his own declaration (Mk. 14:22-24). To the eye and taste they remain bread and wine, but "let your faith be your stay," says St. Cyril of Jerusalem. He continues, "Instead of judging the matter by taste, let faith give you unwavering confidence that you have been privileged to receive the Body and Blood of Christ."[339]

The Eucharist, writes Saint Ignatios of Antioch, "is the flesh of our Savior Jesus Christ, the flesh which suffered for our sins and which the Father in His graciousness raised from the dead."[340] In the Eucharist we are offered Christ's glorified flesh, to which we are joined, without confusion or division, in order to partake of divine life.

In the Eucharist, Christ acts to make us His own Body. According to Saint Nicholas Cabasilas, "the Bread of Life himself changes him who feeds on him and transforms and assimilates him into himself."[341] When we partake of the Holy Gifts we are in Christ and Christ is in us, according to his promise: "He who eats my flesh and drinks my Blood abides in me and I in him" (John 6:56). Eternity penetrates our finitude (John 6:54). The life of the Trinity flows and dwells in us. In the Eucharist we become God-bearers. We become "partakers of the divine nature" (2 Peter 1:4), which is to say we become by grace what God is by nature through the transfiguring, sanctifying, and perfecting power of Christ through the Holy Spirit.

The Eucharist: A vision of the true life and the new humanity

The Eucharist unites the members of the Church both to Christ and to one another. It creates a network of relations, a community. "Because there is one bread, we who are many are one body, for we all partake of the one bread" (I Cor 10. 17). Saint John of Damascus writes: "If union is in truth with Christ and with one another, we are assuredly also united voluntarily with all those who partake with us."[342] Sharing in the life of Christ and energized by the gifts of the Holy Spirit, the Church becomes an epiphany of divine love.

In the Divine Liturgy we are given the vision and the image of true human life as God created it and intended it to become. Through the Eucharist the destructive powers of Satan are being continuously defeated and the life of selfless love is being revealed, learned, and lived. According to Vladimir Lossky, the Divine Liturgy makes manifest the true dimensions of the Christian life as "the way which leads from the multiplicity of corruption, that of individuals which divide humanity, towards the unity of the one, pure nature in which there is disclosed a new multiplicity: that of persons united to God in the Holy Spirit."[343]

The Eucharistic assembly becomes the image of the new humanity gathered around the risen Lord, empowered, nourished, and perfected by His love and mercy. In and through the Divine Liturgy, the members of the community are initiated into the depths of the corporate life of the Church as communion with God. Here we have a glimpse of the Church as an image of the Holy Trinity, the mysterious identity of the monad and of the triad. To quote Lossky again, there is "a single human nature in the hypostasis of Christ, many human hypostases in the grace of the Holy Spirit."[344] And although we are all one in Christ, we are at the same time many, concrete, unique, and unrepeatable persons in the Holy Spirit. As St. Maximos the Confessor puts it:

> The men, women and children coming into the Church reborn and recreated by her in the Spirit, are just about infinite in number. They are very different from each other in race and appearance; they are of all languages, life-styles and ages. There are great differences in their mentalities, customs and interests, their social station, their skills, and their professions. Their fortunes, their characters, and their abilities are very different, but the Church confers one and the same divine character and title equally on all: that they be, and be called, Christians… The holy Church is an image of God; she works the same unity in the faithful as God, even though the people unified in her through faith vary in their peculiarities and come from different places and different ways of life. It is God's nature to work this unity himself in the substance of things, without fusing them. He softens down the diversity in them and unifies them, as has already been shown, through their relationship and union with him, their cause, beginning, and end.[345]

In Christ, through baptism and the Eucharist, we can 'subsist' and affirm our existence as personal not on the basis of the immutable laws of our nature, but on the basis of our living relationship with God.[346] The Eucharistic assembly in its communal and ecclesial character is the eschatological community of God, a community which experiences the new life in Christ and witnesses to the presence of God's Kingdom in history. In the words of Metropolitan John Zizioulas, at the Divine Liturgy we "subsist in a manner different from the biological, as members of a Body which transcends every exclusiveness of a biological or social kind... In [our] ecclesial identity we exist not as that which [we] are, but as that which [we] will become, not as a result of an evolution of the human race, whether biological or historical," [347] but as the result of the victory of Christ. "Salvation is not a matter of moral perfection, an improvement of nature, but a new hypostasis of nature, a new creation."[348]

The newness of life in Christ is not the result of human effort. It is a gift from God, given freely to all who would accept it freely. Hence, salvation and the acquisition of perfection is neither the product of biological and historical evolution, nor the result of some ethical codes of behavior. It comes through a radical ontological change, which the Scriptures describe as new life, the death of the old man, the putting off of the old nature and the putting on of the new, and the acquisition of a new heart. This change is made accessible to all through baptism. It is maintained, renewed, nourished, and advanced by the Eucharist, when partaken in faith.

The Church is both an eschatological and historical community. The historical, visible community is truly the Church, against which the powers of hell shall not prevail. But it is still located within time. It has not yet crossed the frontier separating us from the age to come. It is still "part of the process whereby the Body gradually reaches completion so that the Head [Christ] may become all in all through the action of the Holy Spirit and in accordance with the plan of salvation."[349] Through the Divine Liturgy the historical community actualizes itself, really and effectively, here and now as the Body of Christ. It becomes the progressive growth of god-manhood to the full stature of Christ. Because "the adversary, the devil, prowls around like a roaring lion, seeking someone to devour" (1 Peter 5:8), the members of the community need to be vigilant and to live in active expectation of the Parousia, so that they may participate in the glorious promises of the age to come.

Now, on this side of death every ascent requires a descent. So it is with our experiences at every celebration of the Divine Liturgy. We climb the rungs of the ladder of the divine ascent, as the Triune God comes to embrace us with his boundless sacrificial love. We sit at table with him to hear the words of life and to partake of the Bread of life. But then, we are sent back, to "depart in peace." We are required to return to the world and to immerse ourselves in the affairs and circumstances of everyday life, bringing the redemptive power of God and the blessings of the Eucharist to our wounded and broken world. Having partaken of the Body of Christ, we must now tend to the needs of the broken human bodies and spirits that are all around us so that the rays of God's Kingdom may shine in the darkness of our fallen world bringing healing, hope, and joy to the hearts of people, until the Lord comes in glory (Rev. 22:20).

10

Some Textual Problems
in the Divine Liturgy – Are Details Important?

I. REGARDING SOME RITUALS OF THE GREAT ENTRANCE

'Remember us all' or 'Remember all of you'… does it really matter?

During the transfer of the unconsecrated Gifts from the Prothesis to the Holy Table at the Great Entrance, the deacon and the priest interrupt the Cherubic Hymn with a brief commemoration. In many of the recent editions of the Divine Liturgy, this commemoration reads as follows: "May the Lord God remember all of *us* in His Kingdom – πάντων ἡμῶν μνησθείη Κύριος ὁ Θεός ἐν τῇ βασιλείᾳ αὐτοῦ." In the manuscripts, the Diataxeis,[350] and the early printed editions of the Divine Liturgy, however, the commemoration has a slightly different form. Instead of the pronoun *us* – ἡμῶν – (the objective case of the first person plural, *we*), the texts employ the plural pronoun of the second person ὑμῶν– *you*.[351] This form of the commemoration is to be preferred over the other, not because it is older or because it is found in most of the liturgical documents, but because it corresponds more faithfully to the role of the clergy, who pray for the people, entreating the Triune God on their behalf. The rubric of the fourteenth century *Diataxis* of Philotheos Kokkinos tells as much. "As they pass through the temple (or the nave), both [deacon and priest] *pray for all [the people]* saying, May the Lord God remember *all of you* in his kingdom – Διερχόμενοι δέ τόν ναόν εὔχονται ἀμφότεροι ὑπέρ πάντων λέγοντες, Μνησθείη, Κύριος ὁ Θεός, πάντων ὑμῶν ἐν τῇ βασιλείᾳ αὐτοῦ."[352]

The issue that concerns us most, however, is not the use of one or the other of the two pronouns *you* or *us* but why the

193

Cherubikon is interrupted at all with a commemoration. What purpose does the commemoration serve? Was it always part of the Great Entrance ritual and, if not, when and why was it introduced into the service? The answer to this question will help us to get a glimpse of what Robert Taft calls, the 'vagaries' of liturgical evolution, and at the same time see why the early manuscripts and the older editions of the Divine Liturgy prefer the pronoun *you* in the commemoration.

The development of the Great Entrance ritual

Our earliest sources indicate that the transfer of the gifts was conducted with little or no fanfare and certainly without commemorations and song. The gifts were prepared in the skeuophylakion (σκευοφυλάκιον) or in a side chamber – on the side of the bema or sanctuary – before the start of the Divine Liturgy. They were carried out from there at the appropriate time in solemn procession. In its primitive form, the procession was performed in silence.[353] Gradually, the ritual of the Great Entrance began to expand. A varying number of secondary formulas, ritual actions, and a chant – sung by the chanters and the people – were added to accompany the procession.[354] Initially, the chant was a Psalm, most probably Psalm 23 (24), with the *alleluia* as a refrain.[355] Soon the Psalm was sung antiphonally, that is, with a troparion, which was added to the original refrain, *alleluia*. Eventually, between the 8th and 10th century, as evidenced by the *Typikon of the Great Church* (ca. 10th century), the Psalm was abandoned in favor of the hymn, a common occurrence in liturgical history.[356] The earliest of these troparia or hymns is the celebrated Cherubikon, which, according to the chronicler George Cedrenos (11-12th century), was introduced into the Divine Liturgy by a decree of Emperor Justin II in the year 573-574.[357] Since then it continues to be sung at every Divine Liturgy, except those of Great Thursday and the Paschal Vigil.

The Cherubikon, as we have said, was originally sung as a refrain several times and without interruption as the prayers and rituals of the Great Entrance were being accomplished. In fact, as Robert Taft says, "A glance at the Greek text of the

Cherubikon is enough to prove that it was meant to be sung continuously; it is a single grammatical unit that allows for no split."[358] We must ask, therefore, what developments in the evolution of the Divine Liturgy led to the practice of interrupting the Cherubic hymn with commemorations and when the practice was introduced. To answer these questions we must examine the perceptions of the people about the meaning of the transfer of the unconsecrated gifts from the Prothesis to the Holy Table, which is the central act of the Great Entrance.

The medieval liturgical commentators began to interpret the simple functional act of preparing and transferring the unconsecrated gifts to the Holy Table with various symbolic or allegorical interpretations, the earliest of which is that of Theodore of Mopsuestia (+428). Theodore saw in the procession of the gifts an image of Christ being led to his passion and burial. The funeral cortege symbolism led to the gradual development of several elements that form part of the ritual of the Great Entrance. For example, Theodore of Mopsuestia informs us that together with the gifts a linen cloth was brought and spread on the Holy Table. The cloth was soon identified with the burial cloth of Christ. In turn, it became the forerunner of the Epitaphios, a large veil, bearing the icon of Christ's burial.

At the height of the development of the ritual of the Great Entrance, the Epitaphios was accorded a place of honor. It was carried in the solemn procession of the gifts and placed upon the Holy Table. The Epitaphios was usually large, especially in cathedral churches, and more than one person was required to carry it. In smaller churches the Epitaphios was smaller in size. It was carried by the deacon or the priest by draping it over the head or tied around the shoulders, in the manner by which the aer is carried today. In time, the use of the Epitaphios was limited to the Paschal period. The aer, also a large veil, took its place. The aer is used to cover the diskos and the chalice and is carried in the Great Entrance procession draped around the shoulders or the arm of the deacon or the priest. Also, hymns from the Vesper service of Great and Holy Friday began to be said inaudibly by the clergy while entering the sanctuary with the gifts. Though the Epitaphios is no longer carried at the Great Entrance, the hymns from the Great Friday service continue to be said silently by the clergy as they place the gifts on the Holy Table. In addition to the gifts and the Epitaphios, other vessels were also carried in the procession, such as the thurible or censer (θυμιατόν), the ripidia or liturgical fans (εξαπτερυγὰ), the lance (λόγχη), candles and various veils. Sometimes, in honor of the gifts, empty chalices and diskoi were also carried in the procession. Of course, the splendor of the procession depended on the size of the Church. Cathedrals and large urban churches differed from the smaller rural and urban ones. Today, altar servers assist the clergy at the Great Entrance, which continues to be an impressive ritual.

Theodore of Mopsuestia was not the only medieval commentator to add allegorical interpretations to the Great Entrance. St. Maximos the Confessor, for example, interpreted the Entrance as a figure of the incarnation, while St. Nicholas Cabasilas saw it as Christ's triumphal entry into Jerusalem. Nicholas of Andida, Pseudo-Sophronios, and St. Symeon of Thessalonike followed the line of thought of Theodore of Mopsuestia, as did St. Germanos of Constantinople who added a second image, Christ's descent into Hades, to that of his funeral cortege.

Clearly, these representational symbolisms, though imaginative and on one level useful for didactic purposes, are in fact artificial and arbitrary and unrelated to the text of the Divine Liturgy. Nevertheless, the allegorical interpretations of the Great Entrance became increasingly popular, and especially the earliest one, namely Christ's funeral cortege. As a result of these interpretations, the simple practical act of transferring the gifts from one place to another grew gradually into the grand ritual of the Great Entrance.

Popular piety and the Great Entrance – the emergence of the commemorations

The growing splendor of the Great Entrance began to have

an effect on the piety of the clergy and the people. The clergy started to introduce a variety of formulas to suit their personal devotion – some of which have been incorporated into the text of the Liturgy – and the people, as Robert Taft notes, were accustomed "to gather around the clergy during the entrance procession, hoping to be touched by the sacred vessels, thereby receiving a blessing... and to beg a remembrance in the liturgy."[359] St. Nicholas Cabasilas' description of the Great Entrance bears this out. While he encourages the people to kneel and entreat the clergy at the Entrance, Cabasilas is also quick to caution the people against mistaking and adoring the unconsecrated gifts as the Body and Blood of Christ. The passage, though long, is worth quoting to help us understand the growth of the procession ritual and the development of the commemorations at the Entrance:

> The priest, having said the doxology aloud, comes to the altar of preparation, takes the offerings, and reverently holding them head-high departs. Carrying them thus, he goes through the nave of the church. *The faithful chant during this procession, kneeling reverently and devoutly, and praying that they may be remembered when the offering is made.* The priest goes on, surrounded by candles and incense, until he comes to the altar. This is done, no doubt for practical reasons; it was necessary to bring the offerings which are to be sacrificed to the altar and set them down there, and to do this with all reverence and devotion... *During this ceremony we must prostrate ourselves before the priest and entreat him to remember us in the prayers, which he is about to say.* For there is no other means of supplication so powerful, so certain of acceptance, as that which takes place through this most holy sacrifice, which has freely cleansed us of our sins and iniquities. If any of those who prostrate themselves thus before the priest who is carrying the offerings adores them as if they were the Body and Blood of Christ and prays to them as such, he is led into error; he is confusing this entry with that of the entry of the pre-sanctified.'[360]

The commemorations at the Great Entrance came about as a result of the popular piety described by Cabasilas. To assure the people of their prayers, the clergy began to speak quietly the common general commemoration, *"May the Lord God remember all of you in his kingdom."*[361] Gradually, this common commemoration began to be made aloud. In a later stage of development the simple commemoration was amplified to include ecclesial and civil authorities and other classes of the faithful, even when they were not present at the divine service.

While the practice of kneeling at the Great Entrance has all but disappeared today, the commemorations it prompted have been retained, even though the reason for their existence has long since been forgotten.

The first mention of commemorations pronounced aloud by the clergy appears in a Diataxis of the 12-13th century: *"and upon entering, the two (deacon and priest) say to the people, May the Lord God remember you* [plural] *in his kingdom – καί εἰσοδεύ οντες λέγοντες πρὸς τὸν λαόν καί οἱ δύο, Μνησθείη ὑμῶν Κύριος ὁ Θεός ἐν τῇ βασιλείᾳ αὐτοῦ."*[362] The practice, however, became routine only after the fifteenth century with the spread of the printed editions of the Divine Liturgy.

The simple form of the general commemoration noted in the 12-13th century Diataxis is found in other manuscripts and in many of the early and later printed editions of the Divine Liturgy.[363] The expanded commemorations[364] that include church and parish officials, civil authorities, and the living and the dead, though popular in some places, came into use quite late, probably not before the end of the 18th century, first at episcopal and much later at presbyteral liturgies.[365] The expanded commemorations are, in fact, out of place at the Great Entrance and their use should not be encouraged.[366] Unfortunately, however, some bishops and presbyters are inclined to protract the commemorations, making them seem almost interminable.

We have not as yet answered the question about what Taft calls 'the illogical' interruption of the Cherubic hymn. It is not clear from the sources when exactly and where it occurred. Initially, as we have noted, the common or general commemoration was said quietly and probably repeatedly during the course of the entrance procession while the Cherubikon was being sung. Eventually, the commemorations – in their simple or augmented form – were said aloud. Obviously, this required a small change in the rite of the Entrance. Only one of two solutions would be able to accommodate the new practice. The commemorations could be said either after the Entrance and the hymn were concluded, or at some point during the Entrance before the hymn was completed. The latter solution was chosen as the more viable one, probably for two reasons. The commemorations were already being said in a low voice during the procession while the hymn was being sung. It was 'natural' and practical therefore simply to stop the hymn at some point so that the commemorations could be spoken aloud before the procession was concluded. The other factor that probably contributed to the practice was also practical. As we know, it had long been the custom to recite the priestly prayers of the Divine Liturgy inaudibly. By interrupting the Cherubic hymn so that a portion of it would be said after the commemorations, the priest had time to complete the final prayers and rites of the Entrance in the customary inaudible fashion.

From the evidence we have at hand, the practice of interrupting the Cherubikon began sometime between the 13th and 14th century. However, there is no agreement in the manuscripts as to where the hymn was interrupted. The contemporary Greek practice interrupts the hymn after the phrase, "that we may receive the King of all – ὡς τόν Βασιλέα τῶν ὅλων ὑποδεξόμενοι."

The Cherubic Hymn – the text and its interpretation

Often, changes in the liturgical texts were introduced inadvertently through the negligence of some copyist. At other times changes occurred as a result of the deliberate choice of a copyist or an editor. As a result of such changes, the structure, rhythm, emphasis, or meaning of the text is often altered to one degree or another. The Cherubic Hymn presents us with one such example. The entire text of the hymn reads as follows. "We who mystically represent the Cherubim sing the thrice-holy hymn to the life-giving Trinity. Let us now set aside all the cares of life (or all worldly care) that we may receive the King of all invisibly escorted (or escorted unseen) by the angelic hosts. Alleluia. Οἱ τὰ Χερουβεὶμ μυστικῶς εἰκονίζοντες, καὶ τῇ ζωοποιῷ Τριάδι τόν τρισάγιον ὕμνον προσάδοντες, πάσαν νῦν βιωτικὴν ἀποθώμωθα μέριμναν ὡς τὸν Βασιλέα τῶν ὅλων ὑποδεξόμενοι, ταῖς ἀγγελικαῖς ἀοράτως δορυφορούμενον τάξεσιν. Ἀλληλούϊα.

The text of the hymn that now appears in all of the printed editions of the Divine Liturgy reads in part, "let us set aside all *the* cares of life that we may receive the King of all – πά σαν *τήν* βιοτικήν ἀποθώμεθα μέριμναν." In most of the manu-scripts, however, this phrase was worded differently. Instead of the article, "*the* – τήν," we find the adverb "*now* – νῦν."[367] The hymn originally read, "let us *now* set aside all the cares of life – πάσαν *νῦν* βιοτικήν ἀποθώμεθα μέριμναν." The ad-verb is meant to emphasize the need for immediate attention and action, counseling and pressing the worshippers to seize the moment – *now* – to have their hearts on high with God by abandoning all worldly thoughts and household cares. But why is the moment so urgent and in need of vigilance?

The hymn itself, by its very content and by its place and function in the Divine Liturgy, provides the answer. The Cherubikon introduces the second part of the Divine Liturgy, the Eucharist proper.[368] As Robert Taft has shown, it anticipates and is related to the central acts of the Eucharist: the Anaphora and the reception of Holy Communion.[369] I believe that four key phrases in the hymn support this thesis.

The first phrase is the exhortation, "*Let us now set aside all the cares of life.*" This phrase is similar to and anticipates the introductory dialogue of the Anaphora, which begins with the priest's compelling appeal, "*Let us lift up our hearts*" and the people's response, "*We lift them up to the Lord.*" Both the Cherubikon and the opening dialogue constitute a call to the faithful to center their hearts on God, by setting aside all worldly thoughts from their minds.[370] As St. Cyril of Jerusalem says, "God indeed should be in our memory at all times, but if this is impossible by reason of human infirmity, at least in that hour this should be our earnest endeavor."[371]

It is interesting to remember that the hymn and the dialogue have another thing in common. When we recite the Cherubikon or hear the admonition, "Let us lift up our hearts," it is customary for the clergy and the people to lift up their hands, a liturgical gesture that signifies that the heart is on the Lord. The body plays an important role in worship, inasmuch as the whole person – body and soul – participates in the worship of God. Bodily postures and gestures express inner feelings and thoughts. Liturgical prayer calls for various bodily gestures, standing, kneeling, prostrating, bowing, crossing oneself, and the lifting up of hands, among others. The Scriptures make many references to such gestures. We read for example, "I desire therefore that the men pray everywhere, lifting up holy hands, without wrath and doubting" (I Tim. 2:8); and "Let us reach out our hearts toward God in heaven" (Lamentations 3:41). [372]

The second phrase is *"We who mystically represent the Cherubim sing the thrice-holy hymn to the life giving Trinity."* The *Thrice-holy hymn* to which the Cherubikon refers is the *Sanctus*, the hymn of the angels, *"Holy, Holy, Holy, Lord Sabaoth, heaven and earth are filled with Your glory,"* which is noted in the prophecy of Isaiah (6:3) and is sung at every Divine Liturgy as part of the Anaphora.

The third phrase, *"that we may receive the King of all"* refers to the reception of Holy Communion and not to the welcoming of Christ in the form of the unconsecrated elements that are being transferred from the Prothesis to the Holy Table. The Greek original uses the word ὑποδεξόμενοι, the future participle of the verb ὑποδέχομαι (to receive, to welcome). It is usually reserved for the reception of Holy Communion.[373]

Finally, the phrase that concludes the hymn, "that we may receive the King of all, *invisibly escorted by the angelic hosts. Alleluia. Alleluia. Alleluia,"* brings us before the essential eschatological nature of the Eucharist. At the Eucharist the liturgical assembly participates joyously in the marriage supper of the Lamb (Rev. 19:1- 17); it partakes of divine life and experiences in faith the joy of the end times, already here and yet to come in fullness. In the Divine Liturgy we celebrate in joy and thanksgiving the whole mystery of the divine economy from creation to the incarnation, and especially, in the words of the Anaphora, "the cross, the tomb, the resurrection on the third day, the ascension into heaven, the enthronement at the right hand of the Father, and the second glorious coming" of Christ. The Christ who is always with us and whom we receive at the Eucharist is the one who will come again in glory escorted by all the holy angels to judge the living and the dead (Mt. 25:31; 1 Thess. 4:16).

The Cherubikon, therefore, serves a two-fold purpose. It invites the faithful to be watchful and attentive throughout the divine service; and it calls on them to be in a proper state of mind as befits those who will offer the Anaphora and will welcome and receive the Lamb of God, the Lord of lords and the King of kings (Rev. 17:14) in holy Communion.[374]

The Cherubikon and the rite of censing

Let us look briefly at two other items that are related to the Cherubikon, namely, the recitation of the hymn by the celebrant and the rite of censing that accompanies the singing of the hymn. First, let us deal with the question of the censing. Who is responsible for the censing at the Great Entrance: the presiding bishop or presbyter, or the deacon? Of course, the question is moot when a priest serves alone without a deacon. If a deacon is present, however, which of the two should do the censing? The contemporary Greek practice is ambivalent. In some texts the rubrics assign the task to the deacon, while in others it is assigned to the presbyter (or bishop). In the early sources, however, there is no ambiguity. The task is clearly assigned to the deacon,[375] who conducts the censing while the presiding presbyter or bishop recites the prayer of the Cherubikon.[376] This older practice, when applicable, should be restored. Among other things, it permits the deacon to exercise a basic function of his office. It also allows the celebrant to concentrate on the prayer. And, from a practical perspective, it saves time so that other parts of the divine service may be performed more prayerfully and with greater ease.

Let us now turn our attention to the second matter, the multiple recitation of the Cherubic hymn by the celebrant. The early manuscripts and the Diataxeis order the celebrant to recite the hymn only once upon completion of the Prayer of the Cherubikon (Οὐδεὶς ἄξιος.) The present practice, which requires the celebrant to recite it three times, appears to have developed late. The reason for the practice appears to be a misreading of the directives in the *Diataxis* of Philotheos Kokkinos.[377] According to the rubrics in the *Diataxis*, the priest and the deacon were required to recite the hymn once while making three prostrations. "And when the [prayer] has been completed, they stand together and pray the Cherubikon, saying it [quietly] to themselves. And while they are saying it they make three reverences and leave for the Prothesis, the deacon preceding with the censer – Ταύτης δὲ [τῆς εὐχῆς] πληρωθείσης, συστάντες ὁμοῦ εὔξονται τό χερουβικὸν λέγοντες καθ᾽ ἑαυτούς. Καὶ τρὶς ἐν τῷ λέγειν αὐτούς προσκυνοῦντες ἀπέρχονται ἐν τῇ προθέσει, προπορευομένου τοῦ διακόνου μετά τοῦ θυμιατοῦ."[378] At some point in time, this directive was misunderstood and thought to apply to the hymn as well. Hence, through a mistaken interpretation of rubrics a new practice was begun.

The so-called Prayer of the Cherubikon (Οὐδεὶς ἄξιος) is another example of liturgical expansion. Though its origins are uncertain, it appears to derive from the Alexandrine Liturgy of St. Gregory the Theologian, in which we find it after the gifts have been placed on the Holy Table. Not an original element of the Constantinopolitan liturgical tradition, the prayer was borrowed and introduced first into the Liturgy of St. Basil and later into that of St. John Chrysostom, as indicated by the *Barberini Codex, gr. 336*, the earliest extant Euchologion of Constantinople, which includes it in the formulary of Basil but not in Chrysostom. Yet, in another 11-12th century codex, the opposite is true. Also, some 10th century manuscripts have the prayer while others do not. As in other instances, the clergy first used the prayer for personal devotional purposes before it passed into the formularies.

In the Barberini codex the prayer is entitled "Prayer which the priest says to himself while the Cherubika are being said." Other codices have a similar title. However, in some the title and the rubrics indicate that the prayer was said while the gifts were being transferred, an indication that presbyters, at first, did not take part in the procession of the gifts but waited to receive them at the holy doors of the sanctuary, much as a bishop does today.

The prayer of the Cherubikon is addressed to God the Son, a distinguishing characteristic of the Alexandrine Liturgy of St. Gregory, in which the prayers are addressed not to the Father but to the Son. The prayer makes references to the priesthood. Also, it uses the first person singular and not the usual plural as in the other prayers of the Liturgy, a sign of its personal devotional character."

II. 'MERCY, PEACE, A SACRIFICE OF PRAISE'

Which is it: 'a mercy of peace' or 'mercy, peace, a sacrifice of praise?'

Let me cite another example of a change in the text of the Divine Liturgy. This one is from the introductory dialogue of the great Eucharistic Prayer called the Anaphora. The dialogue opens with the deacon's bidding, "Let us stand well. Let us stand in awe. Let us be attentive, that we may present the holy offering in peace." Responding to this command, the people say – according to the received text "a mercy of peace, a sacrifice of praise – ἔλεον εἰρήνης, θυσίαν αἰνέσεως" [380] The manuscripts, however, have several different versions of the response. Some scholars believe that these differences may be due to the fact that the meaning of the response was not always clear. This is especially true of the enigmatic phrase "mercy of peace," which is not found even once in the Scriptures, while the phrase "sacrifice of praise" is commonplace in the Septuagint.[381]

The earliest extant Euchologion of the Constantinopolitan

rite is an eighth century codex known as the Barberini Codex.[382] In the Barberini Codex the response has a very simple form, *"mercy, peace – ἔλεος, εἰρήνη ."*[383] In another eighth century document, however, which is an Armenian version of the Liturgy of St. John Chrysostom, we encounter an augmented form of the response, *"mercy and peace and the sacrifice of praise."*[384] Yet, in another eighth century document, *Ecclesiastical History and Mystical Contemplation –* Ἱστορία Ἐκκλησιαστικὴ καὶ Μυστικὴ Θεωρία, which is a commentary on the Divine Liturgy, written by St. Germanos of Constantinople, the form of the response is the same as in our received text, *a mercy of peace, a sacrifice of praise.*[385]

In later manuscripts and documents the response appears under several forms. In some versions the three words, *mercy, peace,* and *sacrifice* are in the nominative case "ἔλεος, εἰρήνη, θυσία," while in others they are in the accusative, "ἔλεον, εἰρήνην, θυσίαν." The latter form seems to have been favored by the Constantinopolitan redactors for grammatical and stylistic reasons.[386] In either case however, whether in the nominative or in the accusative, the final word of the response, *praise –* αἴνεσις, always appears in the genitive, "αἰνέσεως". Significantly, as far as I know, other than the treatise of St. Germanos, no other early document contains the form of the response with which we are familiar, *a mercy of peace.* The form, *"a mercy of peace – ἔλεον εἰρήνης,"* [387] which was destined to find its way into all the printed editions of the Divine Liturgy, appeared late in a couple of manuscripts of the eleventh and twelfth centuries.[388] The phrase, however, is obscure, if not unintelligible, and was probably created to provide rhetorical and stylistic balance with the phrase θυσίαν αἰνέσεως.[389]

In light of the above, it seems to me that the more primitive form of the response, *"mercy, peace, a sacrifice of praise,"* is the preferred reading. And the accusative form of the words mercy, peace, sacrifice, should be used in the Greek, in order to make clear that the response constitutes the direct object of the diaconal admonition "τὴν ἁγίαν ἀναφορὰν ἐν εἰρήνῃ προσφέρειν."[390] In other words, the response affirms the meaning of the holy offering, which *is* mercy, *is* peace, and *is* a sacrifice of praise.

St. Nicholas Cabasilas makes this point in his *Commentary on the Divine Liturgy* (14th century). For Cabasilas, all expressions of mercy and kindness flow out of a soul that is filled with inner tranquility. Only such a soul, he believes, is capable of offering a sacrifice of praise to God. For him, a soul at peace is itself an offering, a sacrifice pleasing to God. Cabasilas also hints at a linkage between the response and the kiss of peace that precedes the Anaphora:

> Thus, standing firm in faith let our offerings to God proceed as is proper. What does 'as is proper' mean? It means, in peace. Let us take care to offer the holy oblation in peace. Remember the words of our Lord: 'If you bring your gift to the altar, and there remember that your brother has ought against you; leave there your gift before the altar and go your way; first be reconciled to your brother, and then come and offer your gift.'[391] The faithful reply: Not only do we make our offering in peace; it is peace itself that we offer as a gift and a second sacrifice. For we offer mercy to him who said, 'I will have mercy and not sacrifice.'[392] Now mercy is the child of a strong and true peace. For when the soul is untroubled by passion, there is nothing to hinder it from being filled with mercy and the sacrifice of praise.[393]

Robert Taft offers a similar interpretation. "From at least the 8th century our diaconal admonition means: 'Pay attention to the gifts, and to the offering of them that is about to begin.' And the people, as in the other two ratifying responses of the anaphora dialogue ('We have them up to the Lord'), proclaim their willingness with a profession of faith in what the offering is for them: it is God's mercy brought to them in the forgiveness and salvation won by and represented in this sacrifice of Christ; it is peace, that peace of Christ which the world cannot give, of which He spoke in the Gospel of John (14:27; 16:33); it is their sacrifice of praise, offered to the Father through the hands of His Son by the power of His Holy Spirit."[394]

Both the diaconal admonition and the response of the people that introduce the Anaphora serve to remind us that all our prayers and offerings must be characterized by sincere interior dispositions, such as mercy, peace, thanksgiving, and praise. Otherwise, our offerings become empty formalistic acts and our prayers hollow words. This is especially important when we consider the fact that for the Christian, the concept and reality of peace means more than the absence of conflict; and mercy is more than good feelings towards others. Peace and mercy mean, above all, a share in God's infinite, forgiving, healing, compassionate, and steadfast love that breaks through all human perceptions, limitations, and restrictions. This peace and this mercy come from Jesus Christ and result in our communion with God, who is the God of peace and of all mercy. He bestows peace and is the fountain of mercy. Sharing in God's peace and mercy, we share in his own joy in dispensing salvation. In this way we become a eucharistic people, filled with unfeigned love and boundless gratitude for God's gift of communion and life and are made capable of offering him a sacrifice of praise.

III. EXAMINING PORTIONS OF THE ANAPHORA

Offer or Offering? An example of a significant alteration in a liturgical text

Some changes in the liturgical texts, however, were not as innocuous as the ones noted above. To illustrate this point let me refer to the words of offering in the Anaphora of the Divine Liturgies of St. John Chrysostom and of St. Basil.

In all of the printed editions of the two Divine Liturgies, the words of offering are: "*We offer to you these gifts from your own gifts in all places and at all times* – Τὰ σὰ ἐκ τῶν σῶν σοὶ προσφέρομεν κατὰ πάντα καὶ διὰ πάντα." This wording, however, if only in one word, is different from the one that appears in all the early manuscripts of the Divine Liturgy. Instead of the verb "*we offer* – προσφέρομεν," which is found in all of the printed editions, the early manuscripts contain the adverbial participle "*offering* – προσφέροντες."[395]

For the sake of clarity, let me cite the entire passage of the Anaphora in which this phrase is found, as it appears in the early manuscripts. "*Remembering*, therefore, this saving command, and all that came to pass for our sake – the cross, the tomb, the resurrection on the third day, the ascension into heaven, the enthronement at the right hand, the second glorious coming – [and] *Offering* these gifts to you from your own gifts according to all and for all – *We praise you, we bless you, we give thanks to you, and we pray to you, O Lord our God.*"

On the surface, the change in the wording from the adverbial participle *'offering'* to the verb *'we offer'* appears to be harmless and of little significance. But is it?

The unfolding actions of the Anaphora

The plot of the Anaphora, according to Richard McCall, resolves into an unfolding structure of actions that are defined by the verbs of the Anaphora. Through the verbs, he says, we discover the character of the Anaphora and what it *does*.[396]

The Anaphora of the Divine Liturgy of St. John Chrysostom in the early manuscripts contains three actions leading to the consecration of the holy Gifts, as evidenced by the verbs in the text. However, a fourth action was added to the sequence, when the adverbial participle προσφέροντες was changed into the verb form προσφέρομεν. The addition appears to have blurred, if not altered, the meaning of the Church's offering.

The Anaphora, as is commonly known, is addressed to God the Father.[397] It begins with an affirmation: "It is proper and right *to sing to you, bless you, praise you, thank you, and worship you* in all places of your dominion; for you are God ineffable." Then, after recalling and recounting the creative and redemptive activity of the Triune God, the Church offers God thanks: "For all these things *we thank you* [Father] and your only begotten Son and your Holy Spirit; for all things we know and do not know, for blessings seen and unseen that have bestowed upon us. *We also thank you* for this liturgy which you are pleased to accept from our hands…" The first thing that we do through the Anaphora is to offer God thanks for his creative, providential, and redemptive activity in the world. Thanksgiving, then, constitutes the first action of the Anaphora.

The second action unfolds into a proclamation of the holiness of God. The assembly joins the angelic hosts to proclaim the holiness and majesty of the Triune God: "Together with these blessed powers, merciful Master, *we also proclaim and say*: You are holy and most holy... and sublime is your glory."

From the proclamation of God's holiness, the Anaphora proceeds to the *anamnesis* or remembrance of the saving commandment ('Do this') and of God's acts of salvific love in the death, burial, resurrection, ascension, enthronement, and second coming of Christ; and to the *offering* of the sacramental gifts. The remembrance and the offering lead to the third action of the Anaphora, which is the sacrifice of praise. "*Remembering*, therefore, this saving command, and all that came to pass for our sake, the cross, the tomb, the resurrection on the third day, the ascension into heaven, the enthronement at the right hand of the Father, and the second, glorious coming [and] *offering* to you these gifts... *we praise You, we bless You, we give thanks to You, and we pray to You, Lord our God*. As Paul Meyendorff reminds us, this was "all one sentence; and the only active verbs are those which express the action of the gathered assembly and are sung by them: '*We praise, we bless, we give thanks, we pray.*' This is a sacrificial prayer, and we are here performing our sacrifice of praise."[398]

However, when the adverbial participle '*offering*' was changed into the verb form, '*we offer*,' it meant that an additional action was added to the Anaphora. As a result, the object of the remembrance (*Remembering, therefore* – Μεμνημένοι τοίνυν) and of the offering (*offering to You these gifts* – Τὰ σὰ ἐκ τῶν σῶν σοὶ προσφέροντες) was no longer the sacrifice of praise. Now, the object of the remembrance is the offering of the Gifts (*Remembering... We offer*). This represents a dramatic shift.

With the passage of time the holy oblation has become identified not with the sacrifice of praise but with the offering of the holy Gifts. The sacrifice of praise, having lost its original significance, has come to be viewed as a response, a song of praise whose purpose is to cover the voice of the priest who, according to current practice, recites the next part of the Anaphora inaudibly or in a low voice. However, this hymn is more than a song. It is itself an offering, a sacrifice of praise. It is the only possible response of the Church to what she remembers and offers to the Father: the Paschal mystery, which is rendered present not simply to memory but in reality under the sacramental gifts. *"Remembering therefore this saving command and all that came to pass for our sake… [and] offering to you these gifts… We praise you, we bless you, and we give thanks to you."*

To complete our discussion on the actions of the Anaphora we must turn our attention to another detail. The sacrifice of praise unfolds into a petition. "We praise you, we bless you, we give thanks to you, *and we pray to you, Lord our God.*" The object of the petition – *"and we pray to you"* – is the epiclesis, the invocation to the Father to send down his Holy Spirit upon the liturgical assembly and upon the gifts that have been set forth, that they may be changed to be the Body and Blood of Christ. *Remembering and offering – We praise you, we bless you, we give thanks to you, and we pray to you, O Lord our God… Send down your Holy Spirit upon us and upon these gifts here presented. And make this bread the precious Body of Your Christ. (Amen.) And that which is in this cup the precious Blood of your Christ. (Amen.) Changing them by You Holy Spirit. (Amen. Amen. Amen.)*[399] The praise leads to the petition. And the petition leads to the epiclesis, which in turn, through the consecration of the gifts, begins the fulfillment of the Divine Liturgy, the essence of which lies in communion, in our partaking of Christ and in our union with one another.

The sacrifice of praise and thanksgiving

Writing in the fourteenth century, St. Nicholas Cabasilas indicates that the adverbial participle – προσφέροντες – was still being used in the Anaphora during his time and provides us with brief interpretation of the remembrance and the offering.

The Church says: 'We make this oblation mindful of thy benefits.' Surely this is thanksgiving, to honor with our holy offerings the Benefactor for the good things he has given us. Then expressing her thanksgiving even more clearly, she adds: 'In *offering* this oblation, we praise thee, we bless thee, we give thanks to thee, O Lord, and we pray to thee our God.' This then is the purpose of the offering of the holy gifts – to praise, to give thanks, and to supplicate, as we said at the beginning; so the sacrifice we offer is at once eucharistic and supplicatory.[400]

The Church understands sacrifice in a radically new and different way. The initiative for sacrifice is not with us, as most people believe, but with God who continually offers himself to us.[401] Essentially, our sacrifice is always – first and last – a personal response to the personal God, who has revealed himself to us in his Son, our Lord and Savior Jesus Christ. Our sacrifice, as St. Nicholas Cabasilas notes, is an act of praise and thanksgiving, an expression of love and awe, and an acknowledgment of total dependence on God, who alone has life in himself. Thus, the sacrifice offered by the Church is always a response, a sacrifice in return, an antiprosphora – ἀντιπροσφορά.[402] The antiprosphora is, above all, a sacrifice of praise and thanksgiving "for all things that we know and do not know, for blessings seen and unseen that have been bestowed upon us."[403]

At its deepest level the antiprosphora becomes an act of kenosis, an act of self-emptying, the willingness to adopt the condition of a slave – δοῦλος – (Philip. 2:7) and the readiness to lose life in order to gain it (Lk. 9:23-25). At every Eucharist through the bread and wine – the distinctively unique human foods, and therefore symbols of human life – we offer humbly to God our life in exchange for his, which he freely gives to us through the consecrated Eucharistic elements, which are no longer ordinary bread and wine, nor symbols or icons, but the very Body and Blood of the risen Christ, having been sanctified and transformed by the power of the Father through the Holy Spirit. In the Divine Liturgy, as Hugh Wybrew tells it:

[The faithful are] engaged in offering a sacrifice of praise and

thanksgiving to God for all his mighty acts in creation and redemption, and above all for the passion, death, resurrection and
ascension of Jesus Christ, and his coming again in glory... These
saving events [are] commemorated by the offering of the bread
and wine, which through the invocation of the Holy Spirit on
them as well as on the worshippers become the Body and Blood
of Christ, which are received for the remission of sins and eternal life in God's Kingdom... [The faithful] know themselves to
be partakers in the mystical banquet which anticipates the fulfillment of God's plan of salvation.[404]

The altar of God is a table of communion and life

In the Eucharist we come to realize that the altar of God is
always a table of communion and life. In the Eucharist, Christ
draws us into his own sacrificial action to make us partakers
of divine life. In the Eucharist we offer Christ,[405] in order to
receive Christ, the Bread of God (Jn. 6:33). In the Eucharist,
Christ acts to make us members of his own body (Jn. 6:51-58;
1 Cor. 10:16-17) that we may "grow up in every way into
him" (Ephes. 4:15). The mystery of our incorporation into
the body of Christ begins with baptism, through our
immersion in the life-giving font. Through baptism we are
added to the body of Christ; we are grafted and united to
him. We put on Christ in order to participate in his deified
human nature. This wondrous mystery of the ineffable
communion of the created and the uncreated is fully revealed
and continuously realized in the Eucharist – "He who eats
my flesh and drinks my blood abides in me and I in him"
(Jn. 6:56).

In the Eucharist, Christ is forever present and immediate
to his people; and his saving work remains constant and
operative for every generation in every place, until he comes
again in glory to judge the living and the dead. Though the
eucharistic sacrifice is offered many times and in many places,
the reality into which the gifts are changed remains always
the same: the Body of Christ, which was sacrificed once for
all and now lives in glory. In the end, after all is said and
done, our offering in return can only be Christ himself,
because he "alone is the perfect Eucharistic Being. He is the

Eucharist of the world. In and through this Eucharist the whole creation becomes what it always was to be and yet failed to be."[406]

Through the Eucharist we transcend the limitations of our creatureliness. In union with Christ we bear the image of the heavenly Man (1 Cor. 15:49). St. Irenaeus explains the mystery with these words. "Because we are his members and are fed by means of created objects – things he himself provides for us by making the sun rise and the rain fall – he declared that the cup, part of creation, is his own Blood by which our blood is strengthened. He likewise pronounced the bread, part of creation, to be his own Body by means of which our bodies are strengthened… So that our bodies that share in the Eucharist are no longer corruptible, because they have the hope of the resurrection."[407]

The organic unity of the Anaphora

The Anaphora is the great Eucharistic Prayer of the Church. While the celebrant, by virtue of his ordination, is charged with the responsibility to say it, he accomplishes this act for, with, and on behalf of the people. It is not his prayer but the prayer of the Church, of God's holy people. At the Divine Liturgy, as in all the sacraments, the clergy preside and minister – and their role is absolutely essential – but the celebration is the work of all the people of God, clergy and laity together. Hence, in the tradition of the Orthodox Church no bishop or priest may offer the Divine Oblation for or by himself.

The Anaphora is a single prayer and not a series of prayers and hymns. It is composed of several parts, all of which are interdependent and necessary. These include the opening dialogue, the intermittent responses of the people, the praise of the Triune God for his mighty works in creation and in his providential care for the world, and the angelic hymn. The Anaphora also includes the remembrance of the economy of the Son of God, the words of Institution, the offering, the hymn of praise and thanksgiving, the epiclesis, the fruits and benefits of communion, the intercessions, and the concluding doxology and blessing.

The practice of reciting prayers silently, which is centuries old, through time has blurred the organic unity of the Anaphora and has eroded the role of the laity in it. The recitation of prayers silently makes it difficult, if not impossible, for the worshipper to appreciate the unity of the Anaphora or to enter into its profound meanings and implications for the life of faith. By not hearing it, the faithful are robbed of the opportunity to participate actively in this essential prayer of the Church. As a result, they are unable to enter fully into the mystery of Christ's sacrifice that forms the heart of the Christian life and consciousness, or to comprehend correctly the purpose of the Church's antiprosphora in which they are required to play an active role. Practically speaking, the inaudible recitation of the Anaphora prevents the assembly from properly remembering and thanking God for his mighty deeds in history and his wondrous promises.

Reciting prayers silently – losing out on the substance

In our current liturgical practice, most of the priestly prayers of the Divine Liturgy are said inaudibly. As a result, the faithful lose out on the more substantive contents of the Divine Liturgy and find it difficult to comprehend the necessity of and the unity between each component of the rite. For example, the people are called to prayer, "Let us pray to the Lord." The people or the choir responds, "Lord have mercy." Then there is a slight pause after which the priest intones aloud the doxology that concludes the prayer, which he said inaudibly. This, of course, makes the call to prayer superfluous. The problem is further compounded because at the end of the doxology, which the priest intones, the people or the choir must say 'Amen.' The 'Amen,' however, is a very significant word. It is the word of the people. Through the 'Amen' the people give their assent; they approve, seal, and participate in all the actions of the clergy that are done in the name of the people – for, with, and on behalf of the people.[408] However, if the people have not heard the prayer, how can they give their assent? And if by habit they do say the 'Amen,' what are they accepting and sealing as their own?

A similar thing happens with the Anaphora. It is seldom, if ever, said aloud. (This is especially true of the lengthy Anaphora of St. Basil). The people hear only parts of the Anaphora (whether of St. Chrysostom or St. Basil) and the parts they hear have hardly any syntactical connection or logical sequence between them. Thus, for example, at the beginning of the Anaphora the people hear the bidding "Let us give thanks to the Lord." The response, "It is proper and right" is usually dragged out to drown out the voice of the priest who is reading the first part of Anaphora in a low voice. When the choir concludes the response the people hear the priest say, "Singing the victory hymn, proclaiming, crying out and saying," which of course is unconnected to the previous pronouncement. As a result, it makes little sense to the worshipper.

An alert worshipper would ask, "What victory hymn? Who is singing it and why?" The phrase "Singing the victory hymn" concludes the first part of the Anaphora. It refers to the angelic host who constantly praise God with the song, "Holy, Holy, Holy, Lord Sabaoth," which the choir or chanters sing in the unfolding sequence of the Anaphora. The phrase makes sense only if we hear it in its proper context. "… We also thank you for this liturgy which you are pleased to accept from our hands, even though You are surrounded by thousands of Archangels and tens of thousands of Angels, by the Cherubim and Seraphim, six-winged, many-eyed, soaring with their wings… *Singing the victory hymn, proclaiming, crying out, and saying*… Holy, Holy, Holy."

Examples like this can be multiplied. Little wonder then that the worshipper is at a great disadvantage. Through the practice of reciting prayers silently, the more substantive elements and actions of the Divine Liturgy remain hidden under a bushel. The liturgical texts, which express the faith and the vision of the Church and are intended to inspire the mind, energize the will, warm the heart, enliven the faith, and inform the actions of the worshippers, remain inaccessible to their ears.

The practice of reciting prayers silently should be reversed

The recitation of prayers silently has a long and complex history.[409] It is sufficient for our purposes to note only that the practice originated in East Syria among the Nestorians in the sixth century and prevailed throughout the Eastern Church by the end of the eighth century. It was introduced probably out of deep reverence for God; one must not shout but speak softly before him. The practice, however, at first was decried by the Orthodox as an innovation and claimed that it distorted and violated the Church's ethos and piety. In fact, the Emperor Justinian vigorously opposed it, and in 565 he issued a law that forbade it:

> Moreover we order all bishops and presbyters to say the prayers used in the Divine Oblation (Liturgy) and in holy baptism not inaudibly, but in a loud voice that the faithful people can hear, that the minds of those who listen may be excited to greater compunction and may be roused to give glory to the Lord God. For even the divine Apostle teaches, in his letter to the Corinthians, "Otherwise, if you bless with the spirit, how will he who occupies the place of the uninformed say, 'Amen' at your giving of thanks, since he does not understand what you say? For you indeed give thanks well, but the other is not edified" (1 Cor. 14:16-17). And again in his letter to the Romans he says, "For with the heart one believes unto righteousness, and with the mouth confession is made unto salvation" (Rom 10:10). So then, therefore, it befits the reverend bishops and presbyters to say the holy Oblation and the other prayers offered to our Lord and God Jesus Christ together with the Father and the Holy Spirit in an audible voice.[410]

In spite of the imperial decree, the practice prevailed. Vague notions of what constitutes piety, mystery, and mystical contemplation prevailed over an intelligible experience of the holy in the liturgy. The appearance of vague mystical tendencies was not new for the Church. Such tendencies were present in the apostolic era. St. Paul, for example, was careful to admonish the Corinthians that mysterious babble of unintelligible sounds was not a sure sign of the presence or the possession of the Spirit (1 Cor. 14:1-25). He was keen to point out that sound without intelligibility does not edify. For this reason, according to tradition, everything that is said and enacted in the name of the Church must be heard, understood, and tested by the whole Church. The practice of reciting prayers silently – 'sound' without intelligibility – contradicts this fundamental requirement. In the course of time, the practice has effected and altered the Church's liturgical piety and has encouraged and fostered the clericalization of the Church's life and worship.

Happily however, in the last several decades local Churches have attempted – with varying degrees of success – to reverse this practice.[411] When the prayers of the Liturgy, and especially the Anaphora, are said aloud, the people – by hearing them – will, as St. John Chrysostom reminds us, become familiar with "the wonder of the mysteries, what they are, why they were given, and what is their benefit."

A new ritual action – the elevation of the Gifts

The present text of the Anaphora, in which the participle *offering* has been changed into a verb *we offer*, has altered the meaning of the remembrance of the mighty acts of God and the purpose for which the gifts are offered: to give thanks to God for all that we have been given as a result of the saving work of his Son and our Lord, Jesus Christ. Eventually, this change brought about a new liturgical act, the elevation of the discos and the chalice over the Holy Table by the celebrant (or the deacon) as he pronounces the words, "*We offer to You these gifts from Your own gifts*". The elevation is meant to be an act of offering. The liturgical act, however, is a comparatively recent practice. It is first mentioned in two codices of the seventeenth century.[412] The rubrics in the 14th-century *Diataxis* of Philotheos Kokkinos require the priest and the deacon only to point to the holy gifts when the words of offering are said.[413]

The elevation of the Gifts blurs further the meaning of the antiprosphora – ἀντιπροσφορά. The material gifts of bread and wine become the focus of the offering rather than the sacrifice of praise and thanksgiving for the divine economy and our own kenosis before the ineffable mystery of God's boundless mercy and love. In the words of Father Schmemann, "When man stands before the throne of God, when he has fulfilled all that God has given him to fulfill, when all sins are forgiven, all joy restored, then there is nothing else for him to do but to give thanks. Eucharist (thanksgiving) is the state of the perfect man. Eucharist is the life of paradise. Eucharist is the only full and real response of man to God's creation, redemption, and gift of heaven."[414]

The offering of the Gifts constitutes the very pinnacle of our expression of gratitude for everything that God has done and continues to do for the salvation of the world.[415] Indeed as St. Nicholas Cabasilas reminds us, the Liturgy consists in the offering of gifts. Through the bread and wine – the eucharistic gifts – we offer up our life; and our Lord also offers. "He offers himself, that is why he is described both as offering and offerer, and as the receiver of the offering. He is as God the offerer and the receiver and as man the offering."[416] Christ receives our gifts – the bread and the wine – and sanctifies them. He turns them into his own Body and Blood. At the Eucharist God accepts our gifts and gives in return his Son, the most precious and priceless of gifts. In and through the eucharistic gifts we offer Christ and receive Christ, the perfect Eucharist, "in order that, by union with that which is immortal, [we] also might partake of incorruption."[417]

The phrase "κατὰ πάντα καὶ διὰ πάντα" – What does it mean?

The phrase "*Offering to you these gifts*" presents us with an additional problem that is especially troublesome for translators. The first part of the phrase, "*these gifts from your own gifts – Τὰ σὰ ἐκ τῶν σῶν*" is taken from I Chronicles 29:14.[418] The words in the second part of the phrase, "κατὰ πάντα καὶ διὰ πάντα," however, are not sufficiently clear in the Greek original to warrant a definitive translation.

Unfortunately, the beautiful balance and symmetry of the phrase – in its original Greek form – has been achieved at the expense of clarity.[419] Various interpretations have been offered to explain the neuter accusative plural, "*all – πάντα*," the object of both prepositions, κατὰ and διὰ. Panayiotis Trempelas, for example, has suggested the phrase should be interpreted to mean "in all places and for all that you have done for our benefit."[420] Father Schmemann, on the other hand, representing another tradition prefers the rendering, "on (or in) behalf of all and for all."[421]

Another possibility – among others – is to render the Greek literally "*according to all* (you have commanded us) *and for all* (you have done for us)." Basing myself on the comments of St. Nicholas Cabasilas, I had proposed this interpretation to the Liturgical Commission of the Standing Conference of Canonical Orthodox Bishops (SCOBA), on which I was privileged to serve.[422] In his *Commentary on the Divine Liturgy*, Cabasilas writes, "And we do this, says the Church, being mindful of two things – of our Lord's command, when he said: 'Do this in remembrance of me,' and also of all that he has done for us. The mere remembering of the benefits bestowed upon us rouses us to make some sort of return and to offer something at least to him who has showered so many graces upon us... We offer to thee that same offering which thine only-begotten Son himself offered to thee, God, his Father; and we give thanks to thee in offering because he gave thanks... That is why that which we offer thee of those things which thou hast given, is in all things and through all things solely thine."[423]

As I recall, the members of the SCOBA Liturgical Commission grappled long and hard with this enigmatic phrase. After long discussions, the Commission decided to adopt the phrase "*at all times and in all places*," as the one that best represents the meaning of the laconic and enigmatic Greek original, κατὰ πάντα καὶ διὰ πάντα.[424] The decision was based chiefly on two texts, the prophecy of Malachi 1:11 and *The Didache* 14:2, a text that some believe dates to the late first century.

In the prophecy of Malachi we read, "*In all places* incense is offered to his name, and a pure offering –᾽Εν παντί τόπῳ θυμίαμα προσάγεται τῷ ὀνόματι αὐτοῦ καὶ θυσία καθαρά." These words of Malachi were taken by the early Christian writers to refer to the eucharistic sacrifice or to the sacrifice on the cross. Thus, they were destined to become a formulaic expression used in Christian worship, especially with regards to the Eucharist. For example, *The Didache,* which provides us with some details on the eucharistic celebrations of the early Church, contains the words, "For it was of this sacrifice (the Eucharist) that the Lord said, *'In all places and at all times* they will offer me a pure sacrifice – Ev παντί τόπω καὶ χρόνω προσφέρειν μοι θυσίαν καθαράν."[425] There is little doubt that the author(s) of *The Didache* is paraphrasing the words of Malachi. We meet similar phraseology in I Timothy 2:8. "I desire therefore that the men pray *in every place – ἐν παντί τόπω –* lifting up holy hands, without wrath and doubting."

However strong the evidence is from these sources, we are still faced with a problem. There is a marked difference in wording between these sources and our liturgical text. The prophecy of Malachi and *The Didache,* and for that matter I Timothy, use the preposition ἐν *(in),* while our liturgical text uses two different prepositions, κατά and διά, the meaning of which differs from the preposition ἐν. If *"in all places and at all times"* was an early formulaic expression, then we must ask the question, why and when did the anonymous writers of liturgical texts abandon it for the expression "κατὰ πάντα καὶ διὰ πάντα." While the corroborating evidence from Malachi, *The Didache* and the other ancient authorities throws considerable light on the subject, it has not fully solved the meaning of "κατὰ πάντα καὶ διὰ πάντα." In some ways it remains an enigmatic phrase that invites further investigation and reflection.

Nevertheless, if we approach the matter from another perspective, the rendering "in all places and at all times," may be the most viable. Jean Danielou, in his discussion on the Eucharist, makes the following point. "The sacrifice of Christ subsists under three different modes. It is the same priestly action, which took place in a precise moment of history; which is eternally present in heaven;[426] and which subsists under the sacramental appearances. Indeed the priestly action of Christ in its substance is the very action by which creation achieves its end, since by it God is perfectly glorified. It is the action which, since that moment, by unique privilege, is taken from time in order to subsist eternally, and which the sacrament renders present at all times and in all places."[427]

Unlike the sacrifices of the Old Testament that were localized in one place – the Temple of Jerusalem – the Christian eucharistic sacrifice is offered in all places. Furthermore, as Danielou notes, "This food is given daily, which distinguishes the Eucharist, the sacrament of every day, from Baptism, the sacrament which is given only once."[428] With these observations in mind one could argue for the correctness of the phrase "at all times and in all places." This can be supported further when we take into account the fact that "there is only one Eucharist, which is always offered in the name of the 'one, holy, catholic, and apostolic Church."[429]

Another way of looking at the phrase κατὰ πάντα καὶ διὰ πάντα

In a recent article, following the lead of Robert Taft, Father Pavlos Koumarianos has raised another serious question, which may further alter our thinking about this enigmatic phrase. He contends that an historical and literary analysis of the text will show that the phrase "κατὰ πάντα καὶ διὰ πάντα" is related to the hymn of praise – Σὲ ὑμνοῦμεν, and not to the offering – "Τὰ σὰ ἐκ τῶν σῶν."[430] In other words, we remember the mighty works of God and offer the sacramental gifts, so that at all times and in all places we may praise, bless, and give thanks to God and call upon him to send down his Holy Spirit upon us and the gifts that we have set forth.

The connection of the phrase to the hymn emphasizes more clearly the priestly character of the People of God who express their priestly action by singing the sacrificial prayer 'We praise you,' thereby performing the sacrifice of praise.[431]

In the Divine Liturgy, as Paul Meyendorff tells it, "the priestly function is exercised by the entire community, by virtue of their baptism. The function of the ordained clergy is to preside over the priestly community, to unite their priestly prayer… [I]n pagan and Jewish practice only the priest offers sacrifice: here it is clearly the whole assembly the priestly people, which does this."[432] That is why all the prayers of the Divine Liturgy, except for the deprecatory prayers of the clergy, are in the first person plural. "Remembering, therefore, this saving commandment... [and] offering to You these gifts from your own gifts – at all times and in all places we praise You..."

Is the Inclination Prayer a pre-communion prayer?

The prayer of inclination before Holy Communion in the Divine Liturgy of Saint John Chrysostom presents us with a different kind of problem. The text of the prayer reads as follows in the original Greek and in English translation:

Εὐχαριστοῦμέν σοι, Βασιλεῦ ἀοράτε, ὁ τῇ ἀμετρήτῳ σου δυνάμει τὰ πάντα δημιουργήσας καὶ τῷ πλήθει τοῦ ἐλέους σου ἐξ οὐκ ὄντων εἰς τὸ εἶναι παραγαγών, Αὐτὸς, Δέσποτα, οὐρανόθεν ἔπιδε ἐπὶ τοὺς ὑποκεκλικότας σοι τὰς ἑαυτῶν κεφαλάς. Οὐ γάρ ἔκλιναν σαρκὶ καὶ αἵματι, ἀλλά σοί, τῷ φοβερῷ Θεῷ. Σὺ οὖν, Δέσποτα, τὰ προκείμενα πᾶσιν ἡμῖν εἰς ἀγαθὸν ἐξομάλισον, κατὰ τὴν ἑκάστου ἰδίαν χρείαν. Τοῖς πλέουσι σύμπλευσον, τοῖς ὁδοιποροῦσιν συνόδευσον, τοὺς νοσοῦντας ἴασαι, ὁ ἰατρός τῶν ψυχῶν καὶ τῶν σωμάτων ἡμῶν. Χάριτι καὶ οἰκτιρμοῖς καὶ φιλανθρωπίᾳ τοῦ μονογενοῦς σου Υἱοῦ, μεθ' οὗ εὐλογητὸς εἶ, σὺν τῷ παναγίῳ καὶ ἀγαθῷ καὶ ζωοποιῷ σου Πνεύματι, νῦν καὶ ἀεὶ καὶ εἰς τοὺς αἰῶνας τῶν αἰώνων.' Ἀμήν.

We give thanks to You, invisible King. By Your infinite power You created all things and by Your great mercy You brought everything from nothing into being. Master, look down from heaven upon those who have bowed their heads before You; they have bowed not before flesh and blood but before You the awesome God. Therefore, Master, guide the course of our life (or make smooth what lies ahead) for our benefit according to the need of each of us. Sail with those who sail; travel with those who travel; and heal the sick, Physician of our souls and bodies. By the grace, mercy and love for us of Your only-begotten Son, with whom You are blessed, together with Your all holy, good and life giving Spirit, now and forever and to the ages of ages. Amen.

By comparing liturgical texts it can be shown that this

prayer, though found the Barberini Codex, appears to be out of place and is, arguably, unsuitable for the occasion at hand, the preparation for Holy Communion.

To understand the problem we have to look at and clarify the meaning of two key words in the prayer, the noun "προκείμενα" – the plural of "προκείμενον" – and the verb "ἐξομάλισον – ἐξομαλίζω." The noun "προκείμενα" has several meanings. In the Inclination Prayer we are discussing it could refer to the circumstances of life "that are now before us or that lie ahead of us," or it could refer to "that which has been set before us." Some interpreters have understood the word to mean the latter, and therefore believe that it refers to the eucharistic Gifts that are set before us on the Holy Table.[433] However, this interpretation fails to take into account two things. First, in our liturgical texts the word "προκείμενα" never appears alone when it is used to refer to the holy Gifts, as it is in our text. It is always accompanied by one or more words that clearly define its meaning, such as "the gifts here presented or set forth – τὰ προκείμενα δῶρα."[434] Second, the word "ἐξομάλισον," which means, "to make smooth," precludes us from interpreting προκείμενα to mean the holy Gifts.[435] To do so would require of us to change the meaning of the verb, as many translators have done, in order to make sense of it as a pre-communion prayer.[436]

Correctly understood and translated, the prayer means and reads as follows. "Therefore, Master, make smooth what lies ahead as each of us has need. Sail with those who sail; travel with those who travel; and heal the sick, Physician of our souls and bodies."[437]

With all of the above in mind, we may conclude that the prayer is clearly unrelated to the action at hand – the preparation for and the reception of Holy Communion. Therefore, it is appropriate to suggest that it be replaced with another more suitable prayer, perhaps by borrowing the one in the Divine Liturgy of St. Basil the Great, which reads:[438]

Lord Master, the Father of mercies and God of every consolation, bless, sanctify, guard, fortify, and strengthen those who have bowed their heads to you. Distance them from every evil deed. Lead them to every good work and make them worthy to partake without condemnation of these, Your most pure and life-giving mysteries, for the forgiveness of sins and for the communion of the Holy Spirit.

The question, however, remains. How did this prayer make its way into the Divine Liturgy of St. John Chrysostom? Robert Taft provides us with a reasonable answer. To understand the origins of the prayer, he says, we must take into account a standard liturgical unit commonly found in eastern liturgical services. This unit is normally located at the end of a divine service and is comprised of a greeting (Peace be to all), a diaconal command (Let us bow our heads to the Lord) and a prayer of blessing and dismissal said by the presider. [439] Such a pattern of prayer was introduced into the pre-Communion rites of the Divine Liturgy late in the fourth century. [440]

The Inclination Prayer, however, in the Chrysostom Liturgy contains no reference to the Eucharist or to Communion. It was composed for another purpose. That being the case, we must ask, where it came from and why was it placed at this point in the Liturgy?

Although there is no direct evidence Taft, following the lead of Juan Mateos, speculates that the Inclination Prayer was originally located at the end of the Liturgy of the Word, the Third Prayer of the Faithful. [441] And while the sources do not provide us with any direct explanation, it was probably transferred into the pre-Communion rites for one of two reasons. According to Mateos, the word προκείμενα in the text was misapplied at some point in time to the eucharistic elements and resulted in the transfer of the prayer to the pre-communion rites of the Liturgy. [442] Taft on the other hand proposes a different solution. The transfer of this prayer to the pre-communion rites was intended to meet a new need, the withdrawal of non-communicants from the Liturgy before the distribution of Communion.

The gradual decline in the reception of Holy Communion in Late Antiquity eventually introduced a hitherto unfamiliar distinction in the eucharistic assembly: communicants and non-communicants, which is to say people who attend the Divine Liturgy without communicating of the Holy Mysteries. Because the distribution of Communion took a fair amount of time, many non-communicants apparently got into the habit of leaving the Church before the final dismissal of the Liturgy. In Late Antiquity, however, liturgical decorum demanded that no one leave the assembly without being properly dismissed. Catechumens and penitents, for example, who were not permitted to participate in the Eucharist, were dismissed properly with a prayer of blessing after the Readings and before the Great Entrance. According to Taft, the Inclination Prayer in the Liturgy of St. John Chrysostom was transferred to the pre-communion rites to serve as a prayer of blessing for the non-communicants, thereby putting order into their casual and haphazard departure from the Liturgy. The blessing was intended to help them meet the demands and uncertainties of their everyday lives.[443] Whatever the reason for the existence of this prayer in the pre-communion rites, one thing is clear: it is not suitable for the purpose and ought to be replaced, especially since few people today leave before the conclusion of the Liturgy.

Additional examples

One could mention other examples in the Divine Liturgy that require further attention and study. On the list of items one could include the purpose, meaning, and structure of the 'Small Entrance,' the place and meaning of the several litanies, the use of the Antiphons and the Typika, and the deciphering of the several 'dismissals' of the Liturgy. Other items of special concern, though not related to the text and rituals of the Liturgy, are nonetheless significant to the manner by which the Divine Liturgy is understood and celebrated. Such items include: the theological, spiritual, and liturgical education and development of the congregation; the integration of worship and praxis; and the promotion of effective preaching, inasmuch as the homily is a constituent element of the Liturgy. In addition, attention must also be given to such other items as the correctness of the inaudible recitation of the priestly prayers; the manner by which Holy Communion is distributed; the conscious and active participation of the laity in the eucharistic celebration; and the quality of the music being used in worship.

Every day, theological research throws new light on these and other questions. Because we value our origins and our traditions, it is both essential and proper to probe the received tradition, if we are to show the relationship between worship and the realities of the life of faith.

11

The Penthekte Synod and Liturgical Reform

*Prayer, dogmas and canons**

By studying the holy canons of local and ecumenical synods, such as those of the Penthekte Synod of 691-692 AD, I have come to appreciate more fully the pastoral dimensions – the philanthropia – as well as the interrelatedness between the rule of faith, the rule of life, and the rule of prayer.

Prayer is not simply an obligation to be fulfilled mechanically. It is an act of faith, a profound personal encounter with the living God, which results in the illumination of the intellect, the transformation of the passions, and the purification of the heart.

Dogmas are not mere theories about God derived from intellectual inquiry, but in the words of Saint Athanasios, "the actual original tradition, teaching, and faith of the Church, which the Lord bestowed, the Apostles proclaimed, and the Fathers safeguarded."[444] The dogmas of the Church are life.[445] Consequently, they are immediately related to the gifts Christ imparts to us, that is to say, divine knowledge, new life, and immortality. The dogmas both reveal and safeguard an authentic understanding of the ultimate truths about God, creation, and humankind. These revealed truths are deposited in the Scriptures and Tradition, and are embedded in the liturgical and canonical tradition of the Church.

Thus, the holy canons are not lifeless and rigid laws, but the measure and standard for the expression of theological truths and principles in given historical circumstances and situations. Essentially pastoral in nature, the canons are guides, which help both persons and communities promote as well as realize the highest excellence. By setting a standard, the canons uphold the basic truths of the Gospel, as they apply to personal and communal living.

Some may see the Canons of the Penthekte Synod, as they pertain to liturgical matters, as a limiting, negative response to liturgical diversity and creativity. I believe they should be seen as a necessary, tentative corrective response to certain defective practices as well as a creative attempt to organize liturgical activity around a given ethos.

The 'liturgical' canons of the Penthekte Synod

The Penthekte Synod issued one hundred and two canons, thirty-two of which are directly related to liturgical concerns and usages.[446] These 'liturgical' canons (my expression) do not appear in sequence, nor are they listed systematically according to categories. Dispersed throughout the collection, they deal with a variety of problems and issues, none of which strike the modern reader, at least at first glance, as being terribly important. Perhaps this is due to the fact that we are so distanced from the problematics and the political, social, and religious climate of the seventh century. Or, it may be due to the fact that we are simply accustomed to and conditioned by those things in church life, which are commonplace to us now, but were for the Christian faithful of the latter part of the seventh century new developments and expressions. I refer, for example, to such things as the imposition of celibacy upon the episcopate (canon 12)[447] and the promotion of icons portraying Christ not merely in symbolic form as a lamb, but in human form (canon 84).[448]

Initially, some of the canons may appear to be unimportant, curious, and unusual to the modern reader. However, below the surface one can discover a significant theological, liturgical, or disciplinary principle, which has lasting value for the faith community, though it may need to be reinterpreted and expressed differently in the present time.

The 'liturgical' canons touch upon many issues, ranging from proscriptions limiting the practice of private sacramental services in private or home sanctuaries (canon 59)[449] to the condemnation of peculiar local customs and superstitions (canon 79, 67).[450] By seeking to limit the practice of private ceremonies the Synod wished to affirm the communal nature and character of the divine sacraments. By decrying superstitions and faulty customs the Synod sought to relieve worship of illusory myths and release people from the delusions of idolatry. These principles are foundational to authentic Orthodox worship and are always valid and relevant.

The Synod adopted proscriptions to correct abuses in other areas as well, including such things as defective hymnography (canon 81),[451] the improper use of the sign of the cross (canon 73),[452] and the disrespect shown for sacred texts (canon 68).[453]

Several canons were issued to protect the meaning and sanctity as well as the proper use of Holy Communion. These include proscriptions barring laypersons from communicating themselves in the presence of canonical clergy (canon 58),[454] prohibiting the payment of stipends for the distribution of Holy Communion (canon 23),[455] and prohibiting the communication of the dead (canon 83).[456]

Some canons were issued to regulate fasting practices and customs (canons 29, 55, 56, 89).[457] Others sought to regulate and unify the practice in regard to the celebration of the Divine Liturgy of the Pre-Sanctified Gifts (canon 52),[458] the use of wine mixed with water for Holy Communion (canon 32),[459] the prohibition of kneeling on Sundays (canon 90),[460] and the joyful observance of New Week – Διακαινίσιμος Ἑβδομάς (canon 66).[461]

Other canons were adopted to ensure the observance of Sunday through regular church attendance and the frequent reception of Holy Communion (canon 80),[462] the continuity of effective catechetical instruction (canon 78),[463] and the need for good, proper, and effectual chanting in the churches (canon 75).[464]

The Synod also issued canons that were meant to uphold earlier restrictions. These include such things as, prohibiting lay persons from entering the sanctuary (canon 69),[465] requiring women to remain silent in liturgical assemblies (canon 70),[466] abolishing the serving of Agape meals in churches (canon 74),[467] and prohibiting the offering of grapes (canon 28),[468] and milk and honey at the Eucharist (canon 57).[469]

To avoid the creation of illicit assemblies (παρασυναγωγαί) together with the dissensions, divisions, and discord that would follow, the Synod ordered that clergy could not perform liturgical functions in private homes and oratories without the express consent of the local bishop (canon 31).[470] When it came to Holy Communion, the Synod prohibited all persons from receiving the consecrated bread in a vessel, which was usually made of precious metals. It insisted that communicants receive the Bread in their bare hands, as had been the custom from the beginning (canon 101).[471] The purpose of this prohibition was to guard against distinctions between the rich and the poor.

The remaining two 'liturgical' canons help us, at least in part, to understand and appreciate the pastoral nature and dimension of Orthodox canon law. Canon 88[472] absolutely forbids any person from bringing animals into churches. Yet, this same canon allows travelers who have no other recourse, to keep their animal(s) with them when by some necessity they are obliged to take refuge in a temple, for, the canon states, "through it all, it is preferable to consider the salvation and safety of the human being." In a similar vein, although a second baptism is strictly forbidden, canon 84[473] makes a slight concession. It allows persons to be (re)baptized,[474] when their baptism as an infant is in doubt for the lack of evidence by credible and reliable witnesses.

It is clear, from all that we have said, that the Church does not issue canons in the void. Rather, canons are promulgated as a result of particular circumstances and needs. Therefore, to be understood properly, the holy canons must be seen in their historical context. The abolition of the Agape meals is a case in point.

Human beings are susceptible to many temptations, including the exploitation, for personal gain, of sacred events and services. Such, I believe, is the case behind the prohibition of the Agape meals. From the start, these meals were a source of irritation to the community, as evidenced by the admonitions of Saint Paul addressed to the Corinthians (1 Cor 11.20-22). Besides the internal disturbances, which such meals were causing to the community, two other dangers also had to be confronted, the merchandizing of foodstuffs within the precincts of the temple and the hoarding of food by some members of the assembly. To stop these abuses and to protect the honor of the faith community and the good order and dignity of the place of worship, the Agape meals were simply disallowed, having outlived their original purpose and usefullness.

The abolishment of the Agape meal underscores an important liturgical rule. When certain institutions are no longer viable, it behooves the Church to recognize the problem and to act decisively to correct it, by either altering or adapting the institution or removing it completely.

Reforming liturgical practices: An example from the Pedalion.

Of special interest to the liturgist are not only the canons themselves but the commentaries of the medieval canonists,[475] as well as the notes and comments supplied in more recent centuries by the Hieromonk Agapios and Saint Nikodemos the Hagiorite, the compilers of the *Pedalion* (Rudder).[476] The explanatory and critical notes of these many exegetes of the canons provide us with a range of interesting and informative details, which shed light on various liturgical developments, practices, and usages. In addition, they provide us with a basis for reassessing certain practices. Let me cite an example from the *Pedalion*.

Commenting on Canon 28 of the Penthekte Synod, which prohibits both the offering and co-mingling of grapes with the eucharistic elements, Saint Nikodemos provides us with a valuable piece of information regarding the manner by which communion was administered to the sick during times of plague. It appears that in some places, it was the practice to place a portion of the consecrated bread in currants or grapes. These were then administered to those suffering from a contagious disease. Saint Nikodemos denounced this practice as inappropriate and unacceptable. Instead, he offered an alternative method, which indicates clearly that he was sensitive to the issue at hand. He suggested the following remedy:

> Hence, both priests and prelates must employ some shift during the time of a plague, in order to enable them to administer communion to the sick without violating this canon. This must not be done, however, by placing the holy bread in currants, but in some sacred vessel, so that the dying and the sick may take it thence with tongs or the like. The vessel and the tongs are to be placed in vinegar, and the vinegar is to be poured into a funnel, or in any other manner that they can that is safer and canonical.[477]

It is obvious from this account and from no less an authority than Saint Nikodemos, that appropriate methods for the administration of Holy Communion can and ought to be sought in the face of communicable diseases.

In our own day, the fear of AIDS has brought this question into sharp focus once again. Many people, knowing that AIDS is transmitted via body fluids, express concerns about the use of the common communion spoon for the administration of Holy Communion. These concerns and fears should not be dismissed with an air of spiritual superiority or a call to greater faith, as if the fact of communion is void of human considerations and the limitations of the created order.[478]

It is not my purpose here to discuss this controversial issue in depth. I leave the medical considerations to other more qualified persons. I wish to underscore, however, what appears to be the prevailing medical opinion, that the AIDS virus *is not transmitted through saliva*. Nevertheless, the use of the common communion spoon, at least for some people, remains an open issue. With this in mind I wish to raise two points.

First, the Church in her collective wisdom and authority is free to adapt the method by which Holy Communion is administered. For example, at the time of the Penthekte Synod, as evidenced by canon 101,[479] Holy Communion was still being administered according to the ancient practice. Each of the eucharistic elements was received separately and sequentially, the Bread first, placed in the open palm of the right hand held over the left, and then the wine, by sipping from the Cup.[480] The communion spoon, by which a portion of the consecrated bread dipped in the cup is administered to the communicant, was introduced gradually during the course of the eighth century. This method of communicating the laity was generalized after the tenth century.[481] The spoon, however, appeared to have an earlier history in the East, having been used in some localities to administer communion to children and the sick.[482] Its introduction for general use may have been prompted by fears of spilling the elements and in order to curb other abuses.[483] Though this method of administering communion to the laity is now centuries old, it must be remembered that it was itself an innovation, having replaced an older, more venerable practice.

The essential concern of the Church is to uphold always the dignity of the act of communion. Of her own authority, the Church has the right to manage – as warranted by needs and circumstances – the method by which Holy Communion is administered to the faithful. The introduction of the communion spoon is a case in point. As is the concern of the Church not to expose communicants to unnecessary risks, as evidenced by the comments of Saint Nikodemos.

Second, whatever other method may be used for the distribution of communion, it is important that it convey clearly the idea of unity and togetherness. From a liturgical perspective, the single bread of the Eucharist, the common cup, and the common communion spoon are all significant sacramental signs. They bring to the worshipping community a heightened awareness of intimate familial relations and communion. In ordinary, everyday human experiences such kinds of sharing, as those we encounter at the eucharistic assembly, are experienced only between family members, close friends, and lovers. In addition, these same symbols, the one bread, the common cup, etc., allow the believers to perceive the sacramental action as a gift from God. The method, therefore, by which communion is administered must always manifest in a significant way the fundamental experience of the Eucharist as an act of intimate communion.

Perhaps no further change in the present method is required to suit the hygienic sensibilities of the faithful, if the recipients of the sacrament were to receive communion with the head held back, the mouth opened wide and the tongue inside. The celebrant then simply drops the communion into the mouth without the spoon touching the person's lips or mouth. In fact, this method has been in use for several decades in many Orthodox parishes in the United States.[484]

This brief encounter with the liturgical and canonical tradition of the Church makes evident the dynamic character of Orthodox worship and the need for an ongoing assessment of liturgical practice. The Church is obliged to be alert to the changing historical and cultural circumstances in which she finds herself. She must accept the challenges and be responsive to the needs of the people who worship now. The task of liturgical renewal and reform, though sensitive and complex, is nonetheless necessary. It has but one objective, to make worship meaningful, effective, and relevant to the people of God.

12

Invigorating and Enriching the Liturgical Life of the Parish

*Creating a healthy liturgical environment**

The need for worship is innate. Human beings, whether consciously or unconsciously, crave authentic worship. This craving is best fulfilled when "the experience of worship engages our minds, memory, imagination, feelings, body, heart, masculinity/femininity, and other people."[485] Hence, each parish is responsible for providing suitable and effective liturgical experiences capable of inducing the inner and exterior involvement of the people.[486]

The forms of worship operate best when they stir the minds and the hearts of the people and engage them actively in the liturgical action. Worship becomes most attractive when it is performed with faith and is characterized by simplicity, beauty, clarity, directness, solemnity, and joyful dignity. Thus we are obliged to pay special attention to the several essential elements that constitute the liturgical experience, namely, time, space, action, speech, art, and song.

Many factors contribute to the creation of a healthy liturgical environment and a meaningful liturgical experience. An inspired priestly celebration and a coherent and persuasive homily are basic elements. The reading of Scripture lessons and other liturgical texts with care and conviction is another. The graceful and dignified performance of liturgical actions is also important. The prayerful attentiveness of the congregation and its ability to respond gracefully with voice and bodily posture is another. Finally, because singing is so central to our liturgical tradition, the quality of our liturgical music and singing is crucial. Songs intensify speech, heighten action, and evoke memories.[487] Therefore, the parish is obliged to both secure the services of qualified chanters and music directors, while at the same time efforts are expanded to return to the assembled worshippers their ministry of song.[488]

Liturgical reductionism – The 'Sunday Church'

A perplexing problem, at least for most Orthodox parishes in North America, is the fact that the rich liturgical tradition of the Church in many instances has been reduced, as Professor Paul Meyendorff observes, to the Sunday morning eucharistic liturgy.[489] "We have become a 'Sunday Church,' peopled by 'Sunday Christians.' The Eucharist," he notes, "has lost its connection to the Orthodox liturgical corpus, of which it is supposed to be the climax – something akin to reducing a fifteen-course banquet to dessert alone."[490]

Professor Meyendorff is certainly correct to lament the fact that we have reduced our liturgical experiences to a Sunday morning Liturgy. However, the greater problem – if not sin – is that in many places even this one experience is less than lofty and less than adequate to meet the spiritual needs of the people, let alone to sustain the vibrancy of their faith.

How and why have we become a Sunday parish? What has happened to make the parish lose the vibrancy of its liturgical life? We claim – and rightly so – that the Church is primarily a worshipping community. Why then do those in charge of parish life pay so little attention to the liturgical needs of the parish? How can this occur even when a parish has spent hundreds of thousands of dollars erecting a new beautiful church edifice or renovating an old one? To answer these and other related questions, I think, we must take into account several historical, social, and cultural factors.

The early immigrant communities

To our immigrant forebears America appeared like a turbulent sea of opposing worldviews and lifestyles. To survive in such a situation, they organized themselves into communities or clubs with administrative forms that mirrored the realities of the political structures of their towns and villages. The community became the lifeboat that promised survival for cherished cultural values and institutions. One of those highly valued institutions of the community was the Church. Thus, churches were established in order to help the community preserve its Orthodox faith and to help people in their spiritual and other needs. But the church was also viewed as the foremost instrument for the preservation of ethnic identity and the cultivation and transmission of the community's cultural heritage. Parenthetically, it must be remembered that the Church is respectful of ethnic identities and the cultural heritages of her people, because they are, after all, an integral part of human life and history. The Church, however, condemns all forms of phyletism, which idolizes and makes absolute individual identities conditioned by history. While the world tends to isolate people according to their identities, the Church welcomes all. In the Church natural, social, and spiritual divisions are transcended. Christ gives unity to all in his Body, the Church (Gal. 3:28).

In time, as it matured and became integrated into the fabric of American life, the dynamics and the focus of the Orthodox community began to shift. Without loosing its ethnic coloration or betraying the legacy of its heritage, the community gradually took on an ecclesial identity. The adoption of the new Uniform Parish Regulations of the Greek Orthodox Archdiocese by the Clergy Laity Congress in 1964 registered clearly the change in the primary identity of the community as an ecclesial entity.[491]

However, the sense of being Church is not always and fully operative in the parish. Its early beginnings linger on. Thus, for example, parish membership is often thought to be more of a commercial transaction rather than a faith commitment. One considers himself a member of the community and a good Christian, even if he does not share in the sacraments and attend Church regularly, as long as he contributes to the financial support of the community.

The process of adaptation, acculturation, and assimilation

As I have written elsewhere, Orthodox Christians in America need not abandon their roots nor be apologetic about the fact that they carry with them cultural values that have been hammered out in places and times other than their own.[492] Indeed, this very fact should remind us of our own responsibility and mission to be active and creative participants in the historical process. As heirs of an excellent legacy, we are compelled to understand and appreciate it. We are also required to define it and live it in accordance with our responsibility to the historical realities in which we find ourselves.

In America, no cultural tradition is able to remain completely autonomous or unaffected by the lure of the mainstream of American life. Indeed, acculturation becomes easier with each succeeding generation. All immigrant groups that come to America enter consciously into the stream of American life. They learn the language and the customs of the land and make the necessary adjustments that will allow them to preserve their cultural identity – and all that it entails by way of religion, values, ideals, language, customs, and traditions – while adopting part of American culture. This is what sociologists call the process of *adaptation*.

The offspring of the immigrant and every succeeding generation – as well as the immigrant himself after prolonged contact – experiences the merging of cultures, the inevitable modifications that come as a result of the impact of one culture upon the other. This is the process of *acculturation*, which is inevitable, relentless, and inexorable, but also acceptable and necessary.

Assimilation, on the other hand, is a matter of deep concern and every effort should be made to keep it at bay. Assimilation is that process by which an individual, for any reason, no longer identifies with his or her cultural group. As a result, all the advantages of an ecclesial, social or cultural influence are lost. Uprooted from such stabilizing influences, an individual is obliged to look for and restart a belief system, moral standards, values, and ideals.

The best remedy against the corrosive inroads of assimilation is a vibrant community of faith, in which the religious values are not compromised by vague survival techniques but are enlivened by the transmission and practice of the true faith in all of its expressions. The high rate of mixed marriages makes it all the more necessary to strengthen the ecclesial ties of the Orthodox family member and to facilitate the acculturation process of the non-Orthodox family member in his or her encounter with the Orthodox Church, her rich history and unique Tradition.

Whenever the ecclesial identity of people becomes weak or dormant, the practice of the Orthodox faith is obviously uncertain and ambiguous, and the desire for worship is severely impaired. To address this and similar problems the parish must be willing to mount a broad-based, multifaceted evangelical endeavor to reach both those within and those who are outside the Church. Certainly, good pastoral work, strong liturgical preaching, inspiring liturgical services, and effective community-building and social justice programs can facilitate this process.

Changing cultural and social realities

Another factor that has contributed to the gradual decline of the liturgical life in many of our parishes, are the changing cultural and socio-economic realities of church life in America. The social mobility of vast numbers of Orthodox people has made the neighborhood urban parish almost a thing of the past. New suburban parishes have taken their place and are thriving. But in both the inner-city church and in the suburban parish, one notices a decline in liturgical life. For one thing, the suburban parish is usually located in an isolated place away from public transportation, not readily accessible even to those parishioners who care to experience a fuller traditional corporate prayer life. For many people who live in the suburbs, going to church has become a chore, especially for families with young children who have to travel long distances and for older folks who lack the means of transportation to get to the church. Also, the modern parish – and this is a crucial point – is no longer the foremost place for social gathering and interaction.

The modern family is not like the immigrant family. The families in today's parish are mostly nuclear and, in many instances, not ethnically or even religiously homogeneous. Mixed marriages have been on the rise, altering the character and composition of the parish. Traditional family structures have also been altered. Single-parent families and blended families are more common today then ever before. And oftentimes the parish has failed to recognize, let alone to meet, these needs and respond to the expectations and challenges of the modern family.

In times past, most families lived around or near the Church. More often than not, the families that the parish catered to were extended families, with grand-parents and other relatives living in close proximity to each other. Devotion to the Church was usually expressed by regular attendance at all – or most – of the divine services by at least one or more members of the family. Today, the extended family is a rare phenomenon. Today, both parents usually work and the pressures of work, of family commitments, and of school and after-school activities of children severely limit the family's leisure time. As a result, the time allotted to church attendance has been limited and devotion to the Church is often expressed differently than in the past. For example, increased monetary contributions or the offering of talents for special parish activities and projects often take the place of church attendance and worship.

The depreciation of worship

Clearly, however, as we shall see below, these substitutes for worship are not simply a radical departure from traditional practice but point to a fundamental misunderstanding of the meaning and role of worship in the life of the faith community and its individual members.[493] This loss of meaning leads finally to the depreciation of worship as an essential element of the Christian life.

In part, this is due to the fact that we have failed to educate and train the people adequately in the ways of Christian living, of which prayer and worship are constitutive elements. We think that people know the significance and the meaning of corporate worship, when in fact they don't. We think that they know the value and the power of personal prayer; or that they know how to pray, but they don't. How can we expect the people to practice consciously that which they do not know or cannot appreciate? We offer them precious little by way of authentic liturgical education and training. We are content to feed them pietistic trifle that has little to do with real life and real liturgy. Also, look at the way we deal with the children in our parishes. For decades the practice has been to exclude them from the liturgical assembly. To this day in many parishes children are whisked away from the Divine Liturgy to attend Sunday School classes, encouraging them to think that worship is, at best, a secondary component of church life.

Spiritless worship does not engender commitment

We are obliged to pose some serious questions. Can, in fact, our people worship in spirit and in truth, when the liturgical services they experience are often times spiritless or pretentious?[494] Can people be attracted to worship when the explanations we give for the sacred rites are woefully inadequate, the language of prayer is incomprehensible, the preaching of the word is uninspiring, and the music is mediocre? Can people relate to worship when the community's commitment to translate its devotional acts into works of justice and loving-kindness is lacking or lukewarm? Simply put, we must come to realize that an aesthetically, intellectually, and spiritually impoverished liturgy only alienates the people from the Church and her worship. This is especially true of the young. It does not take much to disaffect and estrange the younger generation from the Church. Highly mobile, today's young people – *Generation X* – are less likely than the generations that preceded them to be faithful and loyal to an institution – even when the institution is the Church – unless they are convinced of its compelling excellence and value.

Examples of liturgical creativity and vitality

In spite of many obstacles, thanks to the vision and persistence of clerical and lay leadership, many parishes pursue a vigorous liturgical life where the Sunday Church syndrome is held at bay. While the traditional daily cycle of worship in these parishes may not be always and fully operative, there is nevertheless an array of divine services scheduled weekly. More importantly, the Sunday morning experience is so powerful that it carries into the activities of the week.

In addition to a modified daily Orthros, there are, for example, other services such as the Saturday night vespers, the feast day vespers and liturgies, the Wednesday or Friday Paraklesis, and the Monday night Compline. Often, the divine services – whether they are conducted in the morning or evening – are followed by some form of Catechetical instruction for various constituencies of the parish.

In many parishes feast days are celebrated with an evening Divine Liturgy on the eve of the Feast, in order to accommodate working people and their families. Many times, a community dinner allowing for social interaction among the people follows the liturgical service. Various prayer services are also scheduled in the evenings or mornings prior to parish meetings and events. Also, other corporate services are scheduled to meet the special needs of parishioners, including such services as the monthly Agiasmos, periodic celebrations of the sacrament of Holy Unction, and other traditional services. Some parishes hold an early morning weekly service that brings people together on their way to work. A breakfast and an appropriate presentation follow the service.

In addition, many clergy schedule time and find the opportune moments to instruct the people in the ways of worship by teaching them the order and the meaning of the divine services. With the assistance of qualified persons they teach the people how to sing the hymns and how to read the prayers of the divine services and encourage congregational participation. Also, they provide texts of the Service of the Hours for use by the people in their daily devotions and meditations, whether in the privacy of their homes and or in the workplace.

The parish is neither a monastery, nor a laboratory, nor a museum

It is important at this point to make something clear. We cannot and must not turn our parishes into monasteries, or into liturgical laboratories, or for that matter into a Byzantine cathedral or village church frozen in some century long past. The parish is not a monastic community. Therefore any attempt to impose upon it a monastic liturgical model is, in the long run, doomed to failure. Neither is the parish a laboratory where subjective liturgical experiments are carried out. Subjective liturgical experiments usually produce trivial liturgy and result in the making of trivial Christians. Neither is the parish a museum, a place that attempts to replicate some idealized past that never was. The parish is a living organism, pulsating with life. Like any living person, it carries a history but it lives in the present and anticipates and works for a better tomorrow.

Revitalizing the liturgical life of the parish

The revitalization of the liturgical life of the parish requires hard work and long-term commitments. Its success depends on the ability of the clergy to identify the real needs of the people and to motivate qualified parishioners to accept liturgical ministries. Its success also depends on the willingness of the parish to support the liturgical programs through adequate funding. It means that funds are made available for the preparation, production, and/or purchase of materials and, above all, for the training – and when indicated by local conditions the financial support – of lectors, singers, choirs, and other ministries essential to a vibrant liturgical life.

On a broader scale, the success of the parish liturgical renewal program requires that the whole Church engage herself in the effort. It means, especially, that the Church is able and willing to organize, authorize, support and otherwise empower a Liturgical Commission composed of competent theologians, pastors, philologists, and church musicians to deal with the issues and tasks of liturgical renewal and reform. However good these efforts – whether on a parish or on a diocesan or on an archdiocesan level – may be, liturgical renewal will never be truly effective unless we understand and come to grips with the deeper underlying reason for the liturgical impoverishment we are – or seem to be – witnessing in our times.

The deeper problem – a crisis of worship – a crisis of faith

This points us in another direction, where, in fact, we will find the more serious reason for the decline in the vitality of parish life in all of its varied expressions and manifestations. Orthodox theologians[495] have long cautioned us of the dangers of secularism. However, I am obliged to make note of the fact that secularism has also produced some very positive things. Indeed, as Olivier Clement notes, the Church should not be afraid of secularization, but work to preserve it from its exaggerations and seek to orientate it in another direction by exposing the human being to the irreducible and the non-assimilable, to a God who is neither tamable nor consumable but is the very source of salvation;[496] by reminding society of its ethical traditions and the legitimacy of existence; and by speaking boldly in the public square of the antinomy of the cross and the glory, of a God "who comes alongside humankind in death and suffering to open up before him unexpected vistas of resurrection."[497]

However, this is neither the time nor place to talk about the beneficial effects of secularization in western societies, such as the curbing of militant clericalism, the appearance of the non-totalitarian state, the creative advances in technology and medicine, and the acceptance of the other in his or her otherness in an authentic pluralism. Indeed, the very subject of secularism with its positive and negative effects is far too complex an issue to be dealt with properly in this context. Nevertheless, for our purposes it is important that we examine some of the negative aspects of secularism, so that we may better understand the extent and meaning of the crisis of worship that some believe is now gripping the Church.

According to Metropolitan Anthony Bloom, a secular society is marked by two characteristics. First, in a secular society human beings have a blurred, weak, and anemic sense of God. And second, in a secular society people develop an acute awareness of the temporal world. They tend to see the world and life essentially in material terms – inert, opaque, autonomous, and self-sufficient, blind to their own depth. As a result, people in a secular society are inclined to "reject or ignore or be insensitive to the other dimension of the world, its transparency to the Divine Presence, its dimension of immensity and eternity."[498]

Herein lie the tension and the problem, since Christians view the world and life differently. For the Christian, the world is not a timeless self-sufficient entity of recurring cycles void of ultimate meanings; and life is not composed of competing chaotic forces where all forms of violence and death reign supreme and the struggle for the survival of the fittest is waged. Rather, Christians see the world and life in sacramental terms, as having "a calling, a destiny and a vocation, capable of being God-bearing, filled with divine Presence, without being destroyed or ceasing to be itself."[499] For the Christian, the world and every human being in it are deep enough to contain God. At the heart of the Gospel is the truth of God's solidarity with his creatures, of the Presence of his rule and of his gentle mercy and tender love which are the foundation both of salvation and of judgment.

Yet, if we think of it, even Christians can lose sight of God and ignore him. On our journey towards the Kingdom we are all susceptible to failure. Seduced by sin, we too can fall away from God, forsake and lose him. Sin is not only the denial and rejection of God but also an ignorance of him.[500] Therefore, the loss or the absence of the sense of God is a matter of deep concern for the Church.

The tragedy of secularism, which Father Schmemann insists is a Christian heresy, lies in the fact that it distorts, exaggerates and therefore mutilates something true.[501] "Secularism," he writes, "is above all a *negation of worship*. Not of God's existence, not of some kind of transcendence and therefore of some kind of religion. If secularism in theological terms is a heresy, it is primarily a heresy about man. It is the negation of man as a worshipping being, as *homo adorans:* the one for whom worship is the essential act, which both 'posits' his humanity and fulfills it."[502] Herein lies the great fallacy. No one is capable of eradicating the yearning for the wholly Other from one's soul. We have been made to worship, that is, to enter into communion with the living God. Therefore, we either learn to come before the true God in prayer and solemn feast or we delude ourselves with the worship idols.

While there is still much church-going and there are pockets where the dominant cultural tone is religious, modern American culture has freed itself from religious tutelage, values, and authority. As the state of irreligion spreads and more people are drawn into its web, there is a tendency among a broad spectrum of the populace to dismiss worship as outdated, useless, and unproductive.[503] When people – as a society or as individuals – loose sight of God and deny the sacramentality of creation, an air of unreality overtakes the world of faith. As God ceases to be relevant in the lives of people, the need for worship fades away and vanishes. Faith and worship are inseparable. When one withers and dies, so does the other. Worship is centered on God. It is "an epiphany of God, a means of his revelation, presence and power."[504] Hence, when there is little or no faith, we are faced with a crisis of worship, the product of the crisis of faith.

Creating a sound cultural context

Several years ago a Commission of theologians, pastors, and sociologists was established by the Greek Orthodox Archdiocese to examine the needs of the faithful and propose a theological agenda for the Greek Orthodox Church in America as the Church moved into the third millennium of the Christian faith. The Commission Report was published and gained wide circulation. In the first section, entitled 'The Faith Crisis,' the Report maintains the following:

> Despite the resurgence of some religious affiliations, western society is on the whole marked by a cultural crisis of faith, that is, a wholesale drifting away from traditional religious and

moral values which now has become a sociological condition affecting all religious groups... A tendency exists among bona fide Orthodox Church members to limit their religious participation to occasional church attendance. Such casual church membership often leads to a movement away from the Church, not so much in a sense of renunciation or joining another body, but in the sense that Orthodox Christianity no longer is a prime definer of one's identity.[505]

In the process of acculturation, doctrine and liturgy accentuate the separateness or particularity of the group, maintaining its identity. Therefore, to be true to its mission, the parish is obliged to provide for all of its people – both young and old – that cultural context in which faith and worship are vigorously dynamic, are rooted in life, and exemplify the meaning and impact of Christ upon the world. In such a cultural context clergy and lay leaders work hard to make the riches of our doctrinal, ethical, and liturgical tradition available to the people in ways that fill their lives with meaning, purpose, hope, and joy.

The creation of such a cultural context requires unfailing commitment and continuous monitoring. Parish leaders are obliged to evaluate regularly the life and activities of the parish. A parish that is organized in a manner that unites the faithful dynamically, makes Christian truths live in the hearts of people, and integrates these truths into life and acts upon them in concrete ways signifies that the liturgical, evangelical, educational, pastoral, and philanthropic activities of the parish are well focused, vibrant, and effective. However, where the secular mode of living and doing business has crept into the parish, where spiritual identities have been blurred and compromised, and where individual and communal activities have become ambiguous, the parish is obliged to reconsider its agenda, redirect its priorities, and revitalize the theological enterprise.

We must remember that the parish is, above all else, the fundamental eucharistic cell of the Church, where the saving work of the Church is actively pursued and enacted. The parish exists for one essential purpose to bring salvation to

the world through the preaching of the Word and the celebration of the sacraments. Everything the parish is and does
emanates essentially from the weekly celebration of the Divine Liturgy. At the Eucharist the new life in Christ is
continuously advanced and the People of God are inspired,
enabled, and emboldened to celebrate joyously the liturgy
after the Liturgy, to become faithful witnesses of Christ in
their everyday activities both at home and in the workplace,
in the words of St. Gregory the Theologian to be "as instruments played by the Holy Spirit."

The times require that we work diligently and continuously to enrapture the people with the truth and power of
the Gospel, in order to facilitate and effect the transformation of naïve religiosity into conscious Orthodox belief,
practice, and piety. In response to the moral and spiritual
imperative of the Gospel, every parish must strive to remain
faithful to the Orthodox spirit, vision, and ethos, and accept
the challenge to be truly the Church.

1

The Liturgy: The Church's Faith in Motion

[1] The words worship (λατρεία) and liturgy (λειτουργία) are used interchangeably and denote the whole range of the Church's divine rites and services. The term Divine Liturgy (Θεία Λειτουργία) is used to designate the divine service by which the Orthodox Church celebrates the sacrament of the Eucharist.

[2] John D. Zizioulas, *Being as Communion* (Crestwood, NY 1985) p. 132.

[3] Ibid. p. 161.

[4] Boris Bobrinskoy, *The Mystery of the Holy Trinity* (Crestwood, NY 1999) p. 127.

[5] Ibid. p. 153.

[6] St. Basil, *On the Holy Spirit*, translated by D. Anderson (Crestwood, NY 1980) p. 74-75.

[7] Alexander Schmemann, *Introduction to Liturgical Theology* (Crestwood, NY 1996) p. 24.

[8] See Georges Florovsky, "Worship and Every-day Life: An Eastern Orthodox View," in *Studia Liturgica*, II, 4 (1963) p. 266-272; and "The Worshipping Church" in *The Festal Menaion*, translated by Mother Mary and Bishop Kallistos Ware (London 1969) p. 21 – 37.

[9] G. Florovsky, "Worship and Every-day Life," p. 272.

[10] Ibid. p. 267.

[11] Boris Bobrinskoy, "Prayer and the Inner Life in the Orthodox Tradition," in *Studia Liturgica*, III, 1 (1964) p. 31.

[12] Georges Florovsky, "The Worshipping Church," in *The Festal Menaion*, p. 21.

[13] Ibid. p. 34.

[14] Don. E. Saliers, *Worship as Theology: Foretaste of Glory Divine* (Nashville, TN 1994) p. 22.

[15] Origen, *On Prayer*, 10 (PG 11, 448).

[16] Olivier Clement, *The Roots of Christian Mysticism* (New York 1995) p. 199.

[17] I am reminded here of the words of the Psalmist. "Great is the Lord, and greatly to be praised; and his greatness is unsearchable... I will meditate on the glorious splendor of your majesty, and on your wondrous works... All your works shall praise you, O Lord, and your saints shall bless you. They shall speak of the glory of your kingdom, and talk of your power... The Lord is righteous in all his ways, gracious in all his works...

The Lord is near to all who call upon him, to all who call upon him in truth. He will fulfill the desire of those who fear him; he also will hear their cry and save them" (Ps. 144 /145).

[18] Olivier Clement, *The Roots of Christian Mysticism*, p. 191.

[19] Dionysios the Areopagite, *The Celestial Hierarchy*, II, 4 in Colm Luibheid, translator, *Pseudo-Dionysius – The Complete Works* (The Classics of Western Spirituality – New York 1987) p. 151.

[20] Panagiotis Skaltsis, Λειτουργικές Μελέτες (Thessaloniki 1999) p. 24.

[21] The Christological structure of the human being is discussed and explained by Panayiotis Nellas, *Deification in Christ – The Nature of the Human Person* (Crestwood, NY 1987) p. 21 – 42.

[22] Dionysios the Areopagite, *The Celestial Hierarchy*, III, 3.

[23] St. John Chrysostom, *Homilies of First Corinthians*, XXX, 6 in *Nicene and Post Nicene Fathers*, vol. XII, p. 178.

[24] The notion that the Holy Spirit inspires true and right prayer in us is echoed in a number of prayers. For example, the Seventh Prayer of the Orthros contains the following words. "Teach us your statutes, for we do not how to pray properly, unless you guide us, Lord, by your Holy Spirit."

[25] See D. Saliers, *Worship as Theology*, p. 111. The Eucharistic Prayers (Anaphora) of the Divine Liturgy of St. John Chrysostom and St. Basil the Great recount in beautiful doxological form the providential and redemptive activities of God that constitute his gracious self-giving and empowering life.

[26] God sent his Son into the world to reveal the truth and to call all people to salvation. Jesus, the incarnate Son of God, accomplished this task through his teachings, his works and signs, his supreme act of love (when he was lifted up on the Cross), and his resurrection and glorification.

[27] Susan K. Wood, "Participatory Knowledge of God in the Liturgy," in *Studia Liturgica*, 29, 1 (1999) p. 30.

[28] G. Florovsky, "Worship and Every-day Life," p. 269.

[29] Thomas Merton, *Seasons of Celebration* (New York 1977) p. 53. Many Orthodox theologians and liturgists have stressed the formative nature of Orthodox worship. Evangelos Theodorou, for example, published a major study on the *Triodion* with the revealing title Η Μορφωτική Αξία τοῦ Ἰσχύοντος Τριωδίου -The Formative Value of the Current Triodion (Athens 1958). Two more recent examples are the articles of Father Stanley Harakas, "The Holy Week Bridegroom Services: An Ethical Analysis,"in *SVTQ*, 46, 1 (2002) p. 23-61 and Nektarios Paris, "Τό Λειτουργικόν Ασμα," in Γρηγόριος Ὁ Παλαμᾶς, 84, vol. 787, March-April (2001). The words of Bishop Nazarii of Nizhnii-Novgorod who wrote an opinion on issues pertaining to renewal of ecclesial life in Russia at the turn of the 20th century provide us with an eloquent summary of the educative and formative value of Orthodox worship. "The Orthodox faith is acquired, strengthened, and maintained chiefly by means of liturgical worship. Liturgical worship is properly considered to be the best school for teaching faith and morals, for it acts abundantly and salutarily on all the powers and capaci-

ties of the soul." (Cited by Paul Meyendorff, "The Liturgical Path of Orthodoxy in America," in *SVTQ*, 4, 1&2 (1996) p. 47.

[30] Susan J. White, *The Spirit of Worship – The Liturgical Tradition* (Maryknoll, NY 1999) p. 21.

[31] From the Small Litany, which is found in all Orthodox services.

[32] These truths are incorporated in the Prayer before the Gospel in the Divine Liturgies of St. John Chrysostom and St. Basil. It reads as follows, "Shine within our hearts, loving Master, the pure light of Your divine knowledge and open the eyes of our minds that we may comprehend the message of Your Gospel. Instill in us also reverence for Your blessed commandments, so that having conquered all sinful desires, we may pursue a spiritual life, thinking and doing all those things that are pleasing to You. For You, Christ our God, are the light of our souls and bodies, and to You we give glory together with Your Father who is without beginning and Your all holy, good, and life giving Spirit, now and forever and to the ages of ages. Amen."

[33] See Metropolitan John (Zizioulas) of Pergamum, "Συμβολισμός καὶ Ρεαλισμός στὴν Ορθοδόξη Λατρεία," in *Σύναξη*, 71, (July-September 1999) p. 6 – 21.

[34] D. Saliers, *Worship As Theology*, p. 156.

[35] Dom Gregory Dix, *The Shape of the Liturgy* (London 1945) p. 741.

[36] This contrast was first used by the author(s) of the ancient Church Order, *The Didache* or *The Teaching of the Twelve Apostles* to describe (chapters 1-6) Christian ethical teaching in the form of the way of death and the way of life.

[37] B. Bobrinskoy, "Prayer and the Inner Life in Orthodox Tradition," p. 36. See also, John S. Romanides, "Man and His True Life according to the Greek Orthodox Service Book," in *GOTR*, 1, 1 (1954) p. 70-73.

[38] J. Zizioulas, *Being as Communion*, p. 50-56.

[39] Ibid. p. 59.

[40] D. Saliers, *Worship as Theology*, p. 193.

[41] Cf., Ex. 24:10-11; Ez. 37:27; Heb. 10:19-25.

[42] One can find, for example, a pattern or model for a dynamic pastoral ministry to the world in the Anaphoral Intercessions of the Liturgy of St. Basil the Great.

[43] Joseph A. Fitzmyer, "Pauline Theology," in R. Brown, J. Fitzmyer and R. Murphy, eds., *The New Jerome Biblical Commentary* (Englewood Cliffs, NJ 1990) p. 1393.

[44] Ibid.

[45] D. Saliers, *Worship As Theology*, p. 174.

[46] J. Zizioulas, *Being as Communion*, p. 36-49.

[47] Father Ion Bria discusses the dynamic dimensions of the life of faith – both for the Church and for her members – in his study, *The Liturgy after the Liturgy – Mission and Witness from an Orthodox Perspective* (Geneva 1996).

[48] Mark Searle, ed., *Liturgy and Social Justice* (Collegeville, MN.1980) p. 29.

[49] Alexander Schmemann, "Sacrifice and Worship," in *Parabola*, 3, 2 (1978) p. 65.

[50] Emmanuel Clapsis, "The Eucharist as Missionary Event in a Suffering World," in his *Orthodoxy in Conversation* (Geneva/Brookline, MA 2000) p. 195.

2
The Nature and Goal of Liturgical Piety

[51] John D. Zizioulas, Ἡ Κτίση ὡς Εὐχαριστία (Athens 1992) p. 98. This volume contains in Greek translation the three lectures of Metropolitan John (Zizioulas) of Pergamon entitled "Preserving God's Creation: Three Lectures on Theology and Ecology," that were delivered by him at King's College in England and published in the *King's College Theological Review*, volumes 12 and 13 (1989 and 1990).

[52] See John D. Zizioulas, *Being as Communion* (Crestwood, NY 1985) p. 42-49.

[53] In the Bible and the writimgs of the Church Fathers the heart is viewed as the center of our being, the primary organ of our human personhood, the place where we experience the presence of God. See, for example, Bishop Kallistos Ware, *The Inner Kingdom* (Crestwood, NY 2000) p. 61-62, 81-82, and 187-190.

[54] P. Nellas, *Deification in Christ: The Nature of the Human Person* (Crestwood, NY 1987) p. 37.

[55] St. Maximos the Confessor, *Chapters on Knowledge, First Century*, 11, 12 in George Berthold, *Maximus Confessor – Selected Writings* (New York 1985) p. 130-131.

[56] See, for example, Metropolitan John Zizioulas, Ἡ Κτίση ὡς Εὐχαριστία, p. 122-123.

[57] Ibid. p. 102.

[58] Ibid. p. 102-112.

[59] See Donald B. Cozzens, *The Changing Face of the Priesthood* (Collegeville, MN 2000) p. 47-54.

[60] See the Anaphora of the Divine Liturgy of St. John Chrysostom.

[61] Archimandrite George, *The Deification as the Purpose of Man's Life*, p. 24.

[62] Ibid. p. 41-43.

[63] Louis Bouyer, *Liturgical Piety* (Notre Dame, IN 1964) p. 88.

[64] For an excellent introduction to the meaning of the prayer see the essays in, Timothy Ware, ed., *The Art of Prayer – An Orthodox Anthology* (London 1985).

[65] For a brief discussion on the levels of the spiritual life see, John S. Romanides, Ρωμαιοσύνη (Thessalonike 1975) p. 96-99.

[66] See, for example, the well-known second antiphon of the Hymns of Ascent (Ἀναβαθμοί) in the fourth tone: "In the Holy Spirit every soul is quickened and through cleansing is exalted and made radiant by the Triple

Unity, in a hidden, sacred manner."

[67] St. Nicholas Cabasilas, *A Commentary on the Divine Liturgy*, 4:35.

[68] St. Symeon the New Theologian, Εὐχαριστία, 2, 225-233, cited in Archbishop Basil Krivocheine, *In the Light of Christ: St. Symeon the New Theologian- Life-Spirituality-Doctrine* (Crestwood, NY 1986) p. 23.

[69] Early Christian art, for example, was essentially symbolic and emphasized eschatological and soteriological ideas. See Georgios Antourakis, Χριστιανικὴ Ζωγραφικὴ (Athens 1990) p. 21.

[70] Anton Baumstark, *Comparative Liturgy* (Westminster, MD 1958) p. 152-174.

[71] A. Schmemann, "Liturgy and Eschatology" in *Sobornost*, 7 (1985) p. 6-14. The article has been reprinted in Thomas Fisch, ed., *Liturgy and Tradition: Theological Reflections of Alexander Schmemann* (Crestwood, NY 1990) p. 97.

[72] Robert F. Taft, *Beyond East and West – Problems in Liturgical Understanding* (2nd edition – Rome 2001) p. 28.

[73] Jean Danielou, "Le symbolisme des rites baptismaux," in *Dieu Vivant*, 1 (1945), cited in R. Taft, *Beyond East and West*, p. 28-29.

[74] Georges Florovsky, "The Worshipping Church," in *The Festal Menaion*, translated by Mother Mary and Kallistos Ware (London 1969) p. 28 – 29.

[75] In the current Greek liturgical books the Service in Preparation for Holy Communion consists of a canon, whose acrostic is the Greek alphabet. According to the rubrics, this portion of the service is to be recited at the end of the Apodeipnon or Compline. The following morning after the regular morning prayers the service is resumed. It consists of the Trisagion prayers and three Psalms (22/23, 23/24, and 115/116:10-19), which contain eucharistic, Christological, and soteriological themes. The Psalms are followed by several troparia (hymns) and a didactic verse. These, in turn, are followed by a series of nine prayers attributed to various authors: St. Basil the Great (2), St. John Chrysostom (3), St. John of Damascus (2), St. Symeon the Translator (1) and St. Symeon the New Theologian (1). The Service, which is meant for those preparing to receive Holy Communion, developed gradually over a long period of time. It is found in several versions, some of which are shorter than the one in the current Greek liturgical books. The Service originated in monastic circles and reflects the Church's deep reverence for the sacrament of the Eucharist. Hence, everyone who is preparing to receive Holy Communion is encouraged to read at least part, if not all, of it.

[76] A. Schmemann, "Liturgical Theology: Remarks on Method," in Thomas Fisch, ed., *Liturgy and Tradition*, p. 142-143.

[77] T. Fisch, *Liturgy and Tradition*, p. 7.

[78] See for example, Roger T. Beckwith and Wilfrid Stott, *This is the Day* (Greenwood, SC 1978) p. 117-124.

[79] A. Schmemann, *Introduction to Liturgical Theology* (Crestwood, NY 1996) p. 75-86.

[80] Ibid. p. 72-73.

[81] In addition to the study of Beckwith and Stott on Sunday, noted above,

see among others, H. B. Porter, *The Day of Light* (Greenwich, CN 1960). Mark Searle, ed., *Sunday Morning: A Time of Worship* (Collegeville, MN 1982). Konstantinos Athanasopoulos, Ἱστορικὴ Ἐξέλιξις τῆς Κυριακῆς (Thessalonike 1977).

[82] A. Schmemann, "Liturgical Theology: Remarks on Method," in T. Fisch, *Liturgy and Tradition*, p. 143.

[83] A. Schmemann, "Liturgical Theology, Theology of the Liturgy, and Liturgical Reform," in *St. Vladimir's Theological Quarterly*, 13 (1969) p. 217-218.

[84] Ibid. p. 138.

[85] Ibid. p. 138.

[86] Ibid. p. 138.

[87] See A. Calivas, "Challenges in Changing Cultural Realities: A Liturgical Approach," in Nomikos Michael Vaporis, ed., *Rightly Teaching the Word of Your Truth: Studies in Faith and Culture in Honor of Archbishop Iakovos* (Brookline, MA 1995) p. 67-74.

[88] A. Schmemann, "Liturgical Theology: Remarks on Method," in T. Fisch, *Liturgy and Tradition*, p. 143.

[89] A. Schmemann, "Liturgy and Eschatology," in *Sobornost*, 7 (1985) and reprinted in T. Fisch, *Liturgy and Tradition*, p. 95. As Father Schmemann notes eschatology is not merely the last chapter in a theological manual, nor a map of future events, or even a personal hope, but the very essence of the Christian faith and life and of Christian liturgy.

[90] A. Schmemann, *Introduction to Liturgical Theology*, p. 103.

[91] Ibid. p. 103-131. See also Paul F. Bradshaw, *The Search for the Origins of Christian Worship* (Oxford 2002) p. 211-230.

[92] See Louis Bouyer, *Liturgical Piety*, p.16.

[93] More is said about this subject below in the essay on the development of the Typikon, p. 63-66.

[94] A. Schmemann, *Introduction to Liturgical Theology*, p. 127.

[95] Among the medieval liturgical commentaries are: *The Ecclesiastical Hierarchy* of (Pseudo) Dionysios (sixth century). *The Mystagogia* of St. Maximos the Confessor (+662). *The Ecclesiastical History and Mystical Contemplation* of St. Germanos of Constantinople (+circa 733). *The Protheoria* of Nicholas and Theodore of Andida (written about 1055-1063). The incomplete commentary of Pseudo-Sophronios of Jerusalem (twelfth century), which ends with the Great Entrance. *The Commentary on the Divine Liturgy* of St. Nicholas Cabasilas (written around 1350). *The Divine Liturgy* and the other treatises of St. Symeon of Thessalonike (+1429). For a full account of these works see Rene Bornert, *Les Commentaires Byzantins de la Divine Liturgie du VIIe au XVe Siecle* (Paris 1966). See also Hans-Joachim Schulz, *The Byzantine Liturgy* (New York 1986).

[96] Mircea Elaide, *The Sacred and the Profane* (New York 1959) p. 130-131.

[97] Alphonse Mingana, *Commentary of Theodore of Mopsuestia on the Lord's Prayer and on the Sacraments of Baptism and Eucharist* (Woodbrooke Studies 6: Cambridge 1933) p. 67.

[98] See A. Schmemann, "Symbols and Symbolism in the Byzantine Liturgy" in Demetrios Constantelos, ed., *Orthodox Theology and Diakonia* (Brookline, MA 1981) p. 91-102.

[99] Ibid. p. 98.

[100] Robert F. Taft, "The Liturgy of the Great Church: An Initial Synthesis of Structure and Interpretation on the Eve of Iconoclasm," in *Dumbarton Oaks Papers*, 34-35 (1980-1981) p.73.

[101] The Entrance Prayer of the Liturgy of St. John Chrysostom in the *Barberini Codex* reads as follows: "Benefactor and Creator of the entire universe, receive the Church which is advancing, accomplish what is good for each one: bring all to perfection and make us worthy of Your Kingdom, by the grace and mercy and love of your Only-begotten Son, with whom you are blessed..." See Stefano Parenti and Elena Velkovska, *L' Euchologio Barberini gr. 336* (Rome 1995) p. 25.

[102] Paul Meyendorff, *St. Germanus of Constantinople on the Divine Liturgy* (Crestwood, NY 1984) p. 73-75.

[103] Ibid. p. 24.

[104] See A. Schmemann, *Introduction to Liturgical Theology*, 27-32.

[105] Ibid. p. 107.

[106] Paul Bradshaw, *The Search for the Origins of Christian Worship* (New York 1982) p. 66-67.

[107] A. Schmemann, "Liturgical Theology: Remarks on Method," p. 143.

[108] A. Schmemann, *Introduction to Liturgical Theology*, p. 136.

[109] Ibid. p. 141-142.

[110] Justin, *First Apology*, 67. Writing almost two centuries later, Eusebius of Caesarea (ca. 260-340) tells the story of a lapsed Christian, Serapion, who was communed on his deathbed. According to this account Eusebius suggests that by the third century it had become customary to bring Holy Communion to the dying. Eusebius, *The History of the Church*, Book VI, 44.

[111] Alistair Stewart-Sykes, *On the Apostolic Tradition* (Crestwood, NY 2001) p. 156-158. Burton Scott Easton, *The Apostolic Tradition of Hippolytus* (Ann Arbor, MI 1962), 32, p. 60. Geoffrey J. Cumming, *Hippolytus: A Text for Students* (Nottinghamshire 1976), 36-37, p. 27. For a detailed account on the practice of private Communion see Nathan Mitchell, *Cult and Controversy: The Worship of the Eucharist Outside the Mass* (New York 1982).

[112] St. Basil, *Letter 93*.

[113] For more on the Liturgy of the Pre-Sanctified Gifts see, Nicholas Uspensky, *Evening Worship in the Orthodox Church* (Crestwood, NY 1985) p. 111 – 190. Ioannis Fountoulis, *Κείμενα Λειτουργικῆς (8) – Λειτουργία τῶν Προηγιασμένων Δώρων* (Thessaloniki 1971). Demetrios Moraitis, *Η Λειτουργία τῶν Προηγιασμένων Δώρων* (Thessaloniki 1955).

[114] Nonetheless, there were probably individuals who thought of frequent private Communion in lesser terms, as a protection against danger and temptation. Such and other misguided notions led finally to the prohibition of the practice.

[115] A. Stewart-Sykes, *On the Apostolic Tradition*, p. 166.

[116] St. Basil *Homily on the Martyr Julitta*, 3-4.

[117] Olivier Clement, "Life in the Body," *The Ecumenical Review*, 33 (1981) p. 131.

[118] Ibid. p. 165.

[119] Peter Hammond, *The Waters of Marah – The Present State of the Greek Church* (New York 1956) p. 16.

3

The Byzantine Rite

[120] Robert F. Taft, *Beyond East and West* (Rome 2001) p. 143.

[121] Ibid. p. 153-156.

[122] S. H. Cross and O.P. Sherbowitz-Weltzor, *The Russian Primary Chronicle* (Cambridge, MA 1953) p. 111.

[123] See, for example, N. H. Baynes and H. L. B. Moss, *Byzantium* (Oxford 1949) p. xx.

[124] Ephrem Carr, "Liturgical Families in the East," in Anscar J. Chupungco, ed., *Handbook for Liturgical Studies*, vol. I (Collegeville, MN 1997) p. 18.

[125] The Byzantine Rite developed gradually over several centuries. These developments will be discussed in greater detail in the essay that follows. For an excellent concise introduction to the Byzantine Rite see Robert F. Taft, *The Byzantine Rite: A Short History* (Collegeville, MN 1992).

[126] Panayiotis Trempelas, Λειτουργικοί Τύποι Αἰγύπτου καί Ἀνατολῆς (Athens 1961) p. 323-324. Ioannis Fountoulis, Λειτουργική (Thessalonike 1975) p. 75. Ephrem Carr, "Liturgical Families in the East," p. 11.

[127] Liturgical scholars have classified the ancient liturgical rites into several liturgical families. The rites of the East are classified under two families, the Alexandrian, which has two branches, the Egyptian and the Ethiopian; and the Antiochene, which is sub-divided into two main types, the West Syrian and the East Syrian. The West Syrian has four branches, the Antioch/Jerusalem, the Maronite, the Armenian, and the Byzantine. The East Syrian has three branches, the Nestorian, the Chaldean and the Malabar. The classical rites of the West are usually classified under two families, the Roman and the Gallican. The Gallican family has four branches, the Gallican, the Ambrosian (or Milanese), the Mozarabic, and the Celtic. In the late Middle Ages, the Roman rite was imposed upon all of the churches in the West. After the Reformation in the sixteenth century, Protestant worship developed along seven major liturgical traditions, the Lutheran, the Reformed, the Anglican (Episcopalian), the Free Church (Congregationalists, Baptists, Disciples, and others), Methodist, Quaker (which has no liturgies per se), and Pentecostal (an American phenomenon of the twentieth century). See E. Carr, "Liturgical Families in the East," and Gabriel Ramis, "Liturgical Families in the West," and Jordi Pinell I Pons, "History of the Liturgies in the Non-Roman West," in A. J. Chupungco, ed., *Handbook of Liturgical Studies*, p. 11-24; 25-32; and 179-

195. James F. White, *Introduction to Christian Worship* (Nashville, TN 1982) p. 38-43, and *Documents of Christian Worship* (Louisville, KY 1992) p. 1-16. Herman Wegman, *Christian Worship in East and West* (New York 1985) p. 87-93. P. Trempelas, Λειτουργικοί Τύποι Αἰγύπτου καί Ανατολῆς.

[128] R. Taft, *The Byzantine Rite*, p. 16.

[129] Ibid.

[130] Among the many works on the liturgical arts, see the following. (Architecture) Konstantinos Kalokyris, Χριστιανική καί Βυζαντινή Αρχαιολογία (Thessalonike 1970). Richard Krautheimer, *Early Christian and Byzantine Architecture* (Baltimore, MD 1965). Thomas F. Mathews, *The Early Churches of Constantinople: Architecture and Liturgy* (London, 1977). Rowland J. Mainstone, *Hagia Sophia: Architecture, Structure and Liturgy of Justinian's Great Church* (New York 1988). (Iconography) David Talbot Rice, *Byzantine Art* (London 1954). Robin Cormack, *Byzantine Art* (Oxford 2000). John Lowden, *Early Christian and Byzantine Art* (London 1998). Constantine Cavarnos, *Guide to Byzantine Iconography* (Boston 1993). Michael Quenot, *The Icon – Window on the Kingdom* (Crestwood, NY 1991). Paul Evdokimov, *The Art of the Icon* (Rendondo Beach, CA 1990). Peter Galadza, "The Role of Icons in Byzantine Worship," in *Studia Liturgica*, 21, 2 (1991). (Hymnography) Constantine Cavarnos, *Byzantine Chant* (Belmont 1998). Dimitri Conomos, *Byzantine Hymnography and Byzantine Chant* (Brookline, MA 1984). Egon Wellesz, *A History of Byzantine Music and Hymnography* (Oxford 1961).

[131] The development of the Daily Office will be discussed below. For a history of its formation, see Robert F. Taft, *The Liturgy of the Hours in East and West* (Collegeville, MN 1986) p. 273 – 291. Ioannis Fountoulis, Λογική Λατρεία (Thessalonike 1971) p. 147 – 269.

[132] See Bishop Kallistos Ware, "How to Read the Bible," in *The Orthodox Study Bible* (Nashville, TN 1993) p. 762-770. The same volume contains a handy listing of all the pericopes or lections of the Orthodox Church's Lectionary, p. 771-780. See also among others, David M. Petras, "The Gospel Lectionary of the Byzantine Church," in *St. Vladimir's Theological Quarterly (SVTQ)*, 41, 2&3 (1997) p. 113-140. Paul F. Bradshaw, "The Use of the Bible in Liturgy: Some Historical Perspectives," in *Studia Liturgica*, 22, 1 (1992) p. 35-52. W. Jardine Grisbrooke, "Word and Liturgy: The Eastern Orthodox Tradition," in *Studia Liturgica*, 16, 3&4 (1986/1987) p. 13-30. A Monk of the Eastern Church, *The Year of Grace of the Lord* (Crestwood, NY 1980). Georges Barrois, *Scripture Readings in Orthodox Worship* (Crestwood, NY 1977). Thomas Hopko, "The Bible in the Orthodox Church," in *SVTQ*, 14, 1&2 (1970) p. 66-99. Demetrios Constantelos, "The Holy Scriptures in Orthodox Worship," in *The Greek Orthodox Theological Review (GOTR)*, 12, 1 (1966) p. 7-83. Vasileios Exarchos, Τό Παρ"Ημῖν Ίσχῦον Σύστημα Βιβλικῶν Αναγνωσμάτων (Athens 1935).

[133] The Book of Revelation, the last of the twenty-seven Books of the New Testament is not part of the Lectionary. Clergy, however, are permitted to use it in their homilies and in their instruction classes.

¹³⁴ During the weekdays of the Great Lent, for example, we have a course of lections in more or less continuous sequence from the Book of Genesis, the Book of Proverbs, and the Prophecy of Isaiah. The Book of Psalms (the Psalter) permeates Orthodox worship. The entire Psalter is read once weekly, according to the numerical succession of the Psalms. In addition, selected Psalms, chosen on account of their content, are assigned to various parts of the divine services.

¹³⁵ Thomas Hopko, "The Bible in the Orthodox Church," p. 67.

¹³⁶ See for example, Ioannis Fountoulis, Λειτουργικά Θέματα, Γ (Thessalonike 1977) p. 77-79. Alkiviadis Calivas, Χρόνος Τελέσεως τῆς Θείας Λειτουργίας (Thessalonike 1982) p. 188-190.

4
The Typikon:
The Development of the Orthodox Liturgy

¹³⁷ Church Orders were manuals that contained liturgical rites and directives, moral precepts, and canonical regulations. The original Greek text is available in Βιβλιοθήκη Ἑλλήνων Πατέρων καὶ Ἐκκλησιαστικῶν Συγγραφέων (ΒΕΠΕΣ), vol. 2 (Athens 1955) p. 211-220. For an English translation see, F. X. Glimm, *The Fathers of the Church – The Apostolic Fathers* (New York 1947) p. 167-184; and R. Kraft, *The Apostolic Fathers 3: The Didache and Barnabas* (New York 1965). For a more complete description of and a bibliography on the Church Orders see Panayiotes Chrestou, Ἑλληνικὴ Πατρολογία, volume ii (Thessalonike 1978).

¹³⁸ Other important Church Orders that shed light on the development of the liturgy are the following:

• *The Apostolic Tradition* by Hippolytus of Rome (early third century). Gregory Dix, *The Treatise on the Apostolic Tradition of St. Hippolytus* (London 1937). Bernard Botte, *La Tradition Apostolique de Saint Hippolyte* (Munster 1963). G. J. Cuming, *Hippolytus: A Text for Students* (Nottingham 1976). B. S. Easton, *The Apostolic Tradition of Hippolytus* (Ann Arbor, MI 1962).

• *The Didascalia (Teaching) of the Twelve Holy Apostles* (early third century). R. H. Connolly, *Didascalia Apostolrum* (London 1929). F. X. Funk, *Didascalia et Constitutiones Apostolorum* (Paderborn, 1905 and 1979). *The Ante Nicene Fathers*, vol. vii, p. 371-383.

• *The Apostolic Constitutions* (second half of the fourth century). *ΒΕΠΕΣ*, vol. 2, p 5-208. F. X. Funk, *Didascalia et Constitiones Apostolorum. The Ante Nicene Fathers*, vol. vii, 387-508.

• *The Testament (Διαθήκη) of the Lord* (late fourth century). J. Cooper and A. J. Maclean, *The Testament of our Lord* (Edinburgh 1886). G. Sperry-White, *The Testamentum Domini: A text for Students* (Nottingham 1991).

¹³⁹ The earlier dates for the *Didache* have been proposed by J. P. Audet, *La Didache – Instructions des Apotres* (Paris 1958). Panayiotis Chrestou holds the view that the document developed in three stages during the latter

part of the first century, its final compilation occurring in the decade of 90 A.D. Recent views, however, favor a later date, of the middle or late second century, but based on elements of an earlier period. See Frank Hawkins, "The Didache," in Jones, Wainwright, Yarnold, and Bradshaw, *The Study of the Liturgy* (New York 1992) p. 84-86.

[140] The phrase 'any other water' indicates a place where the water would not be flowing, such as a lake, reservoir, or pool.

[141] See *ΒΕΠΕΣ*, vol. One, p. 13-39. F. X. Glimm, *The Fathers of the Church – The Apostolic Fathers*, p. 3-58.

[142] The thanksgiving prayer of Clement is contained in his *First Letter to the* Corinthians, chapters 59-61.

[143] See A. Calivas, "Ἡ Ἀρχή τῆς Νυχθημέρου καί ἡ Λατρεία τῆς Ἐκκλησίας" in Ἀναφορά εἰς Μνήμην Μητροπολίτου Σάρδεων Μαξίμου, vol. 3 (Geneva 1989) p. 93-105.

[144] See A. Calivas, Χρόνος Τελέσεως τῆς Θείας Λειτουργίας (Thessalonike 1982) p. 78-91.

[145] A. Schmemann, *Introduction to Liturgical Theology* (4th edition – Crestwood, NY 1996) p. 43.

[146] For a brief explanation of the Daily Office in its present form see A. Calivas, *Come Before God* (Brookline, MA 1996).

[147] For the origins and development of the Daily Office see George Guiver, *Company of Voices: Daily Prayer and the People of God* (New York 1988). Robert F. Taft, *The Liturgy of the Hours in East and West* (Collegeville, MN 1986). Paul Bradshaw, *Daily Prayer in the Early Church* (New York 1982). Juan Mateos, "The Origins of the Divine Office," in Worship, 41 (1967) p. 477 – 485. Ioannis Fountoulis, Λογική Λατρεία (Thessalonike 1971).

[148] R. Taft, *The Liturgy of the Hours in East and West*, p. 84. For a brief analysis of the cathedral and monastic types of worship see Ioannis Fountoulis, Τελετουργικά Θέματα (Athens 2002) p. 11-24.

[149] The term is used by R. Taft, *The Byzantine Rite*, p. 52.

[150] Anton Baumstark, *Liturgie Comparee* (Chevetogne, Belgium 1940; English translation: *Comparative Liturgy* (Westminster, MD 1958) p. 11-116.

[151] St. Justin the Martyr, for example, writing in the middle of the second century, attests to this fact. In his day each local church was still organized around the bishop. "On the day named after the sun, all who live in city or countryside assemble. The memoirs of the apostles or the writings of the prophets are read for as long as time allows. When the lector has finished, the president addresses us and exhorts us to imitate the splendid things we have heard. Then we all stand and pray. As we have said earlier, when we have finished praying, bread, wine and water are brought up. The president then prays and gives thanks according to his ability, and the people give their assent with an 'Amen.'" (*Apologia, I, 67*).

[152] For more on the episcopocentric and presbyterocentric Eucharists see the excellent study of (Metropolitan) John D. Zizioulas, *Eucharist, Bishop, Church* (Brookline, MA 2001).

[153] Robert Taft, "The Liturgy of the Great Church: An Initial Synthesis of Structure and Interpretation," in *Dumbarton Oaks Papers*, 34/35 (1980-81)

p. 47. For more information on Hagia Sophia and its liturgy see Thomas Mathews, *The Early Churches of Constantinople: Architecture and Liturgy* (London 1977). Rowland Mainstone, *Hagia Sophia: Architecture, Structure and Liturgy of Justinian's Great Church* (New York 1988).

[154] There are two complete manuscripts of the *Typikon of the Great Church*, Hagios Stavros (HS 40) and Patmos 266. The latter is dated around mid-ninth century and was published by Aleksej Dmitrievskij, *Opisanie Liturgitseskich Rukopisej*, I Τυπικά (Kiev 1895, reprinted in Hildesheim, Germany 1965) p. 1-152. HS 40, however, which is dated mid-tenth century, is more complete. It is divided into two parts: the first follows the calendar year (fixed feasts), while the second is based on Pascha and follows the calendar of the movable feasts. Juan Mateos published a critical edition of HS 40, *Le Typikon de la Grande Eglise*, in the series *Orientalia Christiana Analecta* (*OCA*, vols. 165 – 166, Rome 1962-1963).

St. Symeon of Thessalonike, in his treatise *On Divine Prayer* (*PG* 155, 536-669), gave an elaborate description of the ceremonies of the cathedral rite and analyzed the differences between the liturgical practices at St. Sophia and those at the monasteries. He was the last to champion the cathedral rites of the imperial city. By the time of St. Symeon, the cathedral rite had all but disappeared. In Thessalonike itself it was practiced only in St. Sophia, the cathedral church of the city. With the death of St. Symeon in 1429, the cathedral rite of Constantinople fell quietly into oblivion.

For more on the cathedral rite see Ron Grove, "Towards Recovering the Ἀσματικαί Ἀκολουθίαι. What Were the 'Sung Services' of the Great Church(es) Like?" in *Studia Liturgica*, 30, 2 (2000) p. 189 – 195. R. Taft, *The Liturgy of the Hours in East and West*. Paul Bradshaw, *Daily Prayer in the Early Church* (New York 1982). Oliver Strunk, "Byzantine Office at Hagia Sophia," in *Dumbarton Oaks Papers*, 9 & 10 (1956) p. 175 – 202. Evangelos Antoniades, "Περί τοῦ Ἀσματικοῦ ἢ Βυζαντινοῦ Κοσμικοῦ Τύπου τῶν Ἀκολουθιῶν," in *Θεολογία*, 21-22 (1949-1950).

[155] In the monastic office, the Psalms were used in at least two ways. First, specific Psalms were assigned to the various services, as appropriate and suitable for the hour or the feast. Second, the Psalms were also read continuously according to their order in the Scriptures. The entire Psalter was read at least once during the week.

[156] See R. Taft, *The Liturgy of the Hours in East and West*, p. 32.

[157] Paul Bradshaw, *The Search for the Origins of Christian Worship* (Oxford 20022) p. 174.

[158] For the origins and meaning of the stational liturgy see, John F. Baldovin, *The Urban Character of Christian Worship*, in the series *Orientalia Christiana Analecta* (= *OCA*, 228 Rome 1987).

[159] Ibid. p. 184.

[160] Ibid. p. 37.

[161] For a listing and other details of the sixty-eight processions see J. Baldovin, *The Urban Character of Christian Worship*, p. 292 – 303. In addition to these processions, liturgical processions were often held in times of

natural and civil calamities, such as earthquakes and enemy sieges, the translation of the relics of martyrs and saints, and the dedication of churches. Coronation ceremonies also included a public procession.

[162] The word *synaxis* refers to a liturgical assembly, and especially the assembly for the Eucharist. In the *Typikon of the Great Church* the term is also used to indicate a stational liturgy and the place (or places) of the major liturgical celebration the day.

[163] Blachernae was one of the quarters of the city. The temple in honor of the Theotokos at Blachernae was built in the late fifth century and was one of the most important churches of the City. The domed basilica was joined to the palace at Blachernae by a portico. The church also had an adjoining chapel that contained the most famous of the relics of the Theotokos, her robe.

[164] In ancient Greek the word *lite* (λιτή) meant prayer, supplication, and entreaty. In liturgical documents it was used to designate a prayer that was voiced in processions. In the *Typikon of the Great Church* the term was also used to designate an outdoor public liturgical procession.

[165] Usually the evening service was held at twilight, at the lighting of the evening lamps, hence the name λυχνικόν (from λύχνος – lamp). The service later was also called vespers – ἑσπερινός (ἑσπέρας – evening).

[166] This was another of the most important shrines of the Theotokos. The church was built in the early fifth century and was located in the coppersmiths' section of the City (χαλκοπρατεία), from which it got its name. It was located close to Hagia Sophia and the imperial palace.

[167] These verses are taken from the *Magnificat*, Luke 1:46 – 48.

[168] The petitions and prayers for the various divine services are contained in the Euchologion. As mentioned elsewhere, the earliest extant Euchologion of the Byzantine Rite is the eighth century *Barberini Codex*.

[169] The three lessons are the same as those found in the Menaion of August: Gen. 28:10-17; Ezek. 43:27-44:4; and Prov. 9:1-11.

[170] The verses are from Psalm 44/45:10 – 11. These verses are sung at all the feasts of the Theotokos. In the patristic tradition Psalm 44/45, especially verses 9-17, is interpreted as referring to the Theotokos.

[171] The two lessons are: Phil. 2:5 – 11 and Luke 10:38 – 42:11:27 – 28. The numbering of the Gospel chapters listed in the *Typikon* is, of course, different from the conventional numbering with which we are accustomed. The present chapter divisions of the texts were made in the thirteenth century and the numbering of verses three centuries later. The numbering in the Typikon reflects the old Greek patristic tradition, whereby the texts of the individual Scriptures were divided into paragraphs called κεφάλαια – paragraphs (or chapters). The numbering in the *Typikon of the Great Church* appears today in the margins of each pericope (περικοπή) in the official Greek Liturgical Gospel, the Evangelion.

[172] Juan Mateos, *Typicon de la Grande Eglise*, vol. I, p. 368-372.

[173] Louis Bouyer, *The Spirituality of the New Testament and the Fathers* (New York 1960) p. 317.

[174] Ibid. p. 312, 315.

[175] St. John Cassian, *Conferences*, I, 7.

[176] Ordained monks were given the title hieromonk (ἱερομόναχος) or priest-monk to distinguish them from the non-ordained monks. Similarly, monastics, who were ordained to the diaconate, received the title hierodiakonos (ἱεροδιάκονος).

[177] For a description and analysis of early monasticism and monastic rules in the East see John Thomas and Angela Constantinides Hero, editors, *Byzantine Monastic Foundation Documents – A Complete Translation of the Surviving Founders' Typika and Testaments* (Washington, D. C. 2000), vol. I, p. 21 – 41.

[178] See *"Ελληνες Πατέρες τῆς Ἐκκλησίας (ΕΠΕ) – M. Βασιλείου "Απαντα τά "Εργα*, vol. 8, p. 164 – 409 and vol. 9, p. 10 – 393. In this series, the text appears in two forms, the original Greek accompanied by a Modern Greek translation.

[179] For a full explanation of this and other similar canons see the study of Archbishop Peter L' Huiller, *The Church of the Ancient Councils – The Disciplinary work of the First Four Ecumenical Councils* (Crestwood, NY 1996) p. 219-222, from which this translation was taken. For another translation and explanation of the canon see, *The Rudder (Pedalion) p. 248.*

[180] The 'Jesus Prayer' – the continuous repetition of the invocation, 'Lord Jesus Christ, Son of God have mercy on me,' – is widely practiced among Orthodox monastics and devout people. It is often called the Prayer of the Heart. While the Jesus Prayer has its roots in the New Testament, it was fashioned in the fifth century and began to flourish among the desert fathers. It became a hallmark of hesychasm, a spiritual tradition that requires rigorous separation from the world, emphasizes silence, prayer and the mystical life, and pursues specific methods of prayer. For a brief history and an analysis of the Jesus Prayer see A Monk of the Eastern Church, *The Jesus Prayer* (Crestwood, NY 1987).

[181] *The Longer Rules*, 37:3 – 5 (*ΕΠΕ*, p. 346 – 353).

[182] See A. Calivas, *Χρόνος Τελέσεως τῆς Θείας Λειτουργίας* (Thessalonike 1982) p. 201 – 211.

[183] The anchorites Saints Ammoun (+ca 356) and Makarios (+ca. 390) were the first to introduce the system of the lavra into Egypt. St. Chariton established the first lavra in the deserts of Palestine around 320 – 330.

[184] For additional information on this important monastery see John Binns, *Ascetics and Ambassadors of Christ* (Oxford 1994). Y. Hirschfield, *The Judean Monasteries in the Byzantine Period* (Yale 1992). V. and L. Kesich, *Treasures of the Holy Lands* (Crestwood, NY 1985).

[185] On the nature and purpose of monastic Typika see K. Manaphes, *Μοναστηριακά Τυπικά – Διαθῆκαι* (Athens 1970). More recently, several scholars cooperated to produce in five volumes an English translation of extant Byzantine monastic Typika: John Thomas and Angela Constantinides Hero, editors, *Byzantine Monastic Foundation Documents – A Complete Translation of the Surviving Founders' Typika and Testaments.*

Dumbarton Oaks Studies, XXXV (Washington, DC 2000). This monumental project provides both scholars and interested readers with valuable information that sheds light on the development and life of medieval Byzantine monasteries.

[186] For more on the early version of the monastic office and the use of the Scriptures by monastics see Douglas Burton-Christie, *The Word in the Desert – Scripture and the Quest for Holiness in Early Christian Monasticism* (New York 1993). A. Van Der Mensbrugghe, "Prayer in Egyptian Monasticism," in *Studia Patristica*, vol. II (1957) p. 435 – 454.

[187] An additional service, the First Hour, was created and attached to the Orthros to form a single unit.

[188] I. E. Karagiannopoulos, Ἰστορία Βυζαντινοῦ Κράτους, vol. I (Thessalonike 1978) p. 82.

[189] On the founding of this monastery and its liturgical practices see Ioannis Fountoulis, Ἡ Εἰκοσιτετράωρος Ἀκοίμητος Δοξολογία (Athens 1963).

[190] For a brief account of the life of St. Theodore, the history of the Studios Monastery, and a complete translation of the Founder's *Testament* and *Rule* (Ὑποτύπωσις) see John Thomas and Angela C. Hero, *Byzantine Monastic Foundation Documents*, vol. I, p. 67 – 119. The Testament and the Rule are found also in *PG* 99, cols. 1813-1824 and cols. 1704 – 1720 respectively. The Rule was also published by A. Dmitrivskij, *Opisanie Liturggicheskikh Rykopisie*, vol. I, Typika (Kiev 1895) p. 224-238.

[191] See J. Thomas and Angela C. Hero, *Byzantine Monastic Foundation Documents*, vol. I, p. 87.

[192] See footnote 190 above.

[193] For a succinct analysis of the history of the Studite reforms and the development, spread, and decline of the Studite Typikon see, R. Taft, *The Byzantine Rite*, p. 56-60.

[194] The Monastery of the Theotokos Evergetis became the leader of an enormously influential reform movement in Byzantine monasticism. Building on Basilian and Studite precedents, the community at Evergetis succeeded in revolutionizing monastic positions on such important matters as governance and administration and strict financial management. It also promoted the abolition of privilege and the desirability of the cenobitic life. See John Thomas and Angela C. Hero, *Byzantine Monastic Foundation Documents*, vol. II, p. 458.

[195] A translation of the governance and administrative rules of the Typikon of Evergetis, made by Robert Jordan, appears in J. Thomas and A. Hero, *Byzantine Monastic Foundation Documents*, vol. II, p. 454-506. John Klentos, a former colleague at Holy Cross, who is presently affiliated with the Patriarch Athenagoras Orthodox Institute at Berkeley and teaches at the Graduate Theological Union, wrote his doctoral dissertation on this document: *Byzantine Liturgy in Twelfth Century Constantinople: An Analysis of the Synaxarion of the Monastery of the Theotokos Evergetis* (University of Notre Dame 1995). His study of the liturgical Typikon (also known as the

Synaxarion) of the Theotokos Evergetis constitutes an important contribution to our knowledge of the evolution of Orthodox liturgy and monasticism.

[196] The Nine Odes of the Scriptures are included in the Psalter and in the Horologion. Eight of the nine odes are from the Old Testament. The Ninth Ode, which consists of two parts, is from the New Testament. The Nine Odes in their order are: *First Ode*, the Song of Moses (Ex. 15:1-19; *Second Ode*, A Song of Moses (Deut. 32:1-43), which is sung only on Tuesdays of the Great Lent; *Third Ode*, The Prayer of Hannah, the mother of the Prophet Samuel (1 Kings [or 1 Sam.] 2:1-10); *Fourth Ode*, the Prayer of Habakkuk (Hab. 3:2-19); *Fifth Ode*, a Prayer of Isaiah the Prophet (Is. 26:9-20); *Sixth Ode*, a Prayer of Jonah the Prophet (Jon. 2:3-10); *Seventh Ode*, a Prayer of the Three Holy Youths (Dan. 3:26-56); *Eighth Ode*, the Hymn of the Three Holy Youths (Dan. 3:57-88); and the *Ninth Ode*, the Song of the Theotokos (Lk. 1:46-55) and the Prayer of Zacharias, the father of St. John the Baptist and Forerunner (Lk. 1:68-79).

[197] Panayiotes K. Chrestou has published a comprehensive study on Mt. Athos, Τό "Αγιον "Ορος – Άθωνική Πολιτεία – Ιστορία, Τέχνη, Ζωή (Athens 1987). For the more recent history of Mt. Athos see Demetrios G. Tsamis, "Αγιον "Ορος – Προσέγγιση στή Πρόσφατη Ιστορία του (Thessalonike 1986) and the volume published by the Holy Community of Mt. Athos, Τό Καθεστώς τοῦ Ἁγίου "Ορους "Αθως (Mt. Athos 1996).

[198] John Meyendorff, "Mount Athos in the Fourteenth Century: Spiritual and Intellectual Legacy," in *Dumbarton Oaks Papers*, 42, p. 161.

[199] R. Taft, *The Byzantine Rite*, p. 81 – 83.

[200] J. Meyendorff, "Mount Athos in the Fourteenth Century," p. 161, 164.

[201] These two works are the Διάταξις τῆς Ιεροδιακονίας (Diataxis for the Diaconate) and the Διάταξις τῆς Θείας Λειτουργίας (Diataxis for the Divine Liturgy). The Diataxis for the Diaconate is published in *PG* 154:745-766.

[202] The Typikon was published in Constantinople in 1888. The publishing house Saliveros in Athens has printed subsequent editions.

[203] The Committee under Patriarch Dionysios V was comprised of the Metropolitans of Ainos, Samos, Caesarea, and Mytilene, and the Protopsaltis Georgios Violakis.

[204] For a comparison of the two services – a monastic Vespers and the modified Vespers of the new Typikon – see the study of Ioannis Fountoulis, Μοναχικός Εσπερινός (Thessalonike 1977).

[205] For example, let us look at the restructured order of services for Sunday. On Saturday evening in preparation for Sunday the only service assigned is the Great Vespers. The Midnight Service of Sunday (Μεσονυκτικόν τῆς Κυριακῆς), which differs in structure and content from the same service for weekdays and Saturdays and is shorter in length, is assigned to Sunday morning to be sung before the Orthros. However, in most parishes in the United States – if not in all – the Midnight service has long since been abandoned. In the Greek parishes in the United States the Orthros of

Sunday is sung at mid-morning. The Divine Liturgy is celebrated at the conclusion of the Orthros. Of the several services in the daily office, the Sunday Orthros is the longest and the most complicated. If the Sunday Orthros were to be sung and read in its entirety according to the monastic rubrics it would take upwards of three hours. In most parishes in the United States the Sunday Orthros is usually shortened to just over an hour. New situations and circumstances have required further changes and made abbreviations and omissions inevitable in parish usages.

[206] For example, the rite of the Apokathelosis (Ἀποκαθήλωσις – literally the Un-nailing), which takes place at the Holy Friday Vespers, originated in the Church of Antioch. During the course of the nineteenth century it came to Constantinople and was incorporated into the new Typikon. The ceremony of the light at the Paschal Vigil is mentioned only in a footnote in the new Typikon. However, by the end of the nineteenth century it had become a common practice. The Typikon of 1888 also formalized the practice of reading a Gospel Lesson giving an account of the resurrection before the Paschal Orthros. See A Calivas, *Great Week and Pascha in the Greek Orthodox Church* (Brookline, MA 1992 and 1996) p. 70-71, 108-111.

[207] See for example the comment in the *Festal Menaion*, p. 543.

[208] For a detailed analysis of the four schemata see A. Calivas, Χρόνος Τελέσεως τῆς Θείας Λειτουργίας (Thessalonike 1982).

[209] This is highlighted by the fact that the Liturgy of St. Basil is celebrated on the day of the Feasts of Christmas and Theophany when they fall on a Sunday or a Monday. In such an instance the Typikon does not foresee the celebration of a vesperal Divine Liturgy, only a Great Vesper Service on the eve of the feast. Only one Divine Liturgy is celebrated on the morning of the feast.

[210] For example, the 10th century *Typikon of the Great Church* lists the Liturgy of the Pre-Sanctified among the services of Holy Friday. The Liturgy of the Pre-Sanctified Gifts, in a slightly different form, was at one time also associated with the Sacrament of Marriage.

[211] See Robert Taft, *The Byzantine Rite*, p. 81-83.

[212] Aidan Kavanagh, *Elements of Rite* (New York 1982) p. 3.

[213] A. Schmemann, *Introduction to Liturgical Theology,* p. 39-40.

[214] Ibid. p. 37.

[215] Gabriel Braso, *Liturgy and Spirituality* (Collegeville, MN 1971) p. 228.

[216] R. Taft, *Beyond East and West*, p. 153.

5
The Euchologion

* This is an edited version of an article that was published under the title "The Euchologion: A Brief History," in Peter Chamberas, ed., *Agape and Diakonia: Essays in Memory of Bishop Gerasimos of Abydos* (Brookline, MA 1998) p. 155 – 172.

[217] The Euchologion corresponds to the *Sacramentaries* of the Roman Catholic Church, which developed gradually into the complete Missal. The Sacramentaries were books that supplied the bishops and priests with prayers for the sacraments and other liturgical services.

[218] A collection of principal texts related to the liturgy of the Church from the beginning to the fifth century may be found in Lucien Deiss, *Springtime of the Liturgy* (Collegeville, MN 1979). For a critical analysis of the data and the methods used for the study of the early history of Christian worship see Paul F. Bradshaw, *The Search for the Origins of Christian Worship* (Oxford, 1992).

[219] See Robert F. Taft, *The Byzantine Rite: A Short History ((Collegeville, MN 19923)* p. 24-25.

[220] On the Byzantine Rite see chapters 3 and 4 above. For a comprehensive study on the history, theology and practice of Orthodox worship see Alexander Schmemann, *Introduction to Liturgical Theology* (4th edition - Crestwood, NY 1966). See also Herman Wegman *Christian Worship in East and West* (New York 1985).

[221] The Prayer Book of Serapion was first published by A. Dmitrievskij in Kiev in 1894 from an eleventh century manuscript found in the library of the Great Lavra on Mt. Athos. For more on this Prayer Book see F. E. Brightman, "The Sacramentary of Serapion of Thmuis," in *Journal of Theological Studies,* 1 (1899-1900) p. 88-113 and 247-277; Panteleimon Rodopoulos, *The Sacramentary of Serapion* (Thessalonike 1967); John Woodsworth, *Bishop Serapion's Prayer-Book* (London 1899, which was reprinted in Hamden, CT 1964). The most recent study has been published by Maxwell E. Johnson, *The Prayers of Sarapion of Thmuis. A Literary, Liturgical and Theological Analysis* in the series *Orientalia Christiana Aneleacta,* 249 (Rome 1995).

[222] For more on this Church Order see Gregory Dix, *The Treatise on the Apostolic Tradition of St. Hippolytus* (London 1937, a second edition with preface and corrections by Henry Chadwick in 1968); Burton Scott Easton, *The Apostolic Tradition of Hippolytus* (Ann Arbor, MI 1962); Bernard Botte, *La Tradition Apostolique de Saint Hippolyte* (Munster 1963).

[223] See F. X. Funk, *Didascalia et Constituyiones Apostolrum* 1 (Paderborn 1905) p. 2 – 595. James Donaldson, Constitutions of the Holy Apostles, in the *Ante-Nicene Fathers,* vol. VII (Grand Rapids, MI 1951) p. 387-508.

[224] See C. H. Roberts, and B. Capelle, *An Early Euchologium: The Der Balyzeh Papyrus Enlarged and Re-edited* (Louvain 1949).

[225] A critical edition of the Barberini Codex was published recently by Stefano Parenti and Elena Velkovska, *L' Euchologio Barberini gr. 336* (Rome 1995). For a listing and a description of the primary sources of the Orthodox liturgical tradition see for example, Robert F. Taft, *The Great Entrance* (Rome 1978).

[226] Goar was the first to publish the *Barberini Codex 336.*

[227] Goar was sent to the East as a missionary by the Society for the Propagation of the Faith, in order to help convert the Orthodox faithful to

the Roman Catholic Church. The stratagem of the Latin missionaries was simple: facilitate the process of conversion and the spread of Latin doctrines through the use of Byzantine rites and ceremonies, with which the Orthodox people prayed and were comfortable.

[228] A partial list of these translations appears below in note 230.

[229] The early manuscript versions of the Euchologion included the ordination rite for deaconess.

[230] Among these English versions of the Small Euchologion are: Isabel F. Hapgood, *Service Book of the Holy Orthodox Catholic Apostolic Church* (Brooklyn, NY 1956 – Antiochian Archdiocese). *Service Book of the Holy Eastern Orthodox Catholic and Apostolic Church according to the Use of the Antiochian Orthodox Christian Archdiocese of New York and All North America* (1971). Bishop Dimitri, ed., *The Priest's Service Book, I, II* (New York 1973 – Orthodox Church in America). Nomikos Michael Vaporis, ed., *An Orthodox Prayer Book* (Brookline, MA 1977 – Greek Orthodox Archdiocese). Evagoras Constantinides, ed., *The Priest's Service Book* (Thessalonike 1989 – GOA). *The Abridged Book of Needs* (South Canaan, PA 1995 – OCA). Leonidas Contos and Spencer Kezios, *Sacraments and Services, I, II, III* (Northridge, CA 1995 – GOA). *The Great Book of Needs, I, II, III, IV* (South Canaan, PA 2000 – OCA. Together these four volumes constitute a version of the Great Euchologion).

[231] For example, The Orthodox Church in America (OCA) through its Department of Religious Education has published a series of separate volumes for most of the divine services. Fr. John Zanetos and Fr. Harry Hatzopoulos, priests of the Greek Orthodox Archdiocese, have each published two separate bilingual volumes, one containing the Marriage rites the other the Burial rites. Fr. Peter Chambers has published a book containing an introduction to and a bilingual text of the Baptismal rites, *Baptism and Chrismation: Beginning our Christian Life in the Orthodox Church* (Boston, MA n. d.)

[232] For example, the editor did not include the First and Eighth Day Rites for newborn infants, claiming that they had fallen into disuse and were no longer relevant. Regardless of what one may think of the reforms of Bishop Kavadas, one must applaud him for his pastoral instincts, his courage, and his desire to bring about much-needed liturgical reform. Many of his contemporaries, and especially his students, said of him that he was a man ahead of his times.

[233] Many abbreviated forms of the *Ieratikon* have been published here and abroad. They include: *The Divine Liturgy of St. John Chrysostom* (a reprint of the third edition by the Faith Press in London by the Greek Orthodox Theological Institute Press, Brookline, MA 1950). George Mastrantonis, *The Divine Liturgy of St. John Chrysostom* (St. Louis, MO 1966). *The Divine Liturgy* (official text of the OCA 1967). *Holy Liturgy for Orthodox Christians* (The Romanian Orthodox Episcopate Detroit, MI 1975). Nicon D. Patrinacos, *The Orthodox Liturgy* (Garwood, NJ 1976). Archbishop Athenagoras Kokkinakis, *The Liturgy of the Orthodox Church* (London 1978).

George Papadeas, *The Divine Liturgy of St. John Chrysostom* (Daytona Beach,
FL 1981). *The Orthodox Liturgy* (Oxford 1982). *The Divine Liturgy of St. John
Chrysostom* (a translation of the Holy Cross Faculty – Brookline, MA 1985).
Ἡ Θεία Λειτουργία τοῦ Ἁγίου Ἰωάννου τοῦ Χρυσοστόμου (Thessalonike
1989). This book was published by the Brotherhood 'Lydia.' It contains
the original text and a Modern Greek translation. *The Divine Liturgy of St.
John Chrysostom* (Serbian Orthodox Church 1990). Leonidas Contos, *Lenten
Liturgies* (Northridge, CA 1995). Ἱερατικον (in three volumes) published
by the monastic community Simonos Petra at Mt. Athos 1992).

[234] Issues related to jurisdictional unity in America have been discussed
in a previous essay in volume two of the series, *Essays in Theology and
Liturgy – Challenges and Opportunities: The Church in her Mission to the World*
(Brookline, MA 2001) p. 51-68. In addition to their different foundational
charters and parish regulations and bylaws, one could list a number of
diverse practices among the jurisdictions. These include such things as
the way bishops are elected, criteria for ordination to the priesthood, the
reception of converts, the constitution and prerogatives of parish councils, and marriage and divorce procedures. They also include additions
and deletions in the liturgical texts and abbreviations in the order (τάξις)
of the divine services, the use of different Typika further complicated by
local adaptations of rubrics and regulations, diverse fasting practices, different translations of liturgical texts, and other divergent liturgical and
pastoral practices.

[235] John Meyendorff, *The Byzantine Legacy in the Orthodox Church*
(Crestwood, NY 1982) p. 116.

6
The Spirit and Ethos of Orthodox Prayer

* This essay, altered in form and content, first appeared as part of an
article "The Euchologion: A Brief History" published in the festschrift in
memory of Bishop Gerasimos of Abydos edited by Peter A. Chamberas,
Agape and Diakonia (Brookline, MA 1998) p.155-172.

[236] For a discussion on the spirit and ethos of Orthodox worship see for
example, Ioannis Fountoulis, Τό Πνεῦμα τῆς Θείας Λατρείας
(Thessalonike 1964). Ἡ Λειτουργία Μας (Athens 1967), a collection of es-
says by various authors. Robert F. Taft, "The Spirit of Eastern Orthodox
Worship in *Diakonia*, 12 (1977) p. 103-20 and in his *Beyond East and West –
Problems in Liturgical Understanding* (2nd edition Rome, 2001) p. 143-160.

[237] See for example, John Romanides, "Man and his true life according to
the Greek Orthodox Service Book," in *The Greek Orthodox Theological Review*, 1, (1954) p. 63-83. John Meyendorff, *The Byzantine Legacy in the
Orthodox Church*, p. 115-128.

[238] Stephano Parenti, *Praying with the Orthodox Tradition* (London 1989)
p. 100.

[239] Kallistos Ware, "The Preface" in S. Parenti, *Praying with the Orthodox Tradition*, p. xii.

[240] Susan J. White, *The Spirit of Worship – The Liturgical Tradition* (Maryknoll, NY 1999) p. 58.

[241] The worshipper is made aware of this truth through the various prayers and the variable hymns of the several services that comprise the Daily Office. The Anaphora (the Great Eucharistic Prayer) of every Divine Liturgy, and especially that of St. Basil, makes the same point.

[242] The complete text of the prayer may be found in the *Menaion* of January and in the *Ieratikon*. See for example, *The Festal Menaion*, p. 354.

[243] Bishop Kallistos Ware, "The Preface" in S. Parenti, *Praying with the Orthodox Tradition*, p. x.

[244] Liturgical texts include prayers, petitions, hymns, rubrics, Psalms, Biblical Odes, and a lectionary system.

7
Analyzing the History and Content of Liturgical Texts

[245] Sacramental matter designates those material things, which constitute the essential matter of the sacraments, such as water, oil, bread, and wine.

[246] Architecture designates the form and shape of church buildings as well as the decoration, arrangement, and disposition of liturgical space. The stylistic diversity in Orthodox ecclesiastical architecture does not negate its spiritual unity or cancel its basic identifying characteristics. The external appearance and the interior space of the Orthodox temple constitute an expression of doctrine, representing and interpreting the Church's faith about God, humanity, and the cosmos. Among the features of Orthodox Church architecture are such things as proportionality and ratio of dimensions, a particular expression of harmony, a bond with the natural environment, a richly decorated interior space representing the restored and transfigured creation, and an organic unity with the liturgy.

[247] Alexander Schmemann, *Of Water and the Spirit* (Crestwood, NY 1974) p. 11.

[248] Louis Bouyer, *Rite and Man – Natural Sacredness and Christian Liturgy* (Notre Dame, 1963) p. 147.

[249] Ibid.

[250] See for example, Ioannis Fountoulis, Περί Μία Μεταρρύθμισιν τῆς Θείας Λειτουργίας, p. 16. See also, Thomas Pott, *La reforme liturgique byzantine: Etude du phenomene de l'evolutiuon non spontanee de la liturgie byzantine* (Rome 2000).

[251] The *Psalter* was the only liturgical book to be published in the fifteenth century. It was first published in 1486 and reprinted in 1492. The *Horologion* was printed in 1509, the *Oktoechos* or *Parakletike* in 1520 and 1522, the *Triodion* in 1522, and the three *Divine Liturgies* (by Demetrios

Doukas) in 1526. The *Euchologion* was first published in 1526. The *Evangelion* was published in 1539, the *Apostolos* in 1542, the *Pentekostarion* in 1544, and the *Typikon of St. Savas* in 1545. The *Menaia* were published between 1526 and 1548, the *Eirmologion* in 1568, and the *Anthologion* in 1587. For the history of Greek printing see for example, Evro Layton, *The Sixteenth Century Greek Book in Italy – Printers and Publishers for the Greek World* (Venice 1994). Deno J. Geanakoplos, *Byzantium and the Renaisance – Greek Scholars in Venice* (Hamden, CT 1974). N. E. Skiadas, Χρονικόν τῆς Ἑλληνικῆς Τυπογραφίας, Α. (Athens 1976). N. Tomadakis, "Ἡ ἐν Ἰταλίᾳ Ἔκδοσις Ἑλληνικῶν Ἐκκλησιαστικῶν Βιβλίων (κυρίως λειτουργικῶν)," Ἐπετηρίς Ἑταιρείας Βυζαντινῶν Σπουδῶν, 37΄ (1969-70) p. 3-33. Emile Legrand, *Bibliographie Hellenique ou description raisonne des ouvrages publies en grec par des grecs au Xve et XVIe siecles*, 4 vol. (Paris 1885-1906. A. Sigala, Ἱστορία τῆς Ἑλληνικῆς Γραφῆς (Thessaloniki 1934).

²⁵² The famed printing houses of Venice played a pivotal role.

²⁵³ See Evangelos Theodorou, Μαθήματα Λειτουργικῆς (Athens 1975) p. 291-302. Ioannis Fountoulis, Λειτουργικά Θέματα, Ε (Thessalonike 1986) p. 61-78. Elena Velkovska, "Byzantine Liturgical Books," in Anscar J. Chupungco, ed., *Handbook of Liturgical Studies*, vol. I (Collegeville, MN 1997) p. 225-240. *The Festal Menaion*, translated by Mother Mary and Archimandrite Kallistos Ware (London 1977) p. 535-543.

²⁵⁴ Paul Meyendorff, *Russia, Ritual, and Reform* (Crestwood, NY 1991).

²⁵⁵ See A. Calivas, Χρόνος Τελέσεως τῆς Θείας Λειτουργίας (Thessalonike 1982) p. 36-41.

²⁵⁶ The learned Metropolitan Chrysanthos of Trapezon, who later became Archbishop of Athens, chaired the Committee.

²⁵⁷ Trempelas published the first volume of his work, Αἱ Τρεῖς Λειτουργίαι in Athens in 1935. As the title indicates, the book is a critical edition of the three Divine Liturgies of Saint John Chrysostom, of Saint Basil the Great, and of the Pre-Sanctified Gifts. In 1940 he began publishing other critical studies in the periodical of the Church of Greece, Θεολογία. These studies were collected into two volumes. Μικρόν Εὐχολόγιον, vol. 1 (Athens 1950) contains the sacraments of marriage, unction, ordination, and baptism. Μικρόν Εὐχολόγιον, vol. 2 (Athens 1955) contains the services for the Great and the Small Agiasmos (the blessing of water), the Consecration of churches, the Orthros, and the Vespers.

²⁵⁸ Lawrence Hoffman, "How Ritual Means: Ritual Circumcision in Rabbinic Culture and Today," in *Studia Liturgica*, 23 (1993) p. 78-97.

²⁵⁹ Ibid. p. 79-80.

²⁶⁰ Ibid. p. 80.

²⁶¹ Among the medieval writers who authored liturgical commentaries and interpreted many of the liturgical actions and rituals in symbolic, allegorical, or representational terms are Theodore of Mopsuestia, Pseudo-Dionysios the Areopagite, St. Maximos the Confessor, St. Germanos of Constantinople, Nicholas and Theodore of Andida, St. Nicholas Cabasilas, St. Sophronios of Jerusalem, and St. Symeon of Thessalonike.

[262] L. Hoffman, "How Ritual Means," p. 80.

[263] Ibid. p. 79.

[264] See A. Calivas, *Theology: The Conscience of the Church* (Brookline, MA 2002) p. 23-24.

[265] Theodore Stylianopoulos, *The New Testament – An Orthodox Perspective* (Brookline, MA 1997) p. 184-185.

[266] L. Hoffman, "How Ritual Means," p. 81.

[267] Ibid. p. 82.

[268] Ronald Grimes, *Ritual Criticism* (Columbia, SC 1990) p. 44. Grimes calls normative meanings 'paradigmatic,' because of their capacity to form values and encourage action.

8
Why Textual Reform Is Necessary

[269] The three services for a mother and her newborn infant on the first, the eighth, and the fortieth day after birth are found in the *Great* and *Small Euchologion*.

[270] A. Schmemann, *Of Water and the Spirit* (Crestwood, NY 2000), p. 138.

[271] Ioannis Fountoulis, *Τό Ἅγιον Βάπτισμα – Ἱστορικό – Τελετουργική Θεώρηση* (Athens 1999) p. 22.

[272] This notion is supported, for example, by Panagiotes Simigiatos, "Ὁ μετά τήν Γέννησιν Καθαρμός τῶν Γυναικῶν" in *Γρηγόριος ὁ Παλαμᾶς*, 46, 526-527 (1962) p. 108 ff. For a less severe and more balanced approach see *Women and Men in the Church* (Syosset, NY 1980), a study prepared by a Sub-Committee of the Ecumenical Task Force of the Orthodox Church in America.

[273] For an explanation of these rites see Alexander Schmemann, *Of Water and the Spirit*, p. 131-147; Konstantinos Papagiannis, "Αἱ εὐχαί ἐπί τῇ γεννήσει παιδίου" in *Γρηγόριος ὁ Παλαμᾶς*, 79, 763, (1996), p. 487-504; and Ioannis Fountoulis, *Τελετουργικά Θέματα* (Athens 2002) p. 170-177. For a discussion on the development of the rites see Panagiotes Trempelas, Μικρόν Εὐχολόγιον, Α (Athens 1950) p. 259-271 and 318-335.

[274] It can be shown that texts of prayers were often edited to improve their clarity and meaning, while others were deleted in favor of newer formulations. See for example, the comments of Louis Bouyer about the development of the Anaphora in the Divine Liturgies of St. John Chrysostom and St. Basil the Great in his book, *Eucharist – Theology and Spirituality of the Eucharistic Prayer* (Notre Dame, IN 1968) p. 286-303.

[275] According to Jewish law, whenever a person came into contact with someone or something considered 'unclean,' he was obliged to undergo ritual purification. The same was true of clothing and utensils. They too had to be ritually washed before they were put to use again. A similar principle in reverse was applied to the priests of the Old Testament. They were obliged to undergo a ritual purification after their service in the sanc-

tuary, because they had touched holy things. The Law required of human beings to be purified ritually whenever their creatureliness, fallenness, and sinfullness met with and was exposed by the manifest power of God.

276 The designated period (Lev. 12:1-5) of uncleanness for women giving birth was uneven. The designated period for giving birth to a male child was forty days. The days were doubled – to eighty – at the birth of female child. A woman was considered especially unclean the first seven days after the birth of a boy and the first fourteen days after the birth of a girl. The ritual offering was made upon the completion of the days of purification. (See also, Lev. 15:19 – 24).

277 Joanne M. Pierce, "Green Women and Blood Pollution: Some Medieval Rituals for the Churching of Women after Childbirth," in Studia Liturgica, 29, 2 (1999) p. 197. In this informative article, Dr. Pierce analyzes the history and meaning of the Churching of Women in the West and provides the reader with a list of studies on the subject.

278 See Walter von Arx, "The Churching of Women after Childbirth: History and Significance," in David Powers and Luis Maldonado, eds., Liturgy and Human Passage, Concilium (New York 1979) p. 64.

279 See the Pedalion, p. 718-720.

280 Timothy of Alexandria, Question vii. Pedalion, p. 893.

281 John the Faster, Canon xvii, Pedalion, p. 941.

282 See the interpretation of the Canon of Dionysios in the Pedalion, p. 718-720.

283 The Canons of Hippolytus, translated by Carol Bebawi, Alcuin/GROW Liturgical Study 2 (Nottingham 1987).

284 The Canons of Hippolytus exerted influence upon the Western, the Coptic, and the Ethiopian liturgical tradition.

285 See J. Pierce, "Green Women and Blood Pollution," p. 194-195.

286 The Apostolic Constitutions, Book VI, xxvii, in The Ante-Nicene Fathers, volume VII, p. 462.

287 The English translation of Pope Gregory's letter is from Leo Sherley-Price, Bede, A History of the English Church and People (Baltimore, MD 1983), p. 76-79 and is cited in Joanne Pierce, "Green Women and Blood Pollution," p. 196.

288 Pope Gregory the Great is called Pope Gregory the 'Dialogos – Διάλογος' by Eastern writers and is listed by that name in the Hagiologion (list of saints) of the Church. For some unknown reason the Divine Liturgy of the Pre-Sanctified Gifts has been – wrongly – attributed to him.

289 John Klentos, "Rebaptizing Converts into the Orthodox Church: Old Perspectives on a New Problem," in Studia Liturgica, 29, 2 (1999) p. 233.

290 Stefano Parenti and Elena Velkovska, L'Eucholgio Barberini gr. 336 (Rome 1995) p. 96. For the history of this prayer, see Panagiotis Trempelas, Μικρόν Εὐχολόγιον, vol. I (Athens 1950) p. 262-266. Ioannis Fountoulis, Τελετουργικά Θέματα, p, 170-173.

291 See for example, P. Trempelas, Μικρόν Εὐχολόγιον, vol. I, p. 260 and 267. It may be that the rites for the 'churching of the mother' may have

developed through the influence of western liturgical practices. However, this thesis needs further investigation.

[292] This is a hymn from the Lite (Λιτή) of the Feast of the Meeting of our Lord. It is attributed to John the Monk and is sung at the Vesper service.

[293] See P. Trempelas, *Μικρόν Εὐχολόγιον,* vol. I, p. 270-271.

[294] Karen B. Westerfield Tucker, "When the Cradle is Empty: Rites Acknowledging Stillbirth, Miscarriage, and Infertility," in *Worship,* 76, 6 (2002) p. 490.

[295] K. Papayiannis, "Αἱ Εὐχαί ἐπί τῇ Γεννήσει Παιδίου" in *Γρηγόριος ὁ Παλαμᾶς,* 79, 763 (1996) p. 587-504; and "Ο μετά τήν Γέννησιν Καθαρμός τῶν Γυναικῶν" in *Γρηγόριος ὁ Παλαμᾶς* 46, 540/541 (1962).

[296] Spencer T. Kezios, ed., *Sacraments and Services – Book Two* (Northridge, CA 1995) p. 4.

[297] Evagoras Constantinides, *Μικρόν Εὐχολόγιον ἤ Αγιασματάριον – The Priest's Service Book* (Merrilville, IN 1997) p. 14. Besides eliminating the penitential language, the editor reworked the original Greek text. In effect, he produced a different prayer with a more positive tone.

[298] Dragon imagery in the Scriptures is based on the belief of the ancients that monstrous and menacing diabolical powers dwelled in the depths of the waters. Dragons are a personification of the evil forces of the primeval chaos and symbolize chaotic powers. Christ defeated these evil powers by his own baptism in the Jordan. By descending into the waters of Jordan he crushed the heads of the dragons of the sea, the menacing powers of death and chaos. See for example, Jean Danielou, *The Bible and the Liturgy* (Notre Dame, IN 1956) p. 42.

[299] Elena Velkovska, "Funeral Rites according to the Byzantine Liturgical Sources," in *Dumbarton Oaks papers,* 55 (2001), p. 21-51. See also Themistoklis Christodoulou, "L' Ufficio funebre nei manoscritti greci dei secolii X-XII," *Ecerpta ex Dissertatione ad Doctoratum* (Rome 1996) and the insightful article of Peter Galadza, "Lost and Displaced Elements of the Byzantine Funeral Rites: Towards a Pastoral Re-appropriation," in *Studia Liturgica,* 33, 1 (2003) p. 62-74.

[300] See Chapter 4 for the history and the contributions of these two monastic communities to the liturgical life of the Orthodox Church.

[301] E. Velkovska, "Funeral Rites," p. 44.

[302] The service is contained in the *Τυπικόν τῆς τοῦ Χριστοῦ Μεγάλης Ἐκκλησίας,* p. 434-439.

[303] See *Εὐχολόγιον τό Μέγα* published by 'Astir' A. & E Papademetriou (Athens 1980) p. 395-420.

[304] P. Galadza, "Lost and Displaced Elements of the Byzantine Funeral Rites," p. 63.

[305] See Ioannis Fountoulis, *Τό Λειτουργικόν Εργον Συμεών τοῦ Θεσσαλονίκης* (Thessalonike 1966). p. 144-149.

9
An Introduction To The Divine Liturgy

* This essay is based on three previous articles. The first appeared in *The Greek Orthodox Theological Review*, 28, 3 (1983) under the title, "Reflections on the Divine Liturgy," p. 213-219. The second appeared as an introduction to a new translation of the Divine Liturgy of St. John Chrysostom by members of the Faculty of Holy Cross published by Holy Cross Orthodox Press, *The Divine Liturgy of St. John Chrysostom* (Brookline, MA 1985) p. xiii-xxviii. The third, "The Eucharist: The Sacrament of the Economy of Salvation," appeared in Ben F. Meyer, ed., *One Loaf, One Cup* (Macon, GA 1993) p. 117-138.

[306] Justin the Martyr, *The First Apology*, 65-66.

[307] Louis Bouyer, *Eucharist – Theology and Spirituality of the Eucharistic Prayer* (Notre Dame 1968) p. 15.

[308] This formula used at the distribution of Holy Communion is as follows: "The servant of God (N) receives the Body and Blood of Christ for the forgiveness of sins and life eternal."

[309] After receiving Holy Communion in the sanctuary, the clergy exhibit the Holy Gifts and call the people to Holy Communion with the words, "Approach with the fear of God, with faith, and with love."

[310] St. Symeon of Thessalonike, *Dialogos*, 94, *Patrologia Graeca (PG)* 155, 285; see also his *Apokriseis*, PG 155, 877.

[311] The clergy use this formula as they exchange the Kiss of Peace. The one says, "Christ is in our midst," and the other responds, "He is and shall ever be."

[312] St. Irenaeus, *Against Heresies*, 4:18. 5.

[313] St. Nicholas Cabasilas, *A Commentary on the Divine Liturgy*, Chapter 4:36

[314] John Meyendorff, *Byzantine Theology* (New York 1979) p. 209.

[315] See Bishop Kallistos Ware, "'Ενορία καί Εὐχαριστία," in 'Ενορία – Πρός Μία Νέα 'Ανακάλυψη της (Athens n.d.) p. 125-134.

[316] St. Nicholas Cabasilas, *The Life in Christ*, 4:2

[317] St. Theodore the Studite, *Antirrheticos*, 2.

[318] St. Irenaeus, *Against Heresies*, 4. 18:5.

[318a] "Acts of St. Saturninus and Companions," PL 8.66f, cited in M. H. Shepherd, Jr., *The Worship of the Church* (New York, 1963), p. 3-4.

[319] John D. Zizioulas, *Being as Communion* (Crestwood, NY 1985) p. 21.

[320] St. Nicholas Cabasilas, *The Life in Christ*, The Fourth Book, 1, 3.

[321] St. Gregory of Nyssa, *The Great Catechism*, 37.

[322] St. Ignatios of Antioch, *Letter to the Ephesians*, 20.

[323] St. Nicholas Cabasilas, *A Commentary on the Divine Liturgy*, 44.

[324] Alexander Schmemann, *Introduction to Liturgical Theology* (Crestwood, NY 1996) p. 72.

[325] Ibid.

[326] St. Gregory Palamas, *Homily 56*, cited in John Meyendorff, *A Study of Gregory Palamas* (Crestwood, NY 1964) p. 183.

[327] St. Gregory of Nyssa, *The Great Catechism*, 37.

[328] St. Nicholas Cabasilas, *A Commentary on the Divine Liturgy*, 1:3. See also St. Gregory of Nyssa, *The Great Catechism*, 37.

[329] Clement of Alexandria, *Paedagogos*, 1. 6.

[330] St. Nicholas Cabasilas, *A Commentary on the Divine Liturgy*, 49.

[331] Nicholas of Methone, *Refutation of the Writings of Soterichos*, cited by Bishop Kallistos Ware, "Meaning of the Divine Liturgy for the Byzantine Worshipper," in *Church and People in Byzantium* (Birmingham, GB 1990) p.16.

[332] St. Nicholas Cabasilas, *The Life in Christ*, The Third Book, 2, 3.

[333] St. Romanos the Melodist, *Kontakion On Baptism – Εἰς τούς Νεοφωτίστους, Strophe 3, 4.

[334] Melito of Sardis, *Homily on Pascha*, 66, 70, 71, 102, 103.

[335] St. Nicholas Cabasilas, *A Commentary on the Divine Liturgy*, 4.

[336] Archimandrite Vasileios, *Hymn of Entry* (Crestwood, NY 1984) p. 68.

[337] St. Nicholas Cabasilas, *A Commentary on the Divine Liturgy*, 47.

[338] St. Cyril of Alexandria, *Commentary on the Gospel of John*, 10:2.

[339] St. Cyril of Jerusalem, *Mystagogical Catechesis*, 4:6

[340] St. Ignatios, *Letter to the Smyrnaens*, 7:1.

[341] St. Nicholas Cabasilas, *The Life in Christ*, The Fourth Book, 8.

[342] St. John of Damascus, *An Exact Exposition of the Orthodox Faith*, chapter 13.

[343] Vladimir Lossky, *The Mystical Theology of the Eastern Church* (London 1957) p. 182.

[344] Ibid. p. 183.

[345] St. Maximos the Confessor, *Mystagogia*, chapter 1.

[346] J. D. Zizioulas, *Being as Communion*, p. 56.

[347] Ibid., p. 60, 59.

[348] Ibid. p. 58n.

[349] C. Andronikof, "Assembly and Body of Christ: Identity or Distinction," in *Roles of the Liturgical Assembly*, translated by M. J. O'Connell (Denver 1981) p. 17.

10
Some Textual Problems in the Divine Liturgy

[350] The Diataxeis (Διατάξεις) were manuals of rubrics and ceremonials describing how various rituals were to be performed. These manuals, now defunct, began to appear in the tenth century. The purpose of the Diataxeis was to help regulate the liturgical practices. Of the many Diataxeis that made their appearance between the 12 – 14th centuries, none proved to be more influential than the two written by Philotheos Kokkinos, twice Patriarch of Constantinople (1353-1355 and 1364-1376). The rubrics of

Philotheos were eventually incorporated into the texts of the divine services and continue – for the most part – to retain their vitality to this day. The *Diataxis* of Philotheos Kokkinos and another anonymous *Diataxis* of the 12-13th century (Κῶδιξ Ἐθνικῆς Βιβλιοθήκης Η΄. – ἀρ. 662) have been published by Panayiotis Trempelas, *Αἱ Τρεῖς Λειτορυγίαι* (Athens 1935) p. 1-16.

351See Panayiotis Trempelas, *Αἱ Τρεῖς Λειτορυγίαι*, p. 81. See also, Ioannis Fountoulis, *Κείμενα Λειτουργικῆς (12) – Βυζαντιναί Θ. Λειτουργίαι Βασιλείου τοῦ Μεγάλου καὶ Ἰωάννου τοῦ Χρυσοστόμου* (Thessalonike 1978) p. 32.

352 Panayiotis Trempelas, *Αἱ Τρεῖς Λειτορυγίαι*, p. 9.

353 The *Apostolic Constitutions*, Book 8:12, a fourth century Church Order, contains the following simple description of the Entrance of the Gifts and the altar: "Let us stand upright before the Lord with fear and trembling, to offer... When this is done, let the deacons bring the gifts to the bishop at the altar; and let the presbyters stand on his right hand and on his left. But let two of the deacons, one on each side of the altar, hold a fan... and let them silently drive away the small animals that fly about, that they may not come near the cups."

354 Patriarch Eutychios of Constantinople (+ca. 582) is the first to make mention of a Great Entrance chant, which he informs us was a Psalm. For the origins, history, shape, and the manner by which the Great Entrance chant was executed see Robert F. Taft, *The Great Entrance (Orientalia Christiana Analecta – 200 –* Rome 1978) p. 53 – 118; and for the evolution of the Great Entrance procession, p. 178 – 219.

355 It appears that Psalm 50 (51) and Psalm 117 (118) were also used as Great Entrance chants. It may well be that the Cherubic hymn and parts of the devotional prayer of the celebrant at the Cherubic hymn were inspired by Psalm 23 (24), the initial entrance hymn.

356 One could point to other examples in the development of liturgy to show that ecclesiastical compositions – hymns – gradually suppressed the scriptural elements of the liturgy, especially in parochial worship. The odes in the Orthros and the antiphons of the Divine Liturgy are but two examples.

357 G. Cedrenos, *Σύνοψις Ἱστοριῶν*, PG 121, 748. For more on the Cherubic hymn, in addition to R. Taft, *The Great Entrance*, see also, Panayiotes Trempelas, *Αἱ Τρεῖς Λειτορυγίαι*, p. 70 – 71. Cedrenos also mentions that under the same edict the hymn, "*Τοῦ Δείπνου σου τοῦ Μυστικοῦ – At your Mystical Supper*," was introduced into the Divine Liturgy for Great and Holy Thursday as the Entrance and Communion hymn. The Byzantine liturgy has two additional Great Entrance hymns: the *Νῦν αἱ Δυνάμεις – Now the Powers of heaven*," introduced into the Liturgy of the Pre-Sanctified Gifts in the year 615, according to the *Paschalion Chronikon*, PG 92, 989; and the *Σιγησάτω πᾶσα σάρξ βροτεία – Let all mortal flesh be silent*," introduced around the 11-12th century into the Liturgy of the Paschal Vigil from the liturgy of Jerusalem. Its use at the Paschal Vigil, however, was

not solidified until much later. The monastic Typikon of St. Savas, printed in 1545, for example, lists it as an alternate hymn to the Cherubikon.

[358] R. Taft, *The Great Entrance*, p. 72-73.

[359] Robert Taft, *The Great Entrance*, p. 229.

[360] Nicholas Cabasilas, *A Commentary on the Divine Liturgy* (24), translated by J.M. Hussey and P. A. McNulty (London 1960) p. 65-66; and in *PG* 150, 420.

[361] The commemorations the clergy extend to one another at the Great Entrance – 'May the Lord God remember your priesthood (archpriesthood, diaconate) in his kingdom' – are also founded on this practice.

[362] P. Trempelas, Αἱ Τρεῖς Λειτορυγίαι, p. 9.

[363] See Ioannis Fountoulis, Ἀπαντήσεις εἰς Λειτουργικάς Ἀπορίας, Γ (Thessalonike 1976) p. 101-102.

[364] See for example, the editions of the Divine Liturgy of the Apostolike Diakonia of the Church of Greece and the Service Books of the Antiochian Archdiocese of America.

[365] P. Trempelas, Αἱ Τρεῖς Λειτορυγίαι, p. 82.

[366] See Ioannis Fountoulis, Ἀπαντήσεις εἰς Λειτουργικάς Ἀπορίας, Γ (Thessalonike 1976) p. 205-208. The Fervent Litany, which precedes the Great Entrance but is now suppressed in common Greek usage, allows for general and particular commemorations of the living and the dead. We must remember that the Anaphora is comprised, in part, of the diptychs, a series of commemorations of the living and the dead. And, of course, commemorations of the living and the dead are made at the Prothesis when the Gifts are being prepared at the service of the Proskomide.

[367] See P. Trempelas, Αἱ Τρεῖς Λειτορυγίαι, p. 78. Ioannis Fountoulis, Ἀπαντήσεις εἰς Λειτουργικάς Ἀπορίας, Β (Thessalonike 1975) p. 224-227.

[368] See Robert Taft, *The Great Entrance*, p. 65. Hugh Wybrew, *The Orthodox Liturgy*, 85-86.

[369] I believe that this interpretation of the Cherubic hymn is especially edifying, unlike the fanciful allegorical ones that one finds in some explanations of the Divine Liturgy. An example of such an allegorical interpretation of the Cherubikon can be found in C. Kucharek, *The Byzantine-Slav Liturgy of St. John Chrysostom* (Allendale, NJ 1971) p. 482. According to this interpretation, the hymn is directly linked to the procession of the gifts. In the unconsecrated gifts that are being carried by the deacons and priests, the worshipper is supposed to see Christ, the King of all, being carried aloft, escorted invisibly (ἀοράτως δορυφορούμενον) by the angelic hosts and welcomed reverently by the assembled faithful with the joyful song of the angels, 'Alleluia.' This allegorical or representational interpretation is based on the custom of the ancients who carried triumphant kings in procession, borne aloft on the shields of spear-bearing soldiers. The word δορυφορούμενος, which means 'one who is being escorted as by spear-bearing guards,' appears to have prompted the interpretation. The word is derived from the verb δορυφορέω, which means 'to attend as a bodyguard or to keep guard over.'

³⁷⁰ Compare the words of St. Nicholas Cabasilas, *Commentary on the Divine Liturgy* (26) p. 68. He writes, "The priest raises our thoughts saying: 'Let us lift up our hearts' – let us be heavenly-minded, not earthly-minded. The faithful give their consent and say that their hearts are where our treasure is – there where Christ is, who sits on the right hand of the Father. 'We have lifted them up to the Lord." St. Cyril of Jerusalem emphasizes the same idea in his interpretation of the dialogue – "Let us lift our hearts." He writes, "After this the priest cries aloud, 'Lift up your hearts.' For truly ought we in that most awful hour to have our heart on high with God, and not below, thinking of earthly things. The priest then in effect bids all in that hour to abandon all worldly thoughts, or household cares, and to have their heart in heaven with the merciful God. Then you answer, 'We lift them up unto the Lord,' assenting to him, by your avowal. (*Mystagogical Catecheses*, 5:4).

³⁷¹ St. Cyril of Jerusalem, *Mystagogical Catecheses*, 5:4.

³⁷² Cf. Ps. 62 (63):4 and Ps. 140 (141):2.

³⁷³ R. Taft, *The Great Entrance*, p. 64.

³⁷⁴ In the *Protheoria*, 18, (PG 140, 441), Nicholas of Andida writes, "The Cherubic hymn which is sung exhorts everyone to be more attentive from now until the end of the service, rejecting all lower worldly care as befits those that are to receive the Great King in communion." Cited in Robert Taft, *The Great Entrance*, p. 65.

³⁷⁵ See for example, the Διάταξις τῆς Θείας Ἱερουργίας (a 12-13ᵗʰ century codex) "'Εν δέ τῇ μεγάλῃ εἰσόδῳ αἴρει ὁ διάκονος τόν θυμιατὸν καὶ εὐλογήσαντος αὐτόν τοῦ ἱερέως θυμιᾷ ἔμπροσθεν τῆς ἁγίας τραπέζης μόνον. – At the Great Entrance the deacon lifts the thurible and having received the blessing of the priest he censes in front of the Table only." The Διάταξις τῆς Θείας Λειτουργίας of Philotheos Kokkinos, Patriarch of Constantinople (14ᵗʰ century) notes: "Τοῦ δέ χερουβικοῦ ψαλλομένου εἰσέρχεται ὁ διάκονος ἐν τῷ ἁγίῳ βήματι. Καί λαβών τόν θυμιατὸν μετά τοῦ θυμιάματος καί προσελθών τῷ ἱερεῖ καί λαβὼν συνήθως τήν ἐπί τῷ θυμιάματι εὐλογίαν θυμιᾷ τήν τε ἁγίαν τράπεζαν σταυρωειδῶς κύκλωθεν, τὸ ἱερατεῖον ὅλον καί τὸν ἱερέα. Καί μετά τοῦτο ἵστατο ἐξ ἀριστερῶν αὐτοῦ μετά πάσης εὐλαβείας προσμένων τήν συμπλήρωσιν τῆς εὐχῆς. – While the Cherubic hymn is being sung, the deacon enters into the holy bema (sanctuary). And taking the thurible with the incense he comes to the priest and receives the customary blessing over the incense. He circles the holy Table and censes it cross-wise; and censes all the clergy and the priest. After which he stands reverently to the left [of the priest] and awaits the completion of the prayer." Cited in Trempelas, Αἱ Τρεῖς Λειτουργίαι, p. 9. Trempelas cites additional sources related to the incensation on p. 78 of the same volume. See also, R. Taft, *The Great Entrance*, p. 151-154; and I. Fountoulis, Ἀπαντήσεις εἰς Λειτουργικάς Ἀπορίας, Δ, p. 271-273. According to the sources cited in Trempelas, the censing by the priest first appears in a manuscript of the sixteenth century and in three others of the seventeenth century.

³⁷⁶ According to some of the medieval sources cited by Trempelas and Taft (in the previous note), which describe the celebration of the Divine Liturgy by the Patriarch of Constantinople, the task of censing was assigned to the canstrensios – κανστρήνσιος, a church dignitary, who often times was a deacon. The canstrensios performed other duties as well, one of which was to maintain the patriarchal vestments and to assist the patriarch at vesting. For a description of the duties and prerogatives of this and other patriarchal offices (ὀφφίκια) see (Bishop) Iakovos Pililis, *Τίτλοι Ὀφφίκια καὶ Ἀξιώματα ἐν τῇ Βυζαντινῇ Αὐτοκρατορίᾳ καὶ τῇ Χριστιανικῇ Ὀρθοδόξῳ Ἐκκλησίᾳ* (Athens 1985).

³⁷⁷ See P. Trempelas, *Αἱ Τρεῖς Λειτουργίαι*, p. 78.

³⁷⁸ Ibid. p. 9.

³⁷⁹ For more on the Prayer of the Cherubikon see R. Taft, *The Great Entrance*, 119-148. P. Trempelas, *Αἱ Τρεῖς Λειτουργίαι*, 71-76. Ioannis Fountoulis, *Ἀπαντήσεις εἰς Λειτουργικάς Ἀπορίας*, Δ (Thessalonike 1982) p.243-247.

³⁸⁰ For a detailed account of the response see Robert Taft, "Textual Problems in the Diaconal Admonition before the Anaphora in the Byzantine Tradition," in *Orientalia Christiana Periodica* 49 (1983) p. 340-365. See also Panayiotis Trempelas, *Αἱ Τρεῖς Λειτουργίαι*, p. 95 – 96; and Ioannis Fountoulis, "Ἑρμηνεία ἑπτὰ δυσκόλων σημείων τοῦ κειμένου τῆς Θείας Λειτουργίας ἀπό τόν Νικόλαο Καβάσιλα" *Πρακτικά Θεολογικοῦ Συνεδρίου εἰς Τιμὴν καὶ Μνήμην τοῦ Νικολάου Καβάσιλα* (Thessalonike 1984) p.161-163. For a discussion on the various diaconal admonitions in the Divine Liturgy see, Panagiotes Skaltses, *Τά Διακονικά Παραγγέλματα Καὶ ἡ Στάση τῶν Πιστῶν στὴ Θεία Λειτουργία* (Thessalonike 1999).

³⁸¹ R. Taft, "Textual Problems in the Diaconal Admonition," p. 353.

³⁸² A critical edition of the manuscript was published by Stefano Parenti and Elena Velkovska, *L' Eucologio Barberini gr. 336* (Rome 1995)

³⁸³ Ibid. p. 31.

³⁸⁴ Cited by C. Kucharek, *The Byzantine-Slav Liturgy*, p. 564.

³⁸⁵ Professor Paul Meyendorff has published the Greek text of St. Germanos' work together with an English translation, an introduction and a commentary under the title, *St. Germanus of Constantinople on the Divine Liturgy* (Crestwood, NY 1984). The passage in St. Germanos reads as follows, "The people proclaim thanks for the resurrection of Christ: A mercy of peace, a sacrifice of praise. Ὁ λαός βοᾷ τήν τῆς ἀναστάσεως τοῦ Χριστοῦ χάριν, Ἔλεον εἰρήνης, θυσίαν αἰνέσεως," p. 90-91.

³⁸⁶ R. Taft concludes that the accusative was favored in the Constantinopolitan-type sources, while the nominative was an Italo-Greek and Oriental peculiarity. See his article, "Textual Problems in the Diaconal Admonition," p. 353-354.

³⁸⁷ Another, but unfortunate, form of the response, "ἔλαιον (which means olive oil) εἰρήνης," can be found in some isolated instances.

³⁸⁸ R. Taft, "Textual Problems in the Diaconal Admonition," p. 352.

³⁸⁹ Ibid. p. 353. See also I. Fountoulis, "Ἑρμηνεία ἑπτά δυσκόλων

σημείων," p. 162. P. Trempelas, Αἱ Τρεῖς Λειτουργίαι, p. 96.

390 See C. Kucharek, *The Byzantine-Slav Liturgy*, p. 564-565 and R. Taft, "Textual Problems in the Diaconal Admonition," p. 356.

391 In the liturgical tradition of the Orthodox Church the Kiss of Love or Peace is exchanged before the Creed and the Anaphora. The rite and its position in the Divine Liturgy is largely determined by the Gospel passage that Cabasilas is making reference to here, Mt 5:23.

392 Mt. 9:13.

393 Nicholas Cabasilas, *A Commentary on the Divine Liturgy*, chapter 26.

394 R. Taft, "Textual Problems in the Diaconal Admonition," p. 364.

395 See S. Parenti and E. Velkovska, *L' Eucologio Barberini gr. 336*, p. 34. See also P. Trempelas, Αἱ Τρεῖς Λειτουργίαι, p. 110. I. Fountoulis, "Ἑρμηνεία ἑπτα δυσκόλων σημείων," p. 163. Pavlos Koumarianos, "Σύμβολο καὶ Πραγματικότητα στή Θεία Λειτουργία," in Σύναξη, vol. 71 (July-September 1999) p. 35.

396 Richard D. McCall, "The Shape of the Eucharistic Prayer: An Essay on the Unfolding of an Action," in *Worship*, 75, 4 (2001) p. 321 – 333.

397 The only exception to this rule is found in the Anaphora of the Divine Liturgy attributed to St. Gregory the Theologian, in which the Eucharistic Prayer is addressed to the Son rather than to the Father.

398 Paul Meyendorff, "The Liturgical Path of Orthodoxy in America," *SVTQ*, 40, 1&2 (1996) p. 56-57.

399 The text is from the Anaphora of the Divine Liturgy of St. John Chrysostom. The Anaphora concludes with a series of petitions, commemorations, and remembrances.

400 Nicholas Cabasilas, *Commentary on the Divine Liturgy*, 49.

401 For more on the Eucharist as sacrifice and communion see A. Calivas, "The Eucharist: The Sacrament of the Economy of Salvation," in Ben. F. Meyer, ed., *One Cup, One Loaf – Ecumenical Studies of I Cor 11 and Other Eucharistic Texts* (Macon, Georgia 1993) p. 132 – 138.

402 The idea of the ἀντιπροσφορά mentioned by Cabasilas is further developed by Archimandrite Vasileios, *Hymn of Entry* (Crestwood, NY 1984).

403 Anaphora of the Divine Liturgy of St. John Chrysostom. The ἀντιπροσφορά – the sacrifice in return has a multiplicity of forms. It includes commitment to the Gospel, loyalty to the Orthodox faith, fasting, constant prayer, works of charity, and the struggle against the passions (spiritual ascesis). However, the preeminent expression and form of the ἀντιπροσφορά is found in the Eucharist.

404 Hugh Wybrew, *The Orthodox Liturgy – The Development of the Eucharistic Liturgy in the Byzantine Rite* (Crestwood, NY1990) p. 61.

405 See Timothy (Kallistos) Ware, *The Orthodox Church* (London 1997) p. 285-287. Alexander Schmemann, *The Eucharist* (Crestwood, NY 1988) p. 208-211.

406 Alexander Schmemann, *For the Life of the World – Sacraments and Orthodoxy* (Crestwood, NY 1973) p. 38.

[407] St. Irenaenus of Lyons, *Against Heresies,*V, 2, 2 and IV, 18, 5.

[408] The Church inherited from the Old Testament the custom of assenting to prayer by responding 'Amen' (Deut. 27:14-26; 1Chron. 16:7-36; Neh. 5:13 and 8:6).

[409] This subject has been treated exhaustively by G. N. Filias, Ο Τρόπος ᾽Αναγνώσεως τῶν Εὐχῶν στή Λατρεία τῆς᾽ Ορθοδόξου᾽Εκκλησίας (Athens 1997).

[410] Justinian, *Novella* 137 in R. Schoell and G. Kroll, *Corpus Juris Civilis*, III (Berlin 1899) p. 699. Cited by G. Filias, Ο Τρόπος᾽Αναγνώσεως τῶν Εὐχῶν, p. 54.

[411] The Ecumenical Patriarchate, for example, has recommended and has urged its clergy to read the prayers of the Divine Liturgy and especially the Anaphora aloud.

[412] Panagiotis Trempelas, Αἱ Τρεῖς Λειτουργίαι, p. 109-110.

[413] Ibid. p. 11. "Καί ὅταν ἐκφωνῇ τό Τὰ σά ἐκ τῶν σῶν, ὡσαύτως δεικνεί ουσι ἀμφότεροι, ὁ τὲ ἱερεύς καὶ ὁ διάκονος, τὰ ἅγια. – And when he pronounces the words 'Your own of your own,' both the priest and the deacon, together in like manner point to the holy [gifts]."

[414] A. Schmemann, *For the Life of the World*, p. 37.

[415] See, Pavlos Koumarianos, "Πρόθεση, Προσκομιδὴ, Προσφορὰ" in Θεολογία, vol. 70, Β–Γ (1999) p.508-512.

[416] St. Nicholas Cabasilas, *A Commentary on the Divine Liturgy*, 49

[417] St. Gregory of Nyssa, *Catechetical Oration*, 37.

[418] "But who am I and who are my people, that we should have the means to contribute so freely? For all things are from you, and of your own have we given you – ... ὅτι σὰ τὰ πάντα καὶ ἐκ τῶν σῶν δέδωκαμέν σοι."

[419] Casimir Kucharek, *The Byzantine-Slav Liturgy of St. John Chrysostom* (Allendale, NJ 1971) p. 611.

[420] Panayiotes Trempelas, ᾽Απο τὴν᾽ Ορθόδοξον Λατρείαν Μας (Athens 1970) p. 286-288.

[421] A. Schmemann, *The Eucharist*, p. 192. In this and other texts, Father Schmemann uses this phrase repeatedly. It appears from his writings on the Eucharist that the phrase "on behalf of all and for all" is given several interpretations. It could mean "on behalf of the whole body (the Church) and for the whole body." Or, it could mean "for all His benefits and on behalf of all creation." Or, "on behalf of all creation and for all things."

[422] SCOBA appointed a Liturgical Commission in 1990 to undertake the task of producing a pan-Orthodox translation in English of the Divine Liturgy of St. John Chrysostom. The Commission completed its task in 1992 and submitted its work to the secretariat of SCOBA to advance the project Unfortunately, due to several unforeseen circumstances, SCOBA has yet to act on the translation in an official way. However, copies of the translation with limited rubrics (according to Greek, Slavonic, and Arabic usage) have been circulated, though not widely.

[423] St. Nicholas Cabasilas, *A Commentary on the Divine Liturgy*, 49.

[424] The Commission considered several versions, including the follow-

ing: "Always and everywhere," (New Skete Monastery). "In all and for all," (Holy Cross Faculty; the Archdiocese of Thyateira and Great Britain; and St. John the Baptist Monastery, Essex, England). "In behalf of all and for all," (Orthodox Church in America; Antiochian Archdiocese – Service Book and Liturgikon; and the Romanian Episcopate). Two additional translations were also proposed: "According to all (you have commanded) and for all (you have done)," and "Always and for all." More recently (1995), the Archdiocese of Thyateira and Great Britain published a new translation, in which the phrase is rendered, "In all things and for all things."

⁴²⁵ Διδαχή τῶν Δώδεκα Ἀποστόλων, Βιβλιοθήκη Ἑλλήνων Πατέρων, 2, 220 and Didache – The Teaching of the Twelve Apostles.

⁴²⁶ Here, Danielou is referring to Christ's Crucifixion (Heb 7:27, "For this he did once for all when he offered himself up) and to his unique role as Mediator and eternal intercessor (Heb. 7:24, 25; 8:1 – 6; 9:24). Unlike the sacrifices of the Old Testament that were localized in one place – the Temple of Jerusalem – the Eucharist, the sacrifice of the New Covenant, is offered in all places.

⁴²⁷ Jean Danielou, The Bible and the Liturgy (Notre Dame 1956) p. 138.

⁴²⁸ Ibid., p. 149.

⁴²⁹ J. Zizioulas, Being as Communion, p. 133.

⁴³⁰ Pavlos Koumarianos, "Πρόθεση, Προσκομιδή, Προσφορά," p. 510, note 63.

⁴³¹ See Paul Meyendorff, "The Liturgical Path of Orthodoxy in America," p. 10-11.

⁴³² Ibid.

⁴³³ To make the text comply with this meaning, some translators have had to tinker with the meaning of the word ἐξομάλισον (to make smooth or even or to equalize). Here is one example of such a translation that introduces a new verb meaning. "...Therefore, O Lord, distribute (ἐξομάλισον) to all of us for our own good and according to each one's need the offerings set forth here (τὰ προκείμενα): voyage with those sailing upon the sea, journey with those traveling on land, and cure the sick, O Physician of souls and bodies." C. Kuchareck, The Byzantine-Slav Liturgy of St. John Chrysostom (Allendale, NJ 1971) p. 658.

⁴³⁴ See I. Fountoulis, Ἀπαντήσεις εἰς Λειτουργικὰς Ἀπορίας, Δ. (Thessalonike 1982) p. 109-112.

⁴³⁵ See R. Taft, "The Inclination Prayer Before Communion in the Byzantine Liturgy of St. John Chrysostom: A Study in Comparative Liturgy," in Ecclesia Orans, 3 (1986) p. 29-60 and more recently the fifth volume of his A History of the Liturgy of St. John Chrysostom – The Precommunion Rites (Orientalia Christian Analecta – Rome 2000) p. 166.

⁴³⁶ In his Precommunion Rites (p. 166-169), Taft lists several such revisions of the troublesome phrase, "τὰ προκείμενα εἰς ἀγαθὸν ἐξομάλισον," and notes that the word ἐξομάλισον is often stretched out to mean "to give out" or "to distribute." Another example is provided by Panagiotes Trempelas. In his book, Ἀπὸ τὴν Ὀρθόδοξον Λατρείαν Μας (Athens 1970) p. 368, he gives an interesting but improbable interpretation of the

troublesome passage. "The celebrant supplicates (God) in the name of all, that the sacrifice of the holy Eucharist present upon the altar, (ἵνα ἡ ἐν τῷ θυσιαστηρίῳ προκειμένη θυσία τῆς θείας Εὐχαριστίας ἀποβῇ εὐεργετική καὶ σωτήριος) may be beneficial and salutary for all, according to the special need of each."

[437] This is a more literal translation made by the SCOBA Liturgical Commission (1992). It has yet to be published, but may be available through the Secretariat of SCOBA at the Greek Orthodox Archdiocese, New York, NY. The translation by faculty members of the Holy Cross Greek Orthodox School of Theology reads differently and is perhaps more poetic. It gives essentially the same meaning. "…Therefore, Master guide the course of our life for our benefit according to the need of each of us. Sail with those who sail; travel with those who travel; and heal the sick, Physician of our souls and bodies." *The Divine Liturgy of St. John Chrysostom* (Brookline, MA 1985) p. 28.

[438] The Liturgy of St. John Chrysostom in its final redaction contains other prayers that are 'borrowed' from the Liturgy of St. Basil, as for example, the Prayer of the Trisagion Hymn.

[439] R. Taft, *A History of the Liturgy of St. John Chrysostom – The Precommunion Ritres*, p. 157-164.

[440] Ibid. p. 177 and 180.

[441] Ibid. p. 172-173.

[442] Ibid. p. 196.

[443] Ibid. p. 183-184. The departure of non-communicants before the dismissal may also explain the reason for the duplication of the 'Dismissal Litany,' which is now said after the Great Entrance and repeated again – in the received text – after the Anaphora and before Holy Communion. In no other instance do we encounter the repetition of a whole litany.

11
The Penthekte Synod

[*] An edited version of an article originally published in *The Greek Orthodox Theological Review*, 40, 1&2 (1995) p. 125-147, under the same title. The paper was read at a Conference marking the 1300th anniversary of the Penthekte Synod sponsored by the faculty of the Holy Cross Greek Orthodox School of Theology on March 16 and 17, 1992.

[444] Saint Athanasios, *Epistle to Serapion*, 1. 28, PG 26.539.

[445] See (Metropolitan) John Zizioulas, "Χριστολογία καὶ ὕπαρξη" *in* Σύναξη, 2 (1982) pp 9-20.

[446] Although they are not directly related to liturgical matters, one may list several other canons under the rubric 'liturgical.' Among these are canons that speak to: the deportment (2, 3, 4, 1 3, 22, 23), dress (27), and appearance (96) of clergy; the teaching and preaching ministry of clerics (19); false lists of martyrs (63); and respect for sacred scrolls (68).

[447] "This has also come to our knowledge, that in Africa and Libya, and other places, the most God-beloved bishops there do not cease to live with their wives, even after their consecration, thereby giving offense and scandal to the people. Now since it is our concern that all things tend to the benefit of the flock committed to us, it has seemed good that henceforth such a thing shall by no means take place. And we say this, not with the intention of abolishing or overthrowing the things ordained by the Apostles, but as caring for the advancement to better things and the well-being of the people, and not casting any reproach upon the state of affairs of the clergy... If anyone should be shown to be doing such a thing let him be deposed." The English translation of the texts of the canons is from an unpublished manuscript of the canons of the Ecumenical Synods by Dr. John Cavarnos, made available to me by my colleague Dr. Lewis Patsavos, Professor of Canon Law at Holy Cross Greek Orthodox School of Theology.

[448]"We decree that the figure in human form of the Lamb who takes away the sin of the world, Christ our God, be from this time on exhibited in icons, instead of the ancient lamb. By means of it we understand the depths of the humiliation of the Logos of God, and bring back to memory his sojourn in the flesh, as well as his passion and his salvation-giving death, and the redemption that was brought about thereby for the world."

[449] "Do not by any means administer baptism in an oratory which is within a house; but let those who are about to be held worthy of the unde-filed illumination go to the main church, and there let them enjoy this gift."

[450] "...Since, some on the day after the holy Nativity of Christ our God are seen cooking semilan and distributing it to one another, on pretext of honoring forsooth the puerperia of the blameless Virgin Maternity, we decree that nothing of this sort be done by the faithful. For this is not honor for the Virgin, who above mind and speech bore the incomprehensible Logos in the flesh, if we define and describe, from common and ordinary things, her ineffable childbirth."

"The divine Scripture commanded us to abstain from blood, from things strangled, and from fornication. Those who therefore on account of a gluttonous stomach prepare by any art for food the blood of any animal whatever, and thus eat it, we punish fitly."

[451] "In as much as we have learned that in some regions in the Trisagion hymn after "Holy and immortal" there is added the "who was crucified for us, have mercy upon us," and this, as being alien to piety, was cast out of the hymn by the ancient and holy fathers, as were also the heretics who unlawfully introduced these new words, we likewise, confining the things which were in the past piously legislated by our holy fathers, anathematize those who after the present decree still accept in the churches the addition of this or any other phrase to the Trisagion hymn."

[452] "We order that the figures of the cross, which some have made on the floor; be by all means removed, so that the trophy of the victory won for

us may not be desecrated by the trampling of those who walk over it."

[453] "No one at all is permitted to corrupt or cut to pieces books of the Old or New Testament or of our holy and approved preachers and teachers, or to give them up to the book traders or to deliver them to any such persons for destruction; unless, of course, a book is made useless, either by bookworms, or water, or in some other way... Likewise also he who purchases such books, unless he keeps them himself for his own benefit, or gives them to another as a good service and for preservation."

[454] "Let no one belonging to the lay order offer to himself the divine mysteries if a bishop, presbyter, or deacon be present. But he who shall dare such a thing, as acting contrary to what has been declared, let him be excommunicated for one week, and be instructed thereby not to consider himself more highly than he ought to."

[455] "No one, whether bishop, presbyter, or deacon, shall, when administering the immaculate communion, collect fees of any kind from the communicant for the sake of this communion. For grace is not sold, nor do we give for money the sanctification of the Spirit; but it is to be communicated in a guideless manner to those who are worthy of the gift."

[456] "Let no one give the Eucharist to the bodies of the dead; for it is written (Mt 26.26): "Take and eat." But the bodies of the dead can neither take nor eat."

[457] "Certain people eat eggs and cheese on the Saturdays and Sundays of the holy Lent. It, therefore, seems good that the Church of God, which is in all the world should follow the order and keep the first perfect, and just as they abstain from everything that is killed, so also indeed should they from eggs and cheese, which are the fruits and products of the animals we abstain from... The faithful spending the days of the salutary Passion in fasting, prayer, and contrition of heart ought to fast till the midnight of the Great Sabbath; since the divine Evangelists Matthew and Luke have shown how late at night it was [i.e., the time of the resurrection], the former using the words "in the end of the Sabbath" (Mt 28.1: ὀψὲ δὲ σαββάτων) and the latter the words "very early in the morning" (Lk 24.1: ὄρθρου βαθέως)."

[458] "On all the days of the holy fast of Lent, save on Saturday, Sunday, and the holy day of Annunciation, let the sacred Liturgy of the Pre-Sanctified be performed."

[459] "Since it has come to our knowledge that in the land of the Armenians they bring forth only wine on the holy table, and that those who perform the bloodless sacrifice do not mix water with it... In order that they may not be held in ignorance henceforth we unveil the orthodox thought... The holy fathers who assembled at Carthage gave the following verbal reminder: 'That in the holy mysteries nothing more than the body and blood of the Lord should be offered, just as the Lord himself determined, that is bread and wine mixed with water.'"

[460] "We have received from our God-bearing fathers the canon that we are not to kneel on Sundays..."

⁴⁶¹ "From the holy day or the resurrection of Christ our God until the next Sunday, the whole week, in the holy churches the faithful should have leisure, rejoicing in Christ with psalms and hymns and spiritual songs; and celebrating, and applying themselves to the reading of the divine Scriptures, and delighting in the holy mysteries. For in this way shall we be lifted up with Christ and be exalted with him. Therefore on the above days let there be no horse races at all or any other public spectacle."

⁴⁶² "If any bishop, presbyter, or deacon, or any of those who are reckoned in the clergy, or any layman, has no serious necessity or difficult business so as to absent himself from church for a very long time, but residing in town does not go to church three consecutive Sundays in three weeks, if he be a cleric, let him be deposed, but if a layman, let him be cut off from communion."

⁴⁶³ "Those being illumined must learn all about the faith and on fifth feria of the week (Thursday) recite to the bishop or to the presbyter."

⁴⁶⁴ "We will that those whose office it is to chant in the churches do not employ disorderly shouts (βοάς ἀτάκτους), nor force nature to screaming (κραυγάς) nor select anything that is unsuitable and improper for the church; but that they offer the psalmodies to God, who is the overseer of secrets, with great attention and contrition (μετά πολλῆς προσοχῆς καὶ κατανύξεως). For the sacred Scripture taught that the sons of Israel were to be pious."

⁴⁶⁵ "Let no layman be permitted to enter the holy altar..."

⁴⁶⁶ "Women are not permitted to talk at the time of the divine liturgy; but, according to the word of the Apostle Paul, "let them be silent; for they are not permitted to speak, but should be subordinate as even the law says." (1 Cor. 14:34-35).

⁴⁶⁷ "The so-called love-feasts (ἀγάπαι) should not be held in the Lord's houses or churches, nor should there be eating within the house, nor the spreading of couches."

⁴⁶⁸ "Since we have learned that in various churches grapes are brought to the altar, according to a prevailing custom, and the ministers bring this together with the bloodless sacrifice of the offering, and thus distribute both to the people at the same time, we determine that no priest shall do this here after, but shall give the offering alone to the people for the quickening of their lives (ζωοποίησις) and for the remission of their sins. But as for the offering of grapes as first fruits, the priests are allowed to bless them separately and distribute them to the ones who ask for them as an expression of thanks to the Giver of the fruits, by means of which our bodies, according to His divine decree, are increased and nourished."

⁴⁶⁹ "That honey and milk should not be offered at the altars."

⁴⁷⁰ "We decree that the clerics who perform the liturgy or baptize in oratories located in the houses ought to do so with the consent of the bishop of the place. Therefore, if any clergyman shall not observe this regulation, let him be deposed."

⁴⁷¹ "...Wherefore, if anyone should wish to partake of the immaculate

body in the time of the synaxis, and to offer himself for communion, let him arrange his hands in the form of a cross, and thus draw near and receive the communion of grace. But those who, instead of their hands, make vessels of gold or other materials for the reception of the divine gift and by these receive the immaculate communion, we shall by no means allow to come, as preferring inanimate and inferior matter to the image of God."

[472] "Let no one drive into a church any beast whatever, except a traveler, compelled by the greatest necessity, in default of a shed or resting-place, may lodge in said church. For unless the beast had been taken inside, it would have perhaps perished, and he, by the loss of his beast of burden, and thus being without the means with which to continue his journey, would be in peril of death. Since we are taught that the Sabbath was made for man (Mk 2.27), therefore the safety and comfort of man are by all means to be considered preferable."

[473] "...We also decree concerning infants, as often as dependable witnesses are not found who say that these have undoubtedly been baptized, and since the latter are unable on account of their age to answer properly concerning the mystical initiation (μυσταγωγία) given to them; that without any hindrance they ought to be baptized, lest sometime such a doubt might deprive them of the sanctification of such a purification (κάθαρσις)."

[474] The requirements of civil law and circumstances such as the one described in the canon led to the establishment and maintenance of registry books by local dioceses and parishes.

[475] The most prominent medieval canonists are John Zonaras, Theodore Balsamon, Alexios Aristenos, and Matthew Blastaris. See *The Rudder* D. Cummings, trans. (New York, 1957 and 1983) p. XLV – LIII.

In addition to Cummings, an English Translation of the canons may be found in the *Nicene - Post Nicene Fathers*, vol. 14.

[476] *The Pedalion – Πηδάλιον* (Greek for rudder) is an annotated collection of church canons compiled by the monks Agapios and Nikodemos of the Holy Mountain. It was first published in Leipzig in 1800. Several editions followed in 1841, 1864, 1886, 1908, and 1957. The English translation by D. Cummings was based on the 1908 edition. Besides the *Pedalion*, there are two other important collections of the canons: G. A. Ralles and M. Potles, *Σύνταγμα τῶν Θείων καὶ Ἱερῶν Κανόνων*, 6 vols. (Athens, 1852 - 59), and A. Alivizatos, *Οἱ Ἱεροὶ Κανόνες* (Athens, 1923 and 1949).

[477] See *The Rudder, p.* 322 and the *Πηδάλιον* (1957 edition) p. 243.

[478] These arguments usually center on ideas such as: "It is the divine physician himself who is given to the faithful" and "The Eucharist is the divine remedy, the divine medicine that can heal all ills of body and soul." See e.g., Casimir Kucharek, *The Byzantine Liturgy of St. John Chrysostom* (Allendale NJ, 1971) p. 715. These statements, in and of themselves, are true. However, the issue is not the incorruptibly of Christ and the eucharistic elements, but the possible presence of parasitic organisms. The comments of St. Nikodemos point to the possibility of germs and viruses

attaching themselves to the sacred vessels. Hence, he cautioned clerics to take steps to sterilize these vessels in times of a plague.

[479] See above, note 471.

[480] See e.g., Cyril of Jerusalem, *Mystagogical Catechesis.* 5.21-22.

[481] Konstantinos Kallinikos, Ὁ Χριστιανικός Ναός καὶ τὰ Τελούμενα ἐν Αὐτῷ (Athens, 1958) p. 205-08. See also D. N. Moraites, "Λαβίς" in Θρησκευτική καὶ Ἠθική Ἐγκυκλοπαίδεια, 8, p. 56.

[482] Vasilios K. Stephanides, Ἐκκλησιατικὴ Ἱστορία (Athens, 1948) p. 282.

[483] Ibid. p. 282.

[484] The Roman Catholic Church restored communion under both elements in 1965. Four different modes for the distribution of the Chalice were authorized: direct drinking from the cup; intinction; sipping from a tube; and the use of a spoon. The latter two options, though lawful, are hardly ever used in the Latin Church today. See J. M. Huels, "Chalice – Modes of Distribution," in Peter E. Fink, ed., *The New Dictionary of Sacramental Worship* (Collegeville, MN 1990) p. 175-176.

12
Liturgical Life of the Parish

* This essay is a revised version of the paper I read at the Conference sponsored by Holy Cross Greek Orthodox School of Theology in 2001 on "the Orthodox Parish in America." The papers and proceedings of the Conference are being published by the Holy Cross Orthodox Press in a separate volume edited by Dr. Anton C. Vrame.

[485] Charles Gusmer, *Wholesome Worship.* (Washington, DC, 1989) p. 17.

[486] My comments are based chiefly on my experiences as a priest of the Greek Orthodox Archdiocese and as a member of the faculty of Holy Cross Greek Orthodox School of Theology.

[487] Gilbert Osdiek, *Catechesis for Liturgy* (Washington, DC, 1986) pp. 167 - 79.

[488] Gilbert Osdiek, *Catechesis for Liturgy*, p. 178.

[489] Paul Meyendorf, "The Liturgical Path of Orthodoxy in America," in *SVTQ*, 40, 1&2 (1996) p. 54.

[490] Ibid. p. 54.

[491] Some of the issues that pertain to Orthodoxy in America are discussed in two previous articles, "The American Context: A Testing Ground for Orthodox Identity and Mission" and "Particularities of the American Context: Lessons and Responses." These essays are included in the second volume of this series, *Essays in Theology and Liturgy* (Brookline, MA 2001) p. 51-68 and 69-92.

[492] See my article, "The American Context: A Testing Ground for Orthodox Identity and Mission," p. 52 and 151.

[493] For a frank discussion on the liturgical problems that are facing the Church in the changing cultural realities of our times see *Passion and Resurrection* (a publication of New Skete Monastery, Cambridge, NY 1995), p.

xv–xli.

[494] For example, think of the mediocre rendering of the texts by celebrants, lectors, singers, and choirs that we sometimes encounter.

[495] See for example, John Meyendorff, "Worship in a Secular World," in *SVTQ*, 12, 3&4 (1968) p. 120-124. Alexander Schmemann, "Worship in a Secular Age," in *SVTQ*, 16, 1 (1972) p. 3-16. Metropolitan Anthony Bloom of Sourozh, "Worship in a Secular Society," in Wiebe Vos, ed., *Worship and Secularization* (Bussum Holland 1970) p. 120-130. Olivier Clement, "Witnessing in a Secularized Society," in G. Lemopoulos, ed., *Your Will Be Done* (Geneva 1989). P. 117-135.

[496] Olivier Clement, "Witnessing in a Secularized Society," p. 120-132

[497] Ibid. 132.

[498] Metropolitan Anthony, "Worship in a Secular Society," p. 121-123.

[499] Ibid. p. 124 – 125.

[500] Ibid. p. 122.

[501] A. Schmemann, "Worship in a Secular Age," p. 11.

[502] Ibid. p. 4.

[503] See Charles Davis, "Ghetto or Desert: Liturgy in a Cultural Dilemma," in W. Vos, ed., *Worship and Secularization*, p. 10-27.

[504] A. Schmemann, "Worship in a Secular Age," p. 5.

[505] "Report to His Eminence Archbishop Iakovos – Commission: Archdiocesan Theological Agenda," in *GOTR*, 34, 3 (1989), p. 286, 301.